Bureaucratic Dynamics

TRANSFORMING AMERICAN POLITICS
Lawrence C. Dodd, Series Editor

Dramatic changes in political institutions and behavior over the past three decades have underscored the dynamic nature of American politics, confronting political scientists with a new and pressing intellectual agenda. The pioneering work of early postwar scholars, while laying a firm empirical foundation for contemporary scholarship, failed to consider how American politics might change or to recognize the forces that would make fundamental change inevitable. In reassessing the static interpretations fostered by these classic studies, political scientists are now examining the underlying dynamics that generate transformational change.

Transforming American Politics brings together texts and monographs that address four closely related aspects of change. A first concern is documenting and explaining recent changes in American politics—in institutions, processes, behavior, and policymaking. A second is reinterpreting classic studies and theories to provide a more accurate perspective on postwar politics. The series looks at historical change to identify recurring patterns of political transformation within and across the distinctive eras of American politics. Last and perhaps most importantly, the series presents new theories and interpretations that explain the dynamic processes at work and thus clarify the direction of contemporary politics. All of the books focus on the central theme of transformation—transformation in both the conduct of American politics and in the way we study and understand its many aspects.

FORTHCOMING TITLES

Broken Contract? Changing Relationships Between Citizens and Their Government in the United States, edited by Stephen C. Craig

Congress and the Administrative State, Second Edition, Lawrence C. Dodd and Richard L. Schott

The New American Politics, edited by Bryan D. Jones

Young Versus Old: Generational Gaps in Political Participation and Policy Preferences, Susan MacManus and Suzanne L. Parker

Campaigns and Elections, edited by James A. Thurber and Candice J. Nelson

Cold War Politics, John Kenneth White

Congressional Politics, Second Edition, Leroy N. Rieselbach

Governing Partners: State-Local Relations in the U.S., edited by Russell L. Hanson

Bureaucratic Dynamics

THE ROLE OF
BUREAUCRACY
IN A DEMOCRACY

B. Dan Wood

Texas A&M University

Richard W. Waterman

University of New Mexico

Westview Press

BOULDER • SAN FRANCISCO • OXFORD

Transforming American Politics

Copyright © 1994 by Westview Press, Inc.

Published in 1994 in the United States of America by Westview Press, Inc., 5500 Central Avenue, Boulder, Colorado 80301-2877, and in the United Kingdom by Westview Press, 36 Lonsdale Road, Summertown, Oxford OX2 7EW

Library of Congress Cataloging-in-Publication Data
Wood, B. Dan.
  Bureaucratic dynamics : the role of bureaucracy in a democracy /
B. Dan Wood, Richard W. Waterman.
    p.   cm.
  Includes bibliographical references and index.
  ISBN 0-8133-1846-7   ISBN 0-8133-1847-5 (pbk)
    1. Bureaucracy—United States.   2. Democracy—United States.
I. Waterman, Richard W.   II. Title.
JK421.W58   1994
350'000973—dc20   94-8993
                                                                       CIP

Printed and bound in the United States of America

The paper used in this publication meets the requirements
of the American National Standard for Permanence of Paper
for Printed Library Materials Z39.48-1984.

10   9   8   7   6   5   4   3   2   1

To Pat, Dana, and Todd   — B. Dan Wood

To Edith and the memory of Benjamin
— Richard W. Waterman

Contents

Tables and Figures

Tables

Figures

Preface and Acknowledgments

It is hard to imagine in this era of bureaucracy bashing and widespread antipathy toward "big" government that there was ever a time in U.S. history when centralized government and bureaucracy were considered positive forces. Only a few short decades ago citizen demands to remedy such market ills as air, water, and toxic pollution; workplace health and safety; consumer protection; automobile safety; energy underproduction; deficient education; and poverty resulted in the creation of large government bureaucracies. During the Depression of the 1930s government and bureaucracies were looked upon as saviors from the many ills resulting from the collapse of the market economy. And during the Progressive Era (1890–1920) there was a belief that bureaucracies improved the operation of the U.S. system in areas as diverse as predatory pricing, interstate commerce, banking, foods, drugs, and monopolistic practice.

In the 1990s bureaucracy is generally portrayed as the very antithesis of a rational, efficient, and responsive institution. Most citizens, pundits, and politicians agree that the exercise of power by bureaucracy is inherently undemocratic and sometimes arbitrary. Scholars often argue that bureaucracies manifest elite influence and are structured for particularistic, rather than fair, representation. In other words, over the past few decades popular interpretations of the appropriate role for bureaucracy in U.S. democracy have undergone a striking change. Bureaucracy is no longer considered a solution to many public problems; rather, it is seen as a source of public problems.

Given this prevalent view, it is not surprising that several attempts have been made over the past twenty-five years or so to reform the bureaucracy. The Ash Council under President Richard Nixon, reorganization plans under President Jimmy Carter, the Grace Commission under President Ronald Reagan, and Vice President Al Gore's "reinventing government" proposals were but four of the many high-profile attempts to identify or reduce waste in the federal bureaucracy. There have also been various legislative attempts to reform bureaucracy. These have included the enactment of sunset legislation to periodically review an agency's performance; the establishment of ombuds whose role is to help people dissatisfied with the bureaucratic process; and the broad deregulation movement of the 1970s and 1980s, which removed many regulatory functions from bureaucracy's influence and even eliminated some agencies. Most of these reforms were implemented under the assumption that the bureaucratic process is inherently inconsistent with democratic principles. Bureaucracy is typically perceived as an unrepresentative institution. The solution is to make it accountable to such constitutionally designated officials as the president and Congress.

These prevalent attitudes and subsequent reform efforts have been informed by an understanding of bureaucracy developed mostly through rumor and innuendo, not through sound social science theory and systematic empirical evidence. Little or no scholarly research guided these efforts; the scholarly research that did exist was impressionistic, based purely on critical case studies. Most prior studies of the bureaucracy concluded that it was indeed a palpable threat to democracy. Although the reasoning employed was often persuasive, these studies were based purely on subjective evaluation. None involved a systematic analysis of quantitative data across multiple agencies that could have resulted in conclusive findings. That is the primary goal of this book.

We raise and empirically examine a series of questions about the role of bureaucracy in a democracy. Does bureaucracy respond to public preferences and to constitutionally designated representatives? If so, how and how much? Are signals to the bureaucracy from elected representatives always consistent with mass preferences? If they are consistent, then does bureaucracy respond consistently to the intended signals? What particular tools of elected representatives are most effective for changing the bureaucracy? Does the bureaucratic state represent a threat to our constitutional system of separation of powers and checks and balances? If so, what can be done about this threat?

This book provides answers to these questions that are both surprising and disconcerting. Some old controversies are settled, but some new questions are raised about how well public preferences translate into policy outputs. We find that bureaucracies are highly responsive entities, adapting to many distinct and diverse political signals. However, democratically elected officials may not always send the bureaucracy signals that are consistent with public preferences. The question then becomes, How can democratic principals such as the president be held accountable as they attempt to shape the bureaucracy? The last chapter provides some detailed recommendations intended to address this problem.

We believe, and it is our fervent hope, that the analyses presented in this book will elevate the debate over the role of bureaucracy in a democracy to a new level. Rather than concentrating solely on the world of the bureaucrat, as has too often been the case in the past, we focus on the interaction between bureaucracy and the larger political system. We examine how bureaucracy interacts with such diverse political actors as the president, Congress, the courts, the media, and the public. In exposing these interactions, we demonstrate that the threat to bureaucratic accountability and democracy is not confined solely to the bureaucracy. Rather, democratic principals, the president in particular, can also be guilty of abusing the bureacratic process.

We also argue that the bureaucratic process cannot be understood without examining how the bureaucracy interacts with actors in the larger political system. We show that these interactions are far more complex than citizens, pundits, politicians, and most scholars typically suggest. Rather, political-bureaucratic adaptation is a highly dynamic process involving multiple actors and applications of political stimuli for policy change. Bureaucracies are responsive entities that generate some stimuli of their own in creating movements in the policy process. We have named the book *Bureaucratic Dynamics* to emphasize this feature of the political-bureaucratic process. The subtitle, *The Role of Bureaucracy in a Democracy,* is intended to highlight our concern with how well bureaucratic democracy is working.

The book is divided into seven chapters. Chapters 1 and 2 examine popular, journalistic, and scholarly accounts to determine how most people currently view the bureaucratic process. These chapters raise theoretical questions about the role of bureaucracy in a democracy, in particular, the compatibility of bureaucracy with existing notions of democratic representation and separation of powers. Chapters 3 through 5, which constitute the heart of the book, present findings from an empirical study of outputs from eight different federal agencies: the Environmental Protection Agency (EPA), the Nuclear Regulatory Commission (NRC), the Federal Trade Commission (FTC), the Office of Surface Mining and Reclamation (OSM), the Interstate Commerce Commission (ICC), the National Highway Traffic Safety Administration (NHTSA), the Food and Drug Administration (FDA), and the Equal Employment Opportunity Commission (EEOC). Although the results presented in these three chapters are based on rigorous statistical analysis, they are written so that they are accessible to undergraduate and graduate students, practitioners, and scholars interested in better understanding the bureaucratic process. Results from the statistical models are presented in a graphic form for easy understanding and in a tabular form for scholars who want a more advanced presentation. Technical descriptions of the research methods are relegated to the Appendix and the Notes.

Chapters 3 through 5 provide the basis for the policy proposals presented in Chapters 6 and 7. Chapter 6 offers a policy proposal for improving bureaucratic and political accountability that we dub "policy monitoring." Chapter 7 offers a normative assessment of what role bureaucracy should play in a democratic system. This chapter raises some serious concerns that have been largely overlooked by prior bureaucratic theorists, namely, that responsive bureaucracy may not be fully consistent with effective democratic representation. This is especially true if the signals sent by elected representatives are inconsistent with public preferences. Ironically, then, this book argues that bureaucracy can sometimes be more representative by being unresponsive. Chapter 7 also provides some recommendations for future research and suggestions for practitioners interested in promoting change.

In writing this book, we have had the help of many people and organizations. Professor James A. Stimson has been a patient mentor and friend through the years, offering encouragement and advice at various stages of the project. Professors James E. Anderson, James C. Clingermayer, and an anonymous reviewer read the entire manuscript and offered many useful comments and criticisms. Professor Anderson, a good-humored but quintessential critic of quantitative empirical research, was especially helpful with conceptualization and clarification of the presentation. Comments on parts of the manuscript were given by Professors John T. Scholz, Kenneth J. Meier, George C. Edwards III, Joseph Stewart, David Hedge, Susan Hunter, William T. Gormley, David Rohde, Michael S. Lewis-Beck, Samuel C. Patterson, Jonathan Nagler, Bryan D. Jones, Richard Barke, Woodrow Jones, Barry Weingast, Malcolm Goggin, James Desveaux, and Barbara Headrick. We thank faculty at the University of Texas at Dallas for helpful comments in a colloquium. Various other individuals, some of whom are now professors, provided able research assistance. Marcia Bastian gave generously of her time to create the tables for the book. The National Science Foundation and the Center for Presidential Studies at Texas A&M University provided financial support to Wood when most of the analyses for this book were done. Jennifer Knerr of Westview Press offered much-needed advice in developing the manuscript for a general audience. We say thanks to all of these individuals and organizations but acknowledge that the final condition of the book is our own doing.

B. Dan Wood
Richard W. Waterman

1

Toward a More Dynamic Conception of Bureaucracy

U.S. public bureaucracies are dynamic, adaptive entities. They continually respond to diverse, changing, and not entirely predictable political environments. Their responses have various magnitudes and speeds of adjustment, and they eventually settle into equilibria that may (or may not) reflect prevailing public preferences.

This characterization of bureaucracies as dynamic and adaptive is critical to understanding the role of bureaucracies in American democracy. Bureaucracies perform most public functions in the United States, and the eventual levels at which they perform such functions are important for their consistency (or inconsistency) with public preferences. The speed of bureaucratic adaptation is also important. Rapid adaptation may be consistent with democratic values such as responsiveness and accountability but may be inconsistent with public expectations such as stable and effective public policy. Slow adaptation may enhance government stability but thwart democratic preferences as bureaucracy goes against current majority interests.

This book investigates the dynamics of bureaucratic adaptation and its relation to U.S. democracy. The purpose is to expand the body of knowledge on the scope and nature of these processes. Such knowledge is important for stimulating scholarly debate on bureaucracy, an institution that constitutes the so-called fourth branch of U.S. government, and for understanding how bureaucracy functions within the U.S. democratic scheme. This knowledge may even offer suggestions for improving government, as a later chapter argues.

This book shows that bureaucratic adaptation within policy systems is a complex process. At some times bureaucracies respond to external actors; at other times bureaucracies cause external actors to respond. Bureaucracies respond to both top-down and bottom-up influences and cause responses at both the top and bottom of their respective policy systems. Sometimes the behavior of bureaucracies and other actors in a policy system falls prey to outside dramatic events that move them all along beyond control; at other times bureaucracies create their own dramatic events. These bureaucratic adaptation processes occur continually and simultaneously, and understanding them is an integral part of efforts to understand U.S. government generally.

POPULAR PERCEPTIONS OF
BUREAUCRATIC ADAPTATION

Bureaucratic adaptation is a rich phenomenon that requires a rich theory for explanation. Yet past explanations of this phenomenon have been dominated by popular myths and oversimplifications. Consider, for example, the prevailing popular view of bureaucracy. Citizens widely believe that bureaucracies are slow, lumbering giants that accomplish little and are generally unresponsive to public preferences.[1] At the same time, citizens also assume that bureaucracy is omnipotent and can do whatever it pleases. Politicians are often perceived (and sometimes perceive themselves) as powerless in the face of a resistant bureaucracy (see, e.g., Aberbach and Rockman 1976). Likewise, bureaucrats are often considered to be both power hungry and risk averse, seldom accomplishing their public purpose.[2]

Bureaucratic unresponsiveness and inefficiency are a frequent topic of conversation among U.S. citizens. However, interestingly, citizens rarely have firsthand knowledge of such outcomes. To the contrary, most evidence directly observable by citizens suggests that bureaucracy is both responsive and efficient. For example, survey data (summarized in Hill 1992) show that on average about 60 percent of all Americans have personal encounters with bureaucracy each year. In these encounters a large majority say they came away satisfied that their needs had been met expeditiously and fairly (Hill 1992; see also Goodsell 1983).[3] Furthermore, there is abundant anecdotal evidence to suggest that government is efficient in comparison to the private sector. For example, salaries for upperlevel public-sector employees are generally lower than those paid to their private-sector counterparts (Mosher 1968) (pay raises for all public employees have been few and far between in recent years). The offices and amenities of most public-sector employees are very modest compared to their private-sector counterparts. Nonetheless, citizens continue to hold images of wasted tax dollars, multiple programs doing the same job, excessive red tape, and lazy, bumbling bureaucrats.[4]

What is the basis of this popular discontent over the bureaucracy? The preceding discussion suggests that it is not rooted in empirical examination of the facts but rather is a complex phenomenon stemming from multiple sources. These sources include hostile campaign rhetoric, media hyperbole, American political culture, and a natural tension resulting from the marketlike exchanges between citizens and their government.

As James Q. Wilson (1989: 236) noted, "No politician ever lost votes by denouncing the bureaucracy." Consequently, many politicians have eagerly taken up the cause of attacking the allegedly bloated, inefficient, unproductive, and slow federal bureaucracy. Politicians also regularly accuse the bureaucracy of being out of touch and unresponsive to the public—a charge they are, on occasion, guilty of themselves.

In recent years candidates of both political parties have adopted anti-Washington, antibureaucratic rhetoric as standard components of their campaign speeches. Of these politicians, Reagan is perhaps best remembered for attacking the bureaucracy. But such ideologically diverse presidential candidates as Gerald Ford, Jimmy Carter, and Edward Kennedy also found agreement on one central point: Each found it palatable to blame the bureaucracy. In the 1992 presidential election all three presidential candidates, Bill Clinton, George Bush, and Ross Perot, incorporated attacks on the bureaucracy in their standard campaign speeches. Perot's attacks on Washington were by far the most vehement. The fact that he, as a third-party candidate, received some 20 million votes and 19 percent of the vote nationwide likely guarantees that future presidential candidates will adopt similar antibureaucracy/anti-Washington themes.

The media have also contributed to popular perceptions of the bureaucracy as an unresponsive and inefficient institution. On what basis have the media come to this conclusion? Charles Goodsell (1983: 3) argued, "One source the popular critics always draw upon is that item found in almost every edition of every daily newspaper, the bureaucratic horror story." He described these stories as a "graphic and sympathetic account of how some poor citizen has been mistreated by incompetent bureaucrats or how in some other way a great bureaucratic error has been committed." Politicians and other decisionmakers then focus on these accounts in their reelection efforts.

In addition to bureaucratic horror stories, editorial writers and other purveyors of common wisdom have expressed pejorative opinions about the bureaucracy. For example, columnist George Will, in evaluating President Clinton's 1993 plan to reduce the deficit, concluded, "How advanced is a project if bureaucrats in Washington can fathom it?" (*Newsweek*, March 8, 1993: 68). When such popular political pundits as Rush Limbaugh and various other talk-show hosts who have likewise profited at the expense of the bureaucracy are added to this mix, there is clearly no reason to believe that bureaucracy will be presented in a more positive light by the media any time soon.

Another reason citizens perceive bureaucracies in such a negative light is their distinctive political and institutional culture (see, e.g., Wilson 1975;

Nelson 1982; Aberbach, Putnam, and Rockman 1981). In Europe bureaucracies preceded democracy in the evolution of governing processes. Bureaucracies grew as institutions rooted in an elite public service open only to the most educated and able individuals. Responsible party government and a tradition of aristocratic service resulted in citizen characterization of bureaucracies as respectable institutions. In Europe when government changed, the bureaucracy changed, so it was easy to understand that bureaucracies were integral parts of a responsive, representative, democratic system.

However, the opposite conditions existed in this country. In the early years of the nation there was little or no bureaucracy, and public service was not held in particularly high esteem by citizens. During the 1800s bureaucracy was frequently a scandal-ridden, corrupt instrument of patronage and politics. Since at least the Pendleton Act of 1883, there has been a conscious effort at the highest levels of government to separate bureaucracy from political processes. Scholars have frequently extolled the virtues of a separation between politics and administration, arguing for a neutral, technically competent bureaucracy (e.g., Wilson 1987; Goodnow 1900). As a result, Americans are ambivalent about whether they want their bureaucracies to be responsive to or free from political influence. Citizens want administration that is efficient, effective, and evenhanded across cases and through time; however, they also want responsive government. Generally, they fail to see the contradictions between these two desires.

Citizens also tend to question the legitimacy of an institution that is so large, yet consists primarily of nonelected officials. They suspect that alleged bureaucratic rigidity, rules, and red tape are mere excuses for unresponsiveness to public demands. Citizens also often view bureaucracy as an instrument of elite, rather than popular, influence. This may be because so many departments and agencies were established to serve a particular clientele; or it may be because rules and institutions constitute a mobilization of bias that systematically excludes segments of the public (Lowi 1979; Bachrach and Baratz 1970). For whatever reason, bureaucracies have not been viewed as representative institutions.

Other popular perceptions are that the bureaucracy is resistant to change, has too much discretion, and lacks accountability. Elected officials are seen as being more concerned with reelection and personal agendas than with controlling the bureaucracy. According to this view, even if officials are interested in controlling the bureaucracy, it is too large, diverse, and powerful for the task. Thus, in the United States there is much confusion as to the role of bureaucracy in the democratic system.

To be sure, most citizens operate at the symbolic level with regard to the nature of bureaucracy. They lack the sophistication to understand the trade-offs among bureaucratic responsiveness, efficiency, and important social values such as equity, fairness, and quality of life. Most citizens also do not comprehend the limitations placed on bureaucratic responsiveness by laws and administrative procedures. However, citizens do understand that their own pocketbooks are lighter if bureaucracy is unresponsive and inefficient.

Thus, there is a natural marketlike tension between citizens and the bureaucracy. For example, in private markets consumers seek quantity and/or quality at the lowest price possible. Producers seek a higher price in order to extract wealth and profit. In such arrangements consumers and producers have opposing interests. Consumers always think the price should be lower, and producers always think it should be higher. This causes both parties to the exchange to experience a measure of residual dissatisfaction after the bargain has been struck.

Likewise, in the exchange between citizens and bureaucracy there is the same sort of residual dissatisfaction. Bureaucrats usually find it difficult to provide services at the price citizens prefer. Consequently, citizens' dissatisfaction is manifested in their continuing concern over government responsiveness and efficiency. In an important sense, then, citizen discontent with bureaucracy is a natural phenomenon that is unlikely to go away no matter how responsive and efficient government becomes.

LEGITIMACY, THE CONSTITUTION, AND BUREAUCRATIC ADAPTATION

The popular perception of bureaucracy as a lumbering, resistant, out-of-control giant implies that bureaucratic adaptation processes are dysfunctional. That is, bureaucracies are seen as not changing in response to popular preferences or in response to the preferences of duly elected institutions. Rather, bureaucracies are viewed as following their own independent course. This perception, whether true or not, raises serious legitimacy and constitutional questions for American government.

The disaffection of American citizens with electoral politics in the past as well as the renewed disaffection evidenced by the Perot movement in 1992 probably relates to this sense of powerlessness in the face of "big bureaucracy." Voter participation declined or was generally low in the period from 1945 through 1988; during this same period the bureaucracy exhibited dramatic growth. Participation was up during the 1992 elections, as citizens were mobilized by the Perot movement, which campaigned to regain control of government.

Citizens naturally question the legitimacy of government when they feel that they have little or no control over its outputs or expenditures. Most of what is done by the U.S. government is done by bureaucracy.

However, the common perception is that electoral processes have no real impact on the bureaucracy. If duly elected politicians are powerless in the face of the instrument that does most government work, then there is little reason to conduct elections in the first place. Why send politicians to Washington to create more "out-of-control" bureaucracies? Thus, the inability of citizens to see bureaucracy as a representative institution and as part of the democratic process diminishes the legitimacy of government in the United States.

Yet ironically many contemporary features of the U.S. bureaucracy were instituted for the explicit purpose of limiting popular control. The "spoils" era, from 1832 to 1883, has been widely described as a time when government corruption and inefficiency were rampant because of excessive patronage and incompetent personnel. After 1883 the accepted wisdom was that there should be a separation between politics and administration. Administrative efficiency was consciously and deliberately given a higher priority than administrative responsiveness in the ensuing government reforms.

The doctrine of separating politics and administration resulted in the passage of the Pendleton Act of 1883, which created a merit system and career civil service. The merit system assured that many jobs in the bureaucracy would be filled on the basis of expertise rather than on the basis of political affiliation or ideological preferences. The civil service provided limited tenure to administrative personnel, guaranteeing that they could not be removed from office without cause.

In 1921 Congress passed the Budgeting and Accounting Act, which delegated to the president responsibility for formulating an executive budget. This legislation created the Bureau of the Budget, which placed responsibility for administrative efficiency on the president. The primary interest of the president was in the efficient operation of government, not in consistency with popular preferences or campaign agendas. The Administrative Procedure Act passed in 1946 ensured that bureaucratic discretion was more tightly bound in responding to political influences. This legislation also laid down explicit procedures for administrative policymaking and adjudication in virtual isolation from electoral politics. Throughout this same period numerous agencies were also created outside the executive departments for the explicit purpose of insulating them from political control. The 1974 reforms to the budgetary process substantially politicized the budgetary function.

All of these reforms suggest that the magnitude and speed of bureaucratic responsiveness to popular controls have been manipulated at various times throughout U.S. history to produce minimal and creeping bureaucratic adaptation. If citizen perceptions about the nature of bureaucratic adaptation are indeed correct, then these reforms were successful, but they came with the unanticipated effect of reduced government legitimacy.

The growth in bureaucratic power since the Progressive Era also raises constitutional questions about the legitimacy of U.S. institutions. Economic and social development has fostered a society that is increasingly complex, interdependent, and technical. Congress has insufficient expertise, information, or time to legislate specific solutions to many public problems. Nuclear power, public health, the economy, the environment, and discrimination are all issues that require the specialized knowledge and full-time attention of experts in the bureaucracy. As a result, Congress has chosen to delegate much policymaking authority to the executive branch and other agencies, a move that may be politically expeditious given the controversial nature of some policies.

For whatever reason Congress delegated authority, many bureaucracies now exercise executive, legislative, and judicial power. Such plenary abdication of power by Congress to the bureaucracy raises obvious constitutional concerns. The principle of legislative supremacy that is strongly embedded in the Constitution is seemingly violated. The Constitution in Article I invested primary policymaking power in Congress, with no evidence that the founders intended that power to be given away to nonelected officials. Yet modern bureaucracy, which consists almost entirely of nonelected officials, makes most government policy. Lowi (1979) called this development "policy without law" and suggested that it is a subversion of the democratic process. Subversive of democracy or not, there are obvious reasons to be concerned over whether bureaucracy accurately reflects public preferences. The public's perceptions of ineffective representation are obviously crucial to its perceptions of government legitimacy generally.

This extensive delegation of power to the bureaucracy also violates the principles of separation of powers and checks and balances. The founders designed a system of shared powers, with each branch of government having some separate responsibilities. The intent was for each branch to limit the power of the others, making inaction easier than action. For example, legislative power is primarily invested in Congress but is shared with the president through the powers of veto and recommendation. Similarly, the executive power is primarily lodged in the president, but Congress checks the application of executive power through the budget, legislation, and the Senate authority to approve nominations. Likewise, the courts since *Marbury* v. *Madison* (1803) have been the final arbiters of what the Constitution says and have established themselves informally as interpreters of the law. However, both the president and Congress may have their own, quite different interpretations. Through legislative power,

Congress and the president can often jointly overturn judicial interpretations as well as bind the courts to their shared viewpoint.

The principles of separation of powers and checks and balances are violated when the bureaucracy performs all three government functions. That is, they are violated when the bureaucracy makes policy, executes it, and then adjudicates disputes that arise as a result of that policy execution. Such a development is clearly inconsistent with the guiding principles of limited government and curbs on tyranny inherent in the Constitution. A listing of the tasks performed by the bureaucracy should serve to emphasize the potential dangers of such a development. Various government agencies audit private records, seize private property, enter private property, compel testimony, impose fines and fees without hearings, issue licenses to operate, set rates, collect taxes, adjudicate controversies involving themselves, and make rules that apply to individuals and entire industries, among other things. An out-of-control bureaucracy, to the extent that one really exists, could mark a realization of the founders' worst fears.

Nevertheless, a check remains on the bureaucracy in that it is subordinate to the Constitution, Congress, the president, and the courts. The Constitution provides certain rights to citizens in their dealings with the bureaucracy, such as due process and equal protection of the laws. Congress and the president are jointly responsible for establishing policymaking directions and boundaries on the bureaucracy. They also jointly administer the bureaucracy, and the courts adjudicate cases and controversies involving the bureaucracy as a litigant.

Nevertheless, the check on bureaucracy imposed by Congress, the president, and the courts is effective only to the extent that these major institutional actors actually use that check. As previously noted, citizens generally believe that politicians do not use this check. These institutions were not designed to control the bureaucracy since there is no evidence that the founders anticipated its modern development. Thus, there are obvious questions about the ability and motivations of legislative, executive, and judicial actors in performing this task.

Concerning Congress as a check on the bureaucracy, the general perception is that the primary motivation for senators and representatives is a desire for reelection (Fiorina 1981). Oversight of the bureaucracy has a low payoff in terms of political visibility and votes. As a result, oversight hearings may occur too infrequently for effective supervision, with the result that they tend to be responsive to problems only after they occur. Additionally, members of Congress tend to be generalists by education and experience and are therefore ineffective supervisors of the policy experts in the bureaucracy. Responsibility for legislative oversight tends to be fragmented between two congressional bodies, the House and Senate, as well as multiple competing committees and subcommittees in each chamber (Dodd and Schott 1979). Members of Congress may also affect the bureaucracy as individuals through their pursuit of constituent complaints. However, the common perception is that this form of legislative oversight is too diffuse to operate as much of a check on the bureaucracy.

The president is also often viewed as a weak check on the bureaucracy. The president, like Congress, lacks the motivation for effective supervision. There are few benefits to be derived from directing the bureaucracy (though major administration scandals may be costly). The president has often been more concerned with foreign policy than with domestic affairs. Obviously, the president cannot personally supervise the bureaucracy, given its enormous size and diversity. The White House staff is also small relative to the entire federal bureaucracy, which implies that the president has difficulty in obtaining the information necessary to monitor and control the bureaucracy. There are also a substantial number of agencies that exist outside the executive branch and that are therefore farther removed from executive control. Thus, there are serious questions about the effectiveness of presidential supervision.

The courts, too, are of questionable merit in ensuring bureaucratic accountability. Most fundamentally, the federal judiciary itself is a nondemocratic institution consisting of appointed, tenured-for-life personnel. There is therefore little reason to expect that it would have much concern for popular preferences. For the courts to act, there must be a case or controversy involving an individual or entity with standing to sue the bureaucracy. Even though the rules of standing have been substantially liberalized by Congress and the courts in recent years (Melnick 1983), lawsuits are expensive and can take a long time, which suggests that bureaucratic accountability is biased toward elites and may be slow in coming. Moreover, the courts have for the most part deferred to the bureaucracy on matters of policy or adjudication, except where procedural errors or denials of constitutional rights exist. Thus, the judiciary may also be a weak check on bureaucratic power.

Concerns over government legitimacy and the continued viability of constitutional principles suggest that it is important to understand the role played by bureaucracy in a democratic system. This is our purpose in writing this book.

CONCLUSION

This book is concerned with understanding bureaucratic adaptation in response to stimuli coming from various parts of the policy system. Some stimuli flow to the bureaucracy from the president, Congress, and the courts along a top-down path. Ideally, such stimuli should result from popular preferences operating through these institutions; however, they may also result from the particularistic interests of influential actors. Other stimuli flow to the bureaucracy along a bottom-up path from citizens, groups, the media, and political elites. The bureaucracy may also send some stimuli of its own to affect each of these actors, which may (or may not) reflect popular preferences, bureaucratic interests, or both. Still other stimuli may result from dramatic events that affect all actors in the policy system simultaneously.

As this book examines these processes, it addresses several important questions relating to U.S. democracy. Do bureaucracies adapt to political stimuli? If so, then how much and how fast do they adapt? As previously discussed, the popular perception is that bureaucratic adaptation is slow to nonexistent. Most citizens believe that bureaucracies are large, rigid, self-interested entities moving slowly along a predetermined path. Citizens do not control them; neither do politicians. Therefore, bureaucracies are often conceived of as antithetical to the democratic scheme. This common belief diminishes the legitimacy of American institutions. It also raises serious questions about the continued viability of constitutional principles such as legislative supremacy, separation of powers, and checks and balances.

If bureaucracies do adapt, then what do they adapt to? Do they respond mostly to stimuli coming from Congress, the president, and the courts, the major instruments of democratic power in the U.S. system? As previously discussed, these institutions are necessary checks on bureaucratic power if constitutional principles are to have continuing viability. Do bureaucracies respond more directly to citizens, interest groups, the media, or other manifestations of pluralist influence? If so, then bureaucracy can be considered an instrument of direct representation. That is, the bureaucracy is itself a representative institution. Sorting out the paths of political influence on the bureaucracy should increase understanding of how bureaucracy fits into the democratic scheme. Such understanding would enhance the legitimacy of U.S. institutions. It could also provide elected officials with the knowledge necessary to assure future bureaucratic accountability.

To the extent that bureaucracies do adapt, how consistent is that adaptation with majoritarian preferences? Bureaucracies may indeed respond to Congress, the president, the courts, or other actors. However, this does not necessarily mean consistency with majoritarian demands or election mandates. Self-interested politicians may push policy in a direction that is contrary to majority preferences. Or the bureaucracy may move policy away from majority preferences, despite receiving consistent signals from politicians. The occurrence of the first scenario suggests the need for politician accountability; the second scenario reinforces the need for bureau-cratic accountability.

The chapters that follow address all of these questions through the presentation of empirical evidence. Chapter 2 examines past qualitative and quantitative evidence on these issues by reviewing previous scholarly literature on the bureaucracy. This chapter also presents a theoretical framework, called principal-agent theory, that can effectively explain the incentives and constraints that drive bureaucratic adaptation. Chapter 3 presents quantitative case studies of eight different federal agencies to ex-amine bureaucratic responses to elected institutions. This chapter finds that bureaucratic responsiveness to the president and Congress is perva-sive and present in all eight agencies. Chapter 4 presents an intensive case study of one agency to determine the relative importance of various stimuli to bureaucratic adaptation and shows that bureaucratic adapta-tion processes are both instantaneous and distributed through time as well as responsive to top-down and bottom-up forces. Chapter 5 exam-ines two instances in which signals run from the bureaucracy to external actors. This chapter also evaluates the effect of dramatic events on bureau-cratic adaptation processes and shows that they are nonrecursive, with stimuli and responses running in both directions. Chapter 6 presents a policy recommendation, dubbed policy monitoring, for the purpose of improving both bureaucratic and politician accountability. Chapter 7 con-cludes with a commentary on the implications of the findings for bureau-cratic democracy. This chapter also evaluates how well bureaucratic democracy is working and offers suggestions for future improvement.

2

Scholarly Thinking and Research on the Bureaucracy

This chapter surveys scholarly thinking and past empirical research on the relation between politics and the bureaucracy. This discussion of past scholarly work has a twofold purpose. First, the chapter highlights some of the unsettled controversies among academics that are relevant to the analyses presented in subsequent chapters. Although the stated purpose for those chapters is to describe the nature of bureaucratic adaptation and its relation to U.S. democracy, the analyses presented there may also help in resolving some of these past controversies.

Second, past theories on politics and the bureaucracy suggest certain a priori expectations about the nature of bureaucratic adaptation in the U.S. system. For example, some scholars have been very thoughtful in coming to conclusions quite similar to the popular perceptions discussed in Chapter 1, namely, that bureaucracies are large, powerful entities that are resistant to change and are often unresponsive to external pressures. Other scholars claim that bureaucracies do respond to external pressures, but only under certain circumstances. Thus, this chapter emphasizes past scholarly work so that readers can judge whether the empirical analyses presented in later chapters are consistent with that work.

The last part of this chapter presents a theoretical framework, called principal-agent theory, for understanding bureaucratic adaptation in a democratic system. Although this is not the only theory that could be applied in describing political-bureaucratic adaptation processes, it does remarkably well in predicting the incentives and behaviors of various actors in a dynamic, hierarchically oriented policy system.

NORMATIVE CONTROVERSIES
OVER POLITICS AND THE BUREAUCRACY

A long-standing and continuing controversy in political science and public administration concerns the role that politics should play in the administration of public policies. Following the rampant abuses of the spoils era and the Pendleton Act of 1883, which established the U.S. civil service and merit systems, many scholars argued for a separation between policymaking and the administrative functions of government. Policymaking was viewed as a congressional function, with administration considered an executive-branch function. Thus, Woodrow Wilson (1987:18; see also Goodnow 1900) wrote in his now famous essay that "administration lies outside the proper sphere of politics."[1]

The notion behind this proposed politics-administration dichotomy was that policymaking was somehow peculiarly suited to the elected officials in Congress, whereas administration was best left to the policy and implementation experts in the bureaucracy. This view was consistent with the principle of legislative supremacy inherent in the Constitution, which was discussed in Chapter 1. It was also consistent with prevailing judicial views of executive power throughout this period. Thus, Congress was to make laws, and the bureaucracy, under the leadership of the president, was to execute them in a policy-neutral, technically efficient manner.

This proposed politics-administration dichotomy was a normative, not an empirical, debate. There was never any controversy over whether there *is* politics in administration. Even Wilson in his seminal 1887 essay recognized that administration involves politics. These early scholars were simply arguing for a more limited involvement of politicians in the administrative process and a more limited involvement of administrators in the policymaking process. Equally important was the explicit call in Wilson's essay for the development of a "science of administration" because the focus of public administration over the next sixty years was on developing efficiency in administration. This necessarily meant limiting some other values, including responsiveness to political influences.

Various other controversies over politics and the bureaucracy emerged from this proposed politics-administration dichotomy, especially when the prescriptions of the dichotomy are taken to their full conclusions. The dichotomy implies that the relation between elected institutions and the bureaucracy should be purely top-down and essentially static through time. Politics and administration are assumed to be separable, hierarchically arranged endeavors. Elected politicians make policy for administration through their nonelected subordinates in the bureaucracy. However, these subordinates should not be susceptible to any political influence beyond initial lawmaking. The president, and future presidents, should be concerned only with administering efficiently, not with altering established policy. Congress should alter policy through additional lawmaking and the legitimate tools of policy direction (the budget, political appointment, etc.). However, beyond this there should be little involvement of politicians in the administrative process.

This view also implies that congressional policymaking should be detailed and explicit so that policies can be administered without ambiguity by experts in the bureaucracy. According to this argument, the president is not an independent policymaker and should not direct the bureaucracy in a manner that is inconsistent with original legislative intent. Congress should not delegate policymaking authority to the bureaucracy. The underlying assumption is that the bureaucracy is not a representative institution and that all bureaucratic policymaking occurs beyond the Constitution and legitimate democratic channels.

The politics-administration dichotomy has given birth to at least three highly visible continuing normative controversies in political science. In the first controversy scholars have disagreed over how much policymaking authority Congress should delegate to the bureaucracy. The politics-administration dichotomy suggests that none should be delegated.[2] However, this has not been a viable option given the highly technical and interdependent nature of problems in modern society. Beginning as early as 1931, with Sharfman's (1931–1937) four-volume analysis of the Interstate Commerce Commission, scholars were contending that Congress delegated too much authority to the bureaucracy (see also Landis 1939; Galloway 1946; McConnell 1966; Stone 1977; Sundquist 1981). The core of this argument was expressed by George Galloway (1946: 242) when he wrote, "Congressmen generally recognize the need for delegating legislative power as a means of reducing their workload and of taking care of technical matters beyond the competence of Congress. But they believe that the great growth of administrative lawmaking has become a menace to the constitutional function of Congress as the legislative branch of the national government." Likewise, Theodore Lowi (1979) argued that broad, ill-defined delegations of congressional authority left the bureaucracy unaccountable and democracy imperiled. And Wilson (1967) noted that the growth of bureaucratic power had not resulted in the formulation of coherent policies. Wilson (1975) also characterized the expansion of administrative power as the "bureaucratic problem."

Not all scholars agreed, however. For example, Francis Rourke (1984: 37), while also expressing his concerns, stated, "Without administrative discretion, effective government would be impossible in the infinitely varied and rapidly changing environment of twentieth century society." Likewise, Kenneth Davis (1969a, 1969b), Anthony Downs (1967), Gary Bryner (1987), and D. Roderick Kiewiet and Mathew McCubbins (1991) argued that bureaucratic discretion is needed in a modern society. In addition, Joseph Harris (1965) argued that discretion is useful since Congress does not possess the detailed expertise of the bureaucracy. Robert Kagan (1980) and Eugene Bardach and Kagan (1982) argued that bureaucratic discretion provides needed flexibility in the regulatory process. And

Susan Hunter and Richard Waterman (1992; see also Hunter, Waterman, and Wright 1993) argued that the level of bureaucratic discretion is dependent on an agency's regulatory task; some agencies therefore require greater discretion than others. Thus, scholars continue to disagree over the amount of policymaking discretion that should be granted to the bureaucracy.

The second normative controversy concerns whether a purely top-down model of political-bureaucratic relations is really appropriate. In an age of highly technical problems, it may not make much sense for all policymaking to be the exclusive domain of legislators. They are generalists who lack the information and ability to resolve many problems through law. Along these lines, Hugh Heclo (1975) and Terry Moe (1985) have argued the relative merits of "neutral" versus "responsive competence" in the bureaucracy. In other words, do elected officials derive a greater benefit from bureaucrats who are purely responsive or from bureaucrats who share the officials' expertise in the policymaking arena? Those favoring neutral competence believe that the role of politics in administration should be limited, whereas those favoring responsive competence believe that political processes benefit from a bureaucracy that plays a more active role.

The bureaucracy may also perform a representational function in the policy process by reflecting the law and past winning democratic coalitions. If past majorities are important, then the bureaucracy should not be fully subservient to legislative policymakers until law is changed. Of course, stable institutions and effective policy implementation require that some weight be given to past majorities. If policy implementation was *super*sensitive to every whim of pluralist democracy, then little would ever get done in the American system. Majorities come and go from year to year, but policy should have at least some stability until they are sufficiently strong to alter the institutional bias. If one accepts any of these arguments, then a purely top-down model of democracy is seemingly dysfunctional.

The third normative controversy concerns the respective roles of Congress and the president in directing administrative policymaking. The politics-administration dichotomy argues for a strict constitutional interpretation of legislative supremacy, but some scholars have argued for a stronger executive role in administrative policymaking. In recent years some scholars have also argued for congressional dominance, claiming that the legislature has the most legitimate claim to directing administrative policymaking because of the Constitution. These scholars have demonstrated congressional influence on bureaucratic outputs through empirical evidence (e.g., Weingast and Moran 1983; McCubbins and Schwarz

1984). However, they have been unable to demonstrate that congressional influence is pervasive in U.S. bureaucracy or that it should be.

Others have suggested that the presidency also has a legitimate claim to directing administrative policymaking through the evolution of institutions (e.g., Moe 1989). The Constitution gave the president the authority to "faithfully execute" the laws, but this power was limited by congressional approval of laws, appropriations, and appointments. What is unclear is whether the Constitution is an evolving document that through reinterpretation has resulted in a modern presidential ability to *independently* alter established policy.

Those who believe that the presidency is now a legitimate policymaking institution note that modern society has seen the presidency evolve to meet the requisites of the office. Congress has also evolved by delegating much of its policymaking authority to the bureaucracy and much of its budgetary and reorganization authority to the president. A large White House staff helps the president make policy and direct the bureaucracy. Congress is a more diverse and fragmented institution than the presidency, so the principle of unity of command means that the presidency is better suited to direct the bureaucracy. Of course, both Congress and the presidency are democratic institutions, but the president often represents a broader constituency. Such representation implies administrative policymaking in the general interest rather than the particularistic interests of subunits of Congress. Thus, the presidency has developed into a policymaking institution that competes with Congress for control of the bureaucracy, primarily because it is better suited to the task.

All three of these controversies are ongoing and will not end with this book. However, the empirical evidence presented in the next few chapters may help resolve some of the issues. The question of how much politics there should be in administration cannot be answered definitively because it involves a value judgment. However, this book does provide evidence on how much politics there actually is in administration and how politics in administration affects policy outputs. Such knowledge should help in making a more informed judgment on where to draw the line between politics and administration.

Concerning the advisability of a purely top-down model of political control, Chapter 3 provides examples of agencies in which a purely top-down model of political control seemingly operated without impediment. However, Chapter 5 contains examples of clear bottom-up effects. The empirical evidence presented in these chapters facilitates the making of an informed judgment on the relative merits of neutral competence versus responsive competence in the administrative process. Such knowledge therefore informs the debate over top-down versus interactive models of bureaucratic democracy.

Concerning congressional or presidential dominance, Chapter 3 shows that the president was dominant over Congress in controlling the bureaucracy throughout most of the 1980s. Thus, the implications of executive dominance for good government are made clear through examination of the historical record. The evidence presented here does not settle the normative debate, but it does give evidence on the efficacy of presidential dominance for effective democratic representation.

EMPIRICAL CONTROVERSIES
OVER POLITICS AND THE BUREAUCRACY

Academics do not often disagree over whether there is politics in administration, just over whether there should be and how much. As a factual matter, it is widely accepted that administrators are now policymakers, as is the president. There is politics in administration, but academics do not always agree on the form that it takes. Several theories try to explain empirically the forms of political-bureaucratic interaction; that is, they purport to explain how and to what extent bureaucracies adapt to changing political conditions.

One issue concerning the form of political-bureaucratic adaptation is *who*, if anyone, controls bureaucracies. In other words, does the bureaucratic process respond to elite influence, pluralist influence, or neither of these? Since the early 1950s the dominant paradigm, still prevalent in some academic circles, has been that the bureaucratic process is dominated by a triumvirate of policy actors: in its simplest form, an interest group, a bureaucracy, and a congressional committee that oversees the agency.[3] This is the so-called iron triangle, subsystem, or capture theory, to highlight some of the various labels that have been applied to this alleged phenomenon throughout the years.

The idea that bureaucratic politics is dominated by interest groups is not new. It was expressed as early as 1936 by E. Pendleton Herring.[4] Ernest Griffith (1939) also wrote of political "whirlpools," and Phillip Selznick (1949) described the powerful effect that interest groups exerted over the Tennessee Valley Authority. It was not until the early 1950s, however, that the elite-based iron triangle and capture theories became the dominant paradigm in the bureaucratic literature. A central premise of both theories was that politics served the needs of the subsystem's participants rather than the public interest. As Samuel Huntington (1952: 498) wrote in his detailed historical analysis of the Interstate Commerce Commission, the ICC had come to accept "'the public interest' and the 'railroad interest' as synonymous terms."

According to Lawrence Dodd and Richard Schott (1979: 103), the basic idea of these elite-based models is that members of Congress craft legislation favorable to interest groups, encourage agencies to render similarly favorable decisions, and use congressional staff to reduce red tape and other obstacles. In return, interest groups help individual legislators in their reelection bids. Interest groups also cater to agencies, which in turn help both the interest groups (by handing down favorable decisions) and legislators (by allowing them to take credit for agency actions). In return, agencies receive higher budgetary allocations and increased authority.[5]

In this elite-oriented process, the president, Congress (considered as a whole, as opposed to its individual committees and subcommittees), and the courts are assumed to be outside of the policymaking loop. It is further assumed that the president and Congress will intercede only on rare occasions and that the courts, which defer to the greater expertise of the bureaucracy, will be even less likely to intervene. Thus, the iron triangle and capture theories posit that bureaucracies are unresponsive to the major U.S. institutional actors, which are uninterested in or incapable of controlling the bureaucracy. What is striking about these theories is that a diverse group of authors from a wide range of academic disciplines and ideological perspectives have all advanced similar ideas (see, e.g., Huntington 1952; Bernstein 1955; Freeman 1955; Kolko 1963, 1965; Cater 1964; McConnell 1966; Downs 1967; Kohlmeier 1969; Fellmeth 1970; Stigler 1971, 1975; Lowi 1979; MacAvoy 1979).

However, not all scholars agreed with the elite-based model. Charles Morgan (1953) criticized Huntington's analysis of the ICC as one-sided, but was largely ignored by his contemporaries. Richard Posner (1974), Barry Mitnick (1980), Wilson (1980), Paul Quirk (1981), William Gormley (1982, 1983), and Waterman (1989) also provided criticisms of the elite-based model. Other scholars agreed with the basic premises of the elite-based model, but then contended that they were evidence of a pluralist process gone wrong. For example, Lowi (1979) argued that "interest group liberalism" proved that pluralism had failed. Likewise, Douglas Cater (1964) recommended that the administrative state be controlled by a governing elite rather than by the various iron triangles dominating the bureaucratic process.

Most of the empirical analyses that accompanied these theories relied heavily on historical commentaries and normative polemics, not on hard empirical evidence. However, the elite-based models were subjected to a "real-world" empirical test during the 1970s. The deregulation movement of the 1970s challenged one of the theory's basic premises, namely, that regulatory agencies serve the interests of the regulated clientele, not the public interest.[6] The theory could not stand up to the empirical test.

In one industry after another, regulatory agencies aggressively promoted deregulation (see Brown 1987; Waterman 1989: Chapter 4). As Martha Derthick and Quirk (1985: 91–92) wrote, "Prevailing theories of 'capture,' which purported to explain the pro-industry bias of regulatory agencies, could not account for, let alone predict, this development." Likewise, the active participation of the president and Congress in the deregulation movement raised serious questions about the other assumptions of the subsystem models. Had the deregulation movement been confined to one or two agencies, it might easily have been dismissed as a mere exception to a larger rule. But the deregulation movement was broadly based, involving numerous agencies and regulated industries.

As a result of this challenge, new permutations of the subsystem model emerged that allowed for participation by the president, Congress, and various other policy participants (see, e.g., Heclo 1978; Kingdon 1983; Sabatier and Pelkey 1987). These new models relied on such concepts as "issue networks," "policy communities," and "advocacy coalitions" to explain away the obvious permeability of policy subsystems to external influence. However, these models did not assign a primary role to institutional actors. Although many scholars continued to employ the subsystems framework, a new emphasis in the literature also developed. Scholars turned their attention to the more pluralist idea of overhead democracy.

The idea that elected officials, such as the president and members of Congress, are integral participants in the bureaucratic process is anathema to the earlier literature, which emphasized lower-level actors. Although Charles Hyneman (1950) had proposed overhead democracy as a cure for the rapid expansion of the bureaucracy, few scholars believed that it was possible. For example, Emmette Redford (1969: 48) wrote, "The ability of overhead political institutions to prescribe is limited, not only by the complexities of interests pressing for continuous representation through established roles, but also by the complexities of organization itself." Likewise, Randall Ripley and Grace Franklin (1986: 41) wrote that

> governmental bureaucracies are not fully controlled by any superior. The structure of the Constitution—both written and unwritten—is such that they are free to bargain over their own preferences. They have some accountability to Congress and the president, but it is not final. ... This is not a fact to be unthinkably deplored or applauded. But it is a fact that is central to our understanding the behavior of bureaucracy in the United States.

Most scholars believed that overhead democracy could never be achieved, though there were a few exceptions (e.g., Rourke 1984; Wilson 1989; Aberbach 1990). The reason, firmly held, was that neither Congress nor the president had either the interest or the necessary political clout to control the bureaucracy. For example, from the early 1940s, when the congressional oversight literature first began to develop, scholars held little hope that congressional oversight would prove to be an effective tool for enforcing bureaucratic accountability (see Huzar 1942; White 1945; Galloway 1946, 1951). In the decades to follow, this became the dominant scholarly view. For example, Seymour Scher (1960) wrote that members of Congress were more concerned with satisfying electorates than with overseeing the bureaucracy. Likewise, Harris (1965) argued that Congress had limited ability to control the bureaucracy. Dodd and Schott (1979: 173) wrote, "The highly dispersed nature of oversight responsibility, the lack of strong central oversight committees, and the natural conflict among committees all undermine severely the ability of Congress to conduct serious, rational control of administration." More recently, Bryner (1987: 74) wrote, "There are few incentives for members of Congress to invest much time in oversight of agency rule making and other actions." Many other distinguished scholars also criticized the quality and effectiveness of congressional oversight (e.g., Bibby and Davidson 1972; Ogul 1976, 1981; Katzman 1980a, 1980b; Sundquist 1981). In addition, Aaron Wildavsky (1964) and Richard Fenno (1966), noting the incremental nature of the budgetary process, argued that budgets held out limited potential for political control of the bureaucracy. And Lowi (1979: 307) wrote, "Little in the political science literature is clearer than the analysis of Congress showing the shortcomings of efforts to gain administrative accountability through legislative oversight and through the development of legislative intent."

Most scholars also agreed that presidents were incapable of controlling the bureaucracy. For example, Roger Noll (1971: 36) wrote, "Although the president could exercise authority ... there is little evidence that he or his administration makes much of an attempt to do so." Dodd and Schott (1979: 42) added, "The potential for control offered by the power of appointment ... is seldom fulfilled." Bryner (1987: 66) observed, "Presidents have generally had little continued interest in the appointment of individuals to regulatory agencies." These views were shared by such notable presidential scholars as Clinton Rossiter (1956), Fenno (1959), Louis Koenig (1975), and Thomas Cronin (1980) as well as such institutional scholars as Heclo (1977), Barry Weingast and Mark Moran (1983) and Herbert Kaufman (1981).

In comparison to Congress and the president, much less was written about the courts and the bureaucracy. The few studies that did focus on the courts, however, generally agreed that the courts were not effective in securing political control. For example, Peter Woll (1963: 109–110) stated that the "courts have retreated from exercising meaningful oversight." Lowi (1979) recommended more vigilant oversight of congressional legislation by the courts and a return to spirit of the *Schecter* case. Given the views of scholars on the effectiveness of Congress, the presidency, and the courts on controlling the bureaucracy, the clear implication was that overhead democracy was not a feasible option.

THE PRINCIPAL-AGENT MODEL

By 1980 the dominant academic paradigm describing the relation between politics and the bureaucracy was very similar to the popular perceptions discussed in Chapter 1. Most scholars viewed the bureaucracy as a plodding behemoth resistant to change and beyond political control. However, during the early 1980s a new framework emerged called principal-agent theory or, more simply, agency theory. Agency theory explicitly assumed that elected officials (principals), such as the president and members of Congress, had political incentives to control the bureaucracy (agents). Unlike the earlier writings on bureaucracy, which were historical studies based on subjective assessments, most of the agency theory literature was based on hard quantitative evidence. Across a wide range of empirical analyses, scholars demonstrated that elected officials could and did exert control over the bureaucracy.[7] These findings contrasted sharply with themes from the earlier literature.

What is most impressive about these studies is that, unlike the earlier bureaucratic literature, where questions were posed, debated, but rarely answered, in this newly emerging tradition clear and consistent findings emerged. Quantifiable outputs from bureaucracies were shown to covary consistently with the changing preferences of the president, Congress, and the courts. And overhead democracy was shown to be alive and well in the United States.

The principal-agent models underlying most of these studies originated among economists who studied relations between business managers and their employees or contractors (see Moe 1984 for a detailed review of the economics literature; see also Mitnick 1980). These formal models were intended to evaluate the conditions under which managerial efficiency could be obtained through increased employee tendencies to work but not shirk. However, they also soon came to be viewed as applicable to relations between public managers, who are often elected, and their employees in the bureaucracy, who are often tenured.

Like the normative politics-administration dichotomy discussed earlier, agency theory posits that the relationship between elected leaders (principals) and nonelective bureaucracies (agents) is hierarchical. Bureaucracies are bound by contract to serve the law and elected institutions. Concerning this contractual relationship, Charles Perrow (1986: 224) wrote, "In its simplest form, agency theory assumes that social life is a series of contracts. Conventionally, one member, the 'buyer' of the goods or services, is designated the 'principal,' and the other, who provides the goods or service, is the 'agent'—hence the term 'agency theory.' The principal-agent relationship is governed by a contract specifying what the agent should do and what the principal must do in return."

The principal seeks to manipulate and shape the behavior of the agent to perform work in a manner consistent with the principal's preferences. The contractual arrangement is one tool for accomplishing this end. However, the problem is that over time disjunctures develop between the interests of politicians (principals) and the bureaucracy (agents). In the arrangement between politicians and the bureaucracy, political coalitions change from those that existed when legislative institutions first adopted the policies. Likewise, bureaucracies develop separate interests through institutionalization and changing external relationships. Thus, a potentially confrontational setting develops in which the goals and objectives of principals and those of agents are often at odds.

Politicians seek to alter established policy toward their preferred objectives, which may not be the same as those of the original legislation or past political coalitions. However, bureaucracies are bound by past coalitions and legislation, which puts them at odds with current officials. Additionally, bureaucratic interests may diverge through time from the original policy to the extent that bureaucracies develop expertise and constituencies that put them at odds with the original policy. Either way shirking occurs from demands for stability or change by current officials and/or from past statutory mandates.

Agency theory posits a process of interaction between principals and agents that is dynamic, evolving through time. Throughout this process, bureaucracies have distinct informational and expertise advantages over politicians. They understand the policy and the organizational procedures required to implement it. As a result, they have both the opportunity and incentive to manipulate politicians and processes for political gain (see, e.g., Niskanen 1971). For some policies, especially those of a technical nature, bureaucracies are more certain about organizational needs, so politicians are reluctant to intervene. The key question for agency theory, then, is how politicians vested with contemporaneous legitimacy can overcome these uncertainties and the bureaucratic tendency to shirk.

The information asymmetry between the principal and the agent is at the heart of this question. So is uncertainty by the bureaucracy about the intentions of the politician. As Perrow (1986: 224) observed "The principal-agent model is [thus] fraught with the problems of cheating, limited information, and bounded rationality in general." Hence, if the preferences of principals and agents diverge, if there is uncertainty between actors, and if the agent has a distinct information advantage, then the probability of shirking increases. Under these circumstances, the principal must reduce uncertainty by acquiring needed information.

Although the language of agency theory may seem rather abstract and foreign to some political scientists and public administration scholars, the notions of deception, cheating, limited information, and bounded rationality are certainly not new to these disciplines (see, e.g., Simon 1947; Lindblom 1959). For example, U.S. budgetary processes have long been characterized as involving these same features (see, e.g., Wildavsky 1964; Fenno 1966). Bureaucracies often employ budgetary deception by submitting an inflated request to the president for the purpose of obtaining increased resources. Presidents cut those budget requests based on "satisficing decisionmaking rules," but they may also send inflated (or, more recently, deflated) budget requests to Congress for purposes of strategy and bargaining. Congress also operates under conditions of uncertainty and assumes that both the president and bureaucracy are cheating. The process of budgeting as described by mainstream political science and public administration, then, obviously involves all of the preceding elements of agency theory.

Two other important elements are also relevant to agency theory. These are the dual concepts of moral hazard and adverse selection. According to Y. Kotowitz (1989), "Moral hazard may be defined as actions of economic agents in maximizing their own utility to the detriment of others, in situations where they do not bear the full consequences of their actions due to uncertainty and incomplete or restricted contracts which prevent the assignment of full damages (benefits) to the agent responsible." Some party to the principal-agent agreement is often at risk because of hidden information or deception by the other party. For the sake of clarity, consider an example of moral hazard: An insurance company (the agent) may be at risk of selling a life insurance policy to an individual (the principal) with a fatal disease if that individual fails to report the condition. This constitutes a moral hazard for the agent and should be taken into account when the contract is made. The problem is that the hazard often is not reported.

Adverse selection arises from the nonobservability of the information, beliefs, and values on which contractual decisions are based. In particular, a principal can never fully know the attributes of the agent chosen to do a particular job. Adverse selection occurs when the principal makes an error in selecting the agent. In the extreme, adverse selection can refer to the possibility that the principal might select an agent that takes payment but fails to live up to the terms of the agreement. If we use the insurance company example again, the insurance company (the agent) might fail to pay off, even though the client (the principal) has fulfilled the terms of the contract. Thus, both parties to the principal-agent agreement are at risk in the typical relationship.

How, then, can the goal of controlling the bureaucracy be accomplished, according to agency theory? The answer is that control is possible because elected principals create bureaucracies. They design these bureaucracies with various incentive structures to facilitate effective control (McCubbins, Noll, and Weingast 1989). Many of these incentive structures operate automatically and independently of specific actions taken by the principal. In addition, political principals also monitor the activities of their bureaucratic agents. Such monitoring is both active and continual, often triggered by a system of alarms (McCubbins and Schwartz 1984). When bureaucratic activities stray from the principal's preferences, policymakers can then apply sanctions or rewards to bring agents back into line. Thus, agency theory is dynamic, positing that well-informed central decisionmakers systematically mold the preferences of bureaucratic agents through time.

Agency theory clearly posits that overhead democracy is possible in the United States. It is possible for elected officials, such as the president and members of Congress, to keep a watchful eye on the bureaucracy. The central role that agency theory assigns to hierarchy obviously differentiates it from past theories of the bureaucratic process. Whereas the iron triangle and capture theories assumed that elected principals were passive and ineffectual participants in the bureaucratic process, agency theory posits that they are active participants with firmly held policy preferences. Hierarchical control is therefore not only possible but is also the ultimate goal of political principals in the bureaucratic process.

Agency theory differs from much of the existing literature in its emphasis on hierarchy, but its assumptions regarding the role of the bureaucratic agent are not radically different from those of past bureaucratic theory. For example, public administrators have long posited that bureaucrats possess distinct information advantages. Max Weber wrote, "Under normal conditions, the power position of a fully developed bureaucracy is always overtowering. The 'political master' finds himself in a position of the 'dilettante' who stands opposite the 'expert,' facing the trained official who stands within the management of administration" (Gerth and Mills 1946: 232). Similarly Rourke (1984: 15) wrote that the "knowledge that agencies acquire by continuous attention to particular functions puts them in an especially advantageous position to influence policy when the facts they gather cannot be subject to independent verification or disproof."

Public administrators have also examined the tendency of bureaucrats to shirk. For example, James March and Herbert Simon (1958) evaluated organizations as a collection of rational individuals who calculate their self-interest first with regard to whether they should join a particular organization and then with regard to whether they will work or shirk. And Rourke (1984: 102) wrote, "The personal goals of agency employees may gain a distinct priority over the actual purposes for which an organization was created. Public organizations and officials are often in a position to justify their pursuit of power on the basis of disinterested criteria like service to the public, when in fact power is sought only to advance the selfish interests of the organization's members." Thus, agency theory and past bureaucratic theory both enable conceptualizations of the bureaucracy as resistant to change. The major difference is that agency theory postulates a more active role in these relations for political principals.

CONCLUSION

Chapter 1 discussed the popular view of bureaucracy as a nonadaptive or very slowly changing entity. According to typical citizen reactions, bureaucratic procedures and insular behavior often conflict with public values and the democratic principles of responsiveness and accountability. Such negative views by citizens of the bureaucracy cause doubts about the legitimacy of U.S. institutions. The bureaucracy is diminished by the low public esteem held for public service. Elected institutions are diminished in the eyes of the public by their impotence in enforcing bureaucratic accountability and responsiveness. And the Constitution is diminished because its most important principles are violated.

This chapter has observed that some scholars reach similar conclusions about the bureaucracy based on subjective accounts and normative polemics. Proponents of elite theory claim that the bureaucracy serves small segments of the public against the general interest. The constitutional branches of government—the president, Congress, and the courts—are outside the policymaking loop when subsystems, iron triangles, or captures operate to determine public policy. In short, U.S. democracy is dysfunctional because modern government serves particularistic interests rather than the public interest.

However, recent empirical studies suggest a more positive view of bureaucracy in the U.S. system. According to these studies, bureaucracies are indeed adaptive entities that play a role in the democratic process. Agency theory can be used to describe empirically the interactions between bureaucracies and elected institutions in considerable detail.

As Rourke (1984: 1) wrote, "The belief that power in the modern state has come increasingly to be centered in the corridors of bureaucracy is more often asserted or assumed than examined." The recent movement, guided by agency theory, toward an empirical analysis of the bureaucracy provides a basis for challenging many of the existing assumptions about the nature of the bureaucratic process. It also provides a basis for evaluating the many conflicting claims that have been advanced in the literature on bureaucracy. This framework is used throughout the next three chapters to explain the dynamics of political-bureaucratic adaptation for eight different federal agencies.

3

The Dynamics of Political Control of the Bureaucracy

Throughout the 1980s theories of political control of the bureaucracy underwent extraordinary change. This change involved movement away from a paradigm emphasizing that U.S. elected institutions were impotent in directing a massive and lumbering federal bureaucracy to one emphasizing that elected leaders can and do shape bureaucratic behavior in systematic ways. In part this change resulted from the deregulation movement of the 1970s and the subsequent election of a Republican president and Senate in 1980. History demonstrated that political control was possible when the Carter and Reagan administrations seemingly changed many programs. Equally important, however, was social science's development of new tools for evaluating the extent of political control of the bureaucracy. Scholars increasingly viewed the control problem as an economic one involving manipulation of microlevel incentives and constraints. They also used dynamic empirical methods to examine the substance of political-bureaucratic relations.

This chapter and the next two use such methods to evaluate bureaucratic adaptation by eight different federal agencies in response to multiple political stimuli.[1] The findings discussed in this chapter are consistent with recent empirical research on assorted agencies showing that overhead democracy is possible and that bureaucracies do respond to external politics in systematic ways. The findings also run counter to existing literature that asserts that bureaucracy is unresponsive and uncontrollable. Since the sample of agencies is large, the results demonstrate the scope of political influence over bureaucracies. The main purpose of this chapter, however, is to show the causal mechanisms of political control across multiple agencies: *how* political control occurs and what preliminary evidence exists on the relative importance of various political tools (i.e., appointments, budgets, reorganizations, oversight, and legislation). Chapter 4 provides additional evidence on this matter for a single agency, the Environmental Protection Agency. The findings from this study increase scientific knowledge of bureaucracy and democracy. They are also useful in assuring official accountability and in developing monitoring and feedback systems for future democratic control, a subject examined in more detail in Chapters 6 and 7.

THEORIES OF POLITICAL CONTROL

As was noted in the last chapter, before the 1980s most research on political-bureaucratic relations was qualitative, seldom considering actual covariations between political stimuli and measurable bureaucratic outputs. The politics-administration dichotomy, which was the dominant paradigm in the public administration literature until well into the 1940s, dispensed a priori with any possibility of political influence on the bureaucratic state. During the 1950s and 1960s the iron triangle and capture theories, while acknowledging that politics was important, argued that the policy loop excluded major political actors, most notably the president. He was perceived as a disinterested bystander with limited influence. Similarly, the congressional literature described difficulties with legislative control mechanisms.

Qualitative assessments before the 1980s saw neither the presidency nor Congress as an effective institution for central control of the bureaucracy. Two developments led to a change in this perception: an economic theory of political-bureaucratic relations, agency theory, and a growing body of empirical support for that theory. The previous chapter cited several studies that found evidence suggestive of political manipulation of the bureaucracy.

However, despite the broad scope of these studies, the evidence on political manipulation remains indefinite, with many questions still unanswered. What is the *scope* of political control of the bureaucracy? Is it limited to the few agencies examined by past research, or does it pervade the larger U.S. bureaucracy? What are the *causal mechanisms* of political control? Does it occur passively through institutional design or actively through manipulation of agency leadership, resources, personnel, or structure? A related concern is the *relative effectiveness* of tools for political control. Are political appointments, budgets, structure, personnel powers, or oversight most important in affecting bureaucratic responsiveness?[2]

The answers to these questions are important for ascertaining the legitimacy of the bureaucratic state as well as whether bureaucratic government is consistent with the Constitution. Additionally, there is another constitutional issue at stake concerning who should make policy for the bureaucracy. If one democratic principal, say the president, is more effective than others, then we might ask whether it is appropriate for policy implementation to reflect executive preferences over those of Congress or the courts. The principle of legislative supremacy suggests that Congress should make policy and that the president should execute it. Some would argue, though certainly not without opposition, that Congress reflects the public will better than the president does because of decentralized constituencies and more frequent elections. In either case, knowing the mechanisms of political control would reveal the relative capacity of democratic institutions to control policy. Rational political control requires knowing how to manipulate the available instruments. Also, agencies may differ in their responsiveness based on certain design criteria. Future policy direction and design would therefore benefit from improved understanding of the characteristics producing bureaucratic stability or responsiveness. Such knowledge would allow normative debate of constitutional issues to occur in the light of empirical evidence rather than in the darkness of speculation.

PAST RESEARCH

This book is the first to examine outputs from many different agencies in a comparative context for determining political control of the bureaucracy. However, it is not the first to suggest how political control occurs. Institutional scholars offer various explanations for political-bureaucratic responsiveness.

Congressional Control

Some congressional scholars assert that legislators are the most important actors since bureaucrats continually watch the rewards and sanctions flowing from Congress. These same scholars suggest, however, that congressional control is difficult to observe since the mechanisms are automatic and indirect (Calvert, Moran, and Weingast 1987; Calvert, McCubbins, and Weingast 1989; Bendor, Taylor, and Van Gaalen 1987). Congress designs agency structure and incentives to assure a relation between legislative preferences and bureaucratic outputs (McCubbins 1985). Additionally, legislators find it more efficient under time constraints to monitor bureaucratic performance indirectly rather than directly through oversight hearings. That is, legislators rely on program recipients, lobbyists, and interest groups to supply information on agency performance (McCubbins and Schwartz 1984). Should discontinuities occur between legislative preferences and bureaucratic activities, Congress controls resources, legislation, and appointments. Bureaucracies are aware of this and cautiously try to avoid alienating legislative principals. Thus, Congress does not have to engage in active and continual oversight to effect political control. Rather, "anticipative responses" by bureaucracies assure that administrative decisions are consistent with congressional preferences.

Past efforts to model congressional influence confirm the elusiveness of congressional control mechanisms. For example, many studies have considered the effect of committee ideology on bureaucratic performance, with mixed results. Typically, these studies have measured ideology as an index derived from ratings by interest groups (e.g., Americans for Democratic Action, the Chamber of Commerce, the League of Conservation Voters). Using this measure, Weingast and Moran (1983), John Chubb (1985), and Moe (1985) found that ideology scores relate systematically to hypothesized agency outputs. However, John Scholz and Feng Wei (1986) and Marc Eisner and Kenneth Meier (1990) found no effect from committee ideology.

The measure of ideology used in these studies—interest group ratings—is troublesome for discerning the mechanisms of congressional control. For one thing, these ratings do not reflect specific legislative stimuli but are simply an annual average of past mostly voting records. They are not really even annual since the scores change each biennium. Thus, ideology scores lack the spatial or temporal resolution to determine how Congress controls the bureaucracy. Additionally, there are collinearity issues associated with congressional ideology scores. When Congress changes, so do the parts of Congress (see, e.g., Cook and Wood 1989). Thus, it is impossible to determine whether bureaucratic responses are due to the entire body, one or more oversight committees, or a multiplicity of forces in the environment of an agency.

Presidential Control

Presidential studies are less nebulous about why bureaucracies respond to the chief executive. According to Moe (1985; see also Nathan 1983; Waterman 1989), the key mechanism of executive control is the appointment and removal power. Modern presidents select political leaders not only for their expertise, and to reward supporters, but also for their ability to administer the president's plan. The Reagan presidency more than any other epitomized the use of political appointments to effect political control. The Reagan transition team spent months screening those who would serve, emphasizing loyalty and ideology above all other attributes (Pfiffner 1988).

Political appointments are important to the modern presidency, but there are also other tools a president can use to achieve political ends. Through the Office of Management and Budget (OMB), a president has the initiative in controlling the resources of most agencies. The OMB also monitors the activities of bureaucracies, both their efficiency and compatibility with the president's program. Through regulatory review (via such executive orders as 12291 and 12498) and the Paperwork Reduction Act of 1980, the OMB has centralized the rulemaking process (Fuchs 1988). Although the overall effect of these powers is difficult to assess, severe constraints now obviously exist on the independent policymaking ability of the federal bureaucracy.

The president also affects bureaucratic performance through other channels. Using personnel authority resulting from the Civil Service Reform Act of 1978, the president can choose senior career executives for compatibility with an agenda. He can use reductions in force or transfers to adjust lower bureaucratic levels. The president can also reorganize a wayward bureaucracy by centralizing control to administration loyalists. All of these powers sum to an unambiguous ability of the chief executive to shape policy.

The multiple tools of the presidency for controlling the bureaucracy can produce a complex pattern of responses through time. Yet past efforts to model presidential effects with empirical methods were simplistic and unconcerned with capturing this dynamic. The typical analysis used annual data with indicator variables switching on at the first or second year of a presidency to represent all executive effects (e.g., Stewart and Cromartie 1982; Chubb 1985; Scholz and Wei 1986; Scicchitano, Hedge, and Metz 1991; Eisner and Meier 1990). The use of annual data and indicator variables is problematic. Annual data cannot distinguish among the many stimuli that occur early in a presidency. Change can result from appointments, budget changes, reorganizations, congressional effects, or other factors, all occurring at different times. Furthermore, it is incorrect to assume that change in executive influence occurs during only one year of a presidency. Indicator variables so designed may only account for variance but not truly explain it. Clearly, a more complex specification with finely divided data is needed to reveal the underlying dynamic of political-bureaucratic relations.[3]

METHODS AND DATA

This study differs from previous research on political-bureaucratic relations in that the designated purpose is to reveal the scope and specific mechanisms of political control. The research employs an explicitly causal logic, considering both the timing and covariation between independent political events and bureaucratic responses. Qualitative methods are integrated with quasiexperimental time-series analysis. That is, particular events that should have caused change in bureaucratic outputs are identified beforehand through archive searches and/or elite interviews. The characteristics of the events, including the timing, magnitude, and direction of the stimulus, are defined. That the events caused change in related outputs from public bureaucracies at time t or t+n is then put forward as a hypothesis. Box-Tiao (1975) impact assessment methods are used to test the hypotheses. Given a statistically significant response from an event, qualitative methods are used to search for alternative explanations to the observed stimulus-response relationships. The types of events considered are political appointments, resignations, budget increases and decreases, congressional oversight hearings, administrative reorganizations, legislation, and political signals that should produce anticipative responses. Agency outputs include various core regulatory enforcements such as litigations, sanctions, and administrative decisions. (See the Appendix for a fuller discussion of the methodology.)

The sample of agencies included in this analysis consists of the ICC, the EEOC, the FTC, the NRC, the FDA, the NHTSA, the OSM, and the EPA. Time series of agency outputs were obtained through Freedom of Information Act requests. The sample was not random but was selected to maximize differences among agencies in organizational design. Four of the agencies are independent regulatory commissions, and four are executive-branch agencies. The EPA is an independent executive-branch agency. All of the agencies implement regulatory policies (regulatory agencies were selected because outputs from such programs are easy to measure). The agencies differ considerably in administrative discretion, constituency, issue salience, complexity of implementation technology, and organizational esprit. Although the sample was shaped somewhat by which agencies were willing to supply data in the form requested, the reported results are generalizable to the entire federal bureaucracy.

One feature of the data distinguishes this study from previous research. Unlike most past studies that relied on annual data, these data consist of finely divided time intervals, enabling us to explore the underlying dynamic of bureaucratic responses to political events. Most dependent series are monthly observations, but when such data were not available, we relied on quarterly measures. The fine temporal resolution of the data allowed us to establish a much closer correspondence between the timing of political events and subsequent bureaucratic responses. In most cases bureaucratic responses occurred in the same month or the month following a political event. We consider this timing to be strong evidence of causal connections between the application of political tools and subsequent changes in bureaucratic performance.[4]

STUDIES IN POLITICAL CONTROL

The scope and mechanisms of political control of the bureaucracy can be illustrated by the following selected findings from the study.

The Interstate Commerce Commission

The ICC is the nation's oldest independent regulatory commission. Established on February 4, 1887, to regulate railroads involved in interstate transportation, the ICC was initially an agency within the Interior Department. Congress soon reestablished it as an independent regulatory commission following the election in 1888 of President Benjamin Harrison, a strong supporter of railroad interests. In so doing, Congress's clear intent was to limit presidential influence over commission activities. Although presidents were granted authority to appoint the commission's members, they were not delegated authority to remove these members from office. In addition, until 1969 presidents did not have the authority to designate the commission chair.

In 1935 Congress passed the Motor Carrier Act, thus expanding the ICC's focus to include regulation of the trucking industry. Enacted at the peak of the Great Depression, this legislation was explicitly designed *to restrict market entry and protect existing carriers from excessive competition.* The law specified that for an operating certificate to be issued, a new prospective carrier had to demonstrate that it was both fit and able to provide the proposed service. Applicants also had to prove that the service would satisfy a "public need," meaning that no other existing carrier could provide the same service. Operating under the provisions of the 1935 act, the ICC issued only limited numbers of new operating certificates over the next forty years. This occurred despite the fact that the Depression had long ago ended and that more certificates would have provided greater public benefit through a larger choice of carriers and lower market prices.

From 1935 to 1977 the ICC was a quintessential example of what scholars of government regulation have called agency "capture" (e.g., Huntington 1952; Stigler 1975; Moore 1978). With the election of President Carter, however, an effort was begun to deregulate the transportation industry. In accordance with these goals, Carter appointed A. Daniel O'Neal and, later, Darius Gaskins to chair the commission. These appointees initiated various administrative reforms intended to loosen ICC procedures for issuing new operating certificates. The administration also proposed legislation that would make the changes permanent. On July 1, 1980, the president signed into law a new motor carrier act that codified many of the ICC's earlier administrative reforms.

The Motor Carrier Act of 1980 represented a major break with past legislative intent by greatly easing restrictions on entry into the protected motor carrier market. The legislation, however, represented a "fragile compromise" since it did not remove either the fitness or public need provisions delineated in the original 1935 act. That these provisions were not removed provided a potential mechanism for reregulating the trucking industry. So long as Carter and his ICC chairs were in office, entry provisions could be generously interpreted. However, this situation would soon change with the arrival of the Reagan administration.

Ronald Reagan campaigned for president in 1980 as an economic deregulator. He had also been endorsed, however, by the Teamsters Union, which was a vociferous opponent of deregulation since it encouraged fierce competition within the trucking industry and reduced the benefits derived from a protected market. On June 16, 1981, President Reagan appointed Reese Taylor as the ICC's new chair. Taylor was reputed to have close ties with the Teamsters, so his appointment may have signaled a withdrawal from the accelerated pace of deregulation that had characterized the Carter years.

In public appearances Taylor quickly distanced himself from the Carter style of deregulation. Testifying before Congress, he admitted to being neither a "regulator nor a deregulator" (U.S. House 1982b: 3). He also defended the existing fitness and public needs provisions of the 1935 and 1980 Motor Carrier acts (U.S. Senate 1981a: 70; 80–81) and advocated a slower path toward deregulation. Once in office Taylor also removed or transferred (to positions of lesser authority) individuals who had previously supported deregulation.

The year following his appointment, congressional committee members heard testimony that Taylor's ICC had abandoned the goal of deregulation. Taylor's critics argued that the ICC was issuing fewer operating certificates, and as a result the trucking industry was becoming less competitive. The stimulus for this change, critics argued, was political, an alleged reward to the Teamsters Union for support in the 1980 campaign. Taylor and other Reagan administration officials were quick to agree that the number of certificates issued by the ICC had declined during his first year in office. They did not, however, agree with their critic's contention that the stimulus for the change was political. Rather, they argued that market forces encouraged the reduction in the number of operating certificates issued. According to their argument, only so many trucking firms could profitably provide service at any one time. As the trucking market became saturated, fewer companies sought new operating authority.

Traditional oversight identified two rival explanations for the cause of trucking reregulation by the ICC after 1981. One explanation suggested that a political factor (i.e., the Taylor appointment) was the stimulus for change. The other explanation was that natural market forces (i.e., the invisible hand of competition) had limited the demand for new certificates, so fewer were being issued. Yet congressional oversight committees were unable to conclusively determine which, if either, explanation was correct.

Determining which of the two explanations was correct was important because the committees had expressed clear views on how they intended the 1980 Motor Carrier Act to be implemented. At Taylor's confirmation hearing Senator Howard Cannon (D–Nev.) explicitly warned the nominee that the Senate committee would be watching "very closely to insure that transportation legislation is implemented expeditiously." Cannon also warned that "there are strong views on this committee in favor of competition" (U.S. Senate 1981a: 2). Despite these warnings and five years of intensive hearings, the relevant House and Senate committees were unable to determine the stimulus for change in the ICC's regulatory behavior. Thus, bureaucratic accountability could not be enforced because the reason for the ICC's altered regulatory pattern could not be precisely determined.

Nevertheless, we can show empirically how the ICC responded to congressional and presidential stimuli directed at deregulating and reregulating the trucking industry. Through a Freedom of Information Act request, we obtained monthly data running from January 1980 through October 1990 on the number of operating certificates issued by the ICC. We tested two hypotheses relevant to this time series. First, the Motor Carrier Act of 1980 should have increased the number of operating certificates issued by the ICC. This change should have occurred because Congress and the Carter administration intended to bring market forces to bear through deregulating the trucking industry. Second, the Reagan administration should have reduced the number of operating certificates issued. The important question is whether the reduction in the number of certificates issued was gradual or abrupt. A gradual reduction would suggest that the post-1981 reregulation resulted from market forces. An abrupt decline coinciding with the appointment of Taylor to chair the ICC would suggest that politics, not market forces, was the reason for the reregulation of the trucking industry. Results of the statistical analysis are in Table 3.1. Graphs of the actual data and predictions of the statistical model are in Figure 3.1.

Concerning the passage of the Motor Carrier Act of 1980, the analysis shows that the new legislation accomplished its deregulatory purpose. Beginning in the same month the law was signed there was an abrupt increase in the number of operating certificates issued. The magnitude of the increase was about 300 percent from the preintervention equilibrium level. For the next twelve months the number of certificates issued in a single month ranged from a low of a little more than 2,000 to a high of about 6,000; this compared to a preintervention equilibrium level of about 1,000 certificates issued per month. Thus, as Congress and the Carter administration had intended, the Motor Carrier Act of 1980 promoted increased competition for the trucking industry.

Concerning the reasons for the post-1981 reregulation of the industry, the analysis presented in Table 3.1 and Figure 3.1 demonstrates clearly which of the two explanations was correct. Now, according to the argu-

FIGURE 3.1 The Impact of the Motor Carrier Act
and Taylor Appointment on ICC Operating Certificates Issued

TABLE 3.1: The Impact of the Motor Carrier Act and Reagan
Administration on Interstate Commerce Commission
Operating Certificates Issued

Variable	Parameter	Estimate	t-statistic
Motor Carrier Act	ω_0	1.15	9.85
Reagan Appointment	ω_0	-0.26	-4.06
	δ_1	0.76	11.49
Moving Average	θ_1	0.85	16.29

Measures of Fit

RMS (Noise Only)   0.060
RMS (Full Model)   0.039 Change = 54%
Autocorrelation of residuals   Q = 33.71 with 23. D.F.

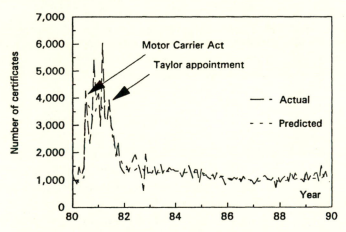

Note: The series was logged and differenced to produce variance
stationarity.   The intervention series were step inputs.   All model
parameters were significant at the 0.05 level or less.

ment advocated by Taylor and the Reagan administration, the motor carrier market could not possibly sustain the new influx of new motor carriers. Eventually market forces would produce a reduction in the number of
certificates issued. If this argument was correct, then we would expect to
see a gradual decline beginning some time after the new legislation was
enacted. What we observe, however, is that the decline in the number of

certificates issued by the ICC was abrupt, corresponding exactly with Taylor's appointment.

The statistical analysis shows that in the month following Taylor's appointment there was a 28 percent decline in the number of operating certificates issued. Furthermore, over the next several months there was a continued steady decline until a new equilibrium was reached, which was some 66 percent below the level established following the passage of the Motor Carrier Act of 1980. Of equal importance, at no point following Taylor's appointment did the number of operating certificates issued ever equal or exceed the level that had existed prior to his appointment. Taylor's appointment was the stimulus for a substantial and immediate reduction in the number of certificates issued by the ICC.

Thus, a political stimulus, not market forces, produced the change in the ICC's regulatory behavior. This knowledge is important for two reasons. First, the ICC case has substantive implications for the interpretations of the Reagan presidency. Although the Reagan presidency is widely viewed as one emphasizing economic deregulation, the ICC case shows that Reagan was actually a reregulator when there was some political benefit to be gained. The case of the ICC represents another regulatory face of Reagan, one in which he was actually an advocate of increased, not decreased, government regulation.

Second, and more relevant to our purpose, the ICC case demonstrates the extent to which an important bureaucracy was responsive/unresponsive to current congressional and executive preferences. Initially, the ICC responded consistently with institutional preferences by deregulating the trucking industry. However, institutional preferences conflicted after the 1980 election, with the president pulling in a different direction from Congress. Despite congressional warnings, Taylor did not enforce the 1980 legislation in a manner consistent with congressional intentions. If Congress had had the capacity to show this during the early 1980s, then it could have taken remedial action. It lacked such an effective monitoring mechanism, however, and as a result both the bureaucracy and executive remained unaccountable.

As this case demonstrates, the president was not accountable to Congress, which, according to the Constitution, is the nation's chief policymaker through the lawmaking power. The president as chief administrator moved policy and the bureaucracy in a direction that was inconsistent with past and current legislative preferences. Furthermore, reregulation of the trucking industry was probably not consistent with citizen preferences, broadly conceived. Certainly many teamsters voted for Reagan in the 1980 election, but they made up only a small proportion of the electorate. Most citizens perceived the new president as a deregulator, not a reregulator. Thus, policy moved in a direction that was wholly inconsistent with public expectations. This theme is mentioned now to emphasize the point and to better establish a theoretical rationale for the last two chapters.

The Equal Employment Opportunity Commission

The EEOC is an independent regulatory commission originally established to administer those sections of the Civil Rights Act of 1964 dealing with employment discrimination. Title 7 of that legislation made it illegal for employers to discriminate on the basis of race, color, religion, sex, or national origin. The primary tasks of the EEOC in these regards are to investigate, conciliate, and remedy complaints of employment discrimination.

Although the EEOC was created as an independent regulatory commission, from the beginning it possessed few of the attributes that could make it a strong and independent law enforcement agency. Before 1972 it had no litigation authority, with power only to negotiate, conciliate, and persuade employers to end employment discrimination. After 1972 the commission's authority was expanded through several legislative and executive actions. The Equal Employment Opportunity Act of 1972 gave the commission authority to file suits on behalf of aggrieved persons. It also guaranteed coverage to federal employees and private enterprises with as few as fifteen employees. A Carter administration reorganization in 1979 gave the commission responsibility for enforcing the Equal Pay Act of 1963, the Age Discrimination Act of 1967, parts of the Vocational Rehabilitation Act of 1973, and various executive orders. Implementation resources, however, were not expanded commensurate with this increased authority (Wood 1990).

Other attributes also suggest that the EEOC was susceptible to political manipulation. Between 1965 and 1977 there were twelve different commission chairpersons, implying that agency leadership was not a strong attribute. The agency mission is controversial, with constituency for agency programs weak at best. The technology of determining and resolving discrimination is fluid and open to interpretation relative to other implementation technologies (e.g., controlling pollution, determining worker safety, or evaluating consumer products). Public support for equal employment opportunity (EEO) is weak because, even though most citizens agree that employment discrimination is wrong, they do not always agree on what constitutes employment discrimination. The clientele served by the EEOC are voting minorities, usually from the lowest socioeconomic strata. In contrast, the goal of ending employment discrimination has economic implications that often arouse intense opposition from powerful business interests.

The early EEOC saw frequent allegations of poor fiscal management, arbitrary charge processing, and high personnel turnover rates (Bullock and Lamb 1984). By 1976 there was a charge backlog exceeding 120,000 unprocessed complaints. Average charge processing time was about two years (U.S. House 1983: 112), with many complainants becoming discouraged and dropping out before the process was completed. More recently a congressional staff report on EEOC district office operations found confusion on complaint processing procedures, little formal personnel training, low personnel morale, poor litigation support services, inadequate resources, and closed door policymaking (U.S. House 1986; see also U.S. House 1983: 35–37, 205–210).

Regulating employment discrimination is a controversial task, which suggests that politicians have motivation to manipulate agency behavior. Moreover, there are clear partisan differences about the appropriate means of remedying employment discrimination. Democrats generally favor affirmative action plans, numerical goals, and timetables, whereas Republicans tend to oppose such approaches. Accordingly, administration of the EEOC through time has reflected these differences.

In 1977 President Carter appointed Eleanor Holmes Norton to chair the commission. During her tenure Norton instituted several reforms, including the reorganization of the commission's internal structure and field offices, the development of new training programs, and the establishment of a "rapid charge processing" system for handling complaints. Additionally, the EEOC under Norton encouraged private employers to develop affirmative action plans to overcome the effects of past and present discrimination. The Norton commission favored the use of goals and timetables in the hiring of minorities and women. In 1978 the commission adopted guidelines to make clear its position that affirmative action did not constitute reverse discrimination. The preferred approach to EEO enforcement was systemic lawsuits directed at entire industries and based on statistical analysis. This was viewed as a more efficient and proactive means of addressing the discrimination problem than the case-by-case approach used by previous administrations.

In contrast, the Reagan administration took the apparent position that the Norton commission had gone beyond the original intent of the law by using such approaches. During the campaign, candidate Reagan implied that the government's affirmative action efforts were in themselves forms of reverse discrimination and that numerical goals and timetables were nothing more than quotas based on illegal criteria. Consistent with this view, President Reagan nominated individuals of a similar persuasion to lead the EEOC.

In February 1981 Reagan nominated William Bell, an African-American conservative from Detroit and a staunch Reagan supporter, to be EEOC chair. Bell was not an attorney, a qualification that had always been considered a prerequisite for being a commissioner. He also had little experience in government or management generally. Civil rights and women's groups lobbied vigorously against the Bell nomination, questioning his competence to lead the agency as well as his commitment to EEO policy. They claimed the nomination was an effort to thrust the agency back into its earlier chaotic years. After it became obvious that the Senate would not approve the nomination, the president withdrew Bell's name.

President Reagan then nominated Clarence Thomas to chair the commission, and he was confirmed by the Senate in May 1982. Thomas was also an African-American conservative who expressed reservations about class action and systemic suits based on statistical analysis (U.S. Senate 1982, 1986). He advocated an end to goals, timetables, and hiring quotas, preferring a policy of case-by-case enforcement. As a result of resignations from the commission, by October 1982 four of the five EEOC commissioners were also Reagan appointees.

The Reagan nominee to be general counsel, Michael Connolly, was equally controversial. Civil rights and women's groups strongly opposed the Connolly nomination; however, he was eminently qualified for the job. As an attorney he had represented major corporations against the government in antidiscrimination suits. The Republican Senate readily confirmed Connolly. Interestingly, soon after the confirmation he aroused further controversy by telling commission staff attorneys that he would no longer be pressing sexual harassment, age discrimination, equal pay, and class action suits (*The Nation*, May 8, 1982).

Additionally, Connolly sent directives to the field reversing former policies without discussing these directives with his own staff or the commission (*Business Week*, August 9, 1982). Connolly's tenure as the EEOC general counsel was contentious, eventually resulting in his resignation in January 1983. His replacement, David Slate, was career oriented and more palatable to Congress and EEO constituencies. Finally, in September 1984 under intense congressional scrutiny, the commission issued a Statement of Enforcement Policy that declared "every case, where violation of an EEOC enforced statute is found and attempts at conciliation have failed, should be submitted to the full Commission for litigation authorization" (Equal Employment Opportunity Commission 1984: 5). This effectively removed the final authority of the general counsel over litigation decisions.

How did the EEOC respond to the sharp changes in philosophy between the Carter and Reagan administrations? If there were changes in agency outputs, what were the reasons for the changes? Were there changes in agency behavior due to the struggle between Congress and the president over commission policy? Our analysis of the EEOC is constrained by the data that the EEOC was willing to provide.[5] However, we can report a time series of monthly litigations from 1981 to 1987. Because the data start in January 1981, we consider only stimuli pertinent to the Reagan administration. Nevertheless, given the stated preference of the Reagan administration for ending employment quotas and affirmative action, the stimuli after January 1981 should have been especially strong.

The EEOC Office of General Counsel handles litigations. Thus, according to the preceding discussion, we should hypothesize three possible stimuli affecting EEOC litigations throughout this period: the Connolly appointment, the Connolly resignation/Slate appointment, and the commission's Statement of Enforcement Policy.

Table 3.2 reports the statistical results. Figure 3.2 contains a graph of the empirical data along with predictions from the model reported in Table 3.2. The commission's Statement of Enforcement Policy produced no change in the number of litigations. The other two interventions, however, were strongly significant. The Connolly appointment produced an immediate decline of 4.57 litigations per month followed by a continued movement to a level 18.28 litigations per month below the preintervention mean. In April 1983, one month after the Slate appointment, there was an abrupt increase of 6.58 litigations per month. The Slate appointment simultaneously produced a trend that increased litigations by an average 0.55 cases filed per month. The lag is reasonable since it takes longer to initiate litigations than it takes to halt them.

Thus, the EEOC initially responded in a fairly predictable fashion to the changing philosophy of the Reagan administration. A Republican appointee (traditionally responsive to business interests) reduced the vigor of enforcement of EEO policy by reducing the number of individual litigations. Interestingly, however, this movement ran counter to the stated intention of the Reagan administration for a return to case-by-case litigations. This early movement also ran counter to congressional intentions and was very controversial with civil rights and women's groups. Accordingly, Congress applied pressure for the EEOC to restore litigations, the most visible bureaucratic output. With the Connolly resignation/Slate appointment, executive influence was counterbalanced by Congress and EEO constituencies, resulting in an upward movement in litigations. Thus, the EEOC responded initially to the president and his appointees and then to Congress and more moderate appointees. In both cases the agency adapted in response to external stimuli.

Using annual data, Wood (1990) showed that all other EEOC outputs besides litigations (e.g., out-of-court settlements, case resolutions, discrimination charges investigated) remained depressed for the remainder of the Reagan administration. Thus, the executive and the bureaucracy

FIGURE 3.2 The Impact of the General Counsel
on EEOC Litigation Activities

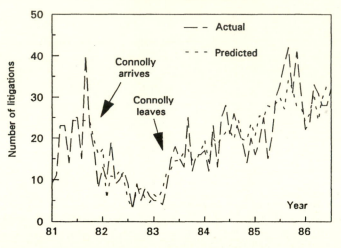

TABLE 3.2: The Impact of the EEOC General Counsel on
Litigation Activities by the Commission

Variable	Parameter	Estimate	t-statistic
Connolly Appointment	ω_0	-4.57	-2.03
Connolly Resignation/Slate Appt.	ω_0	6.58	2.01
	ω_1	0.55	2.27
	δ_1	0.99	44.54
Moving Average	θ_0	0.51	3.69

Measures of Fit

RMS (Noise Only)   80.69
RMS (Full Model)   28.74 Change = 64%

Autocorrelation of residuals   Q = 25.59 with 22 D.F.

Note: The intervention series were step inputs. All model parameters
were significant at the 0.05 level or less.

used deception to curtail equal employment opportunity outputs for most
of the 1980s. As with the ICC case, the bureaucracy was an adaptive entity,
but both the bureaucracy and president were unaccountable to Congress
and citizens.

The Federal Trade Commission

The FTC was established by the Federal Trade Commission Act of 1914 to implement U.S. antitrust policy. Sharing authority for antitrust regulation with the Department of Justice's Antitrust Division, the FTC has responsibility for implementing the Sherman Act of 1890, the FTC and Clayton acts of 1914, and their respective amendments throughout the years. In 1938 Congress passed the Wheeler-Lea Amendment to the original FTC Act to provide some degree of consumer protection to those who had previously been at the mercy of business. The amendment prohibited "unfair and deceptive" business practices, including false advertising, product mislabeling, and mail order fraud. The Robinson-Patman Act of 1936 authorized the commission to regulate unlawful price discrimination.

The FTC operates under vague statutory mandates that offer wide discretionary authority to regulators over what sorts of activities to pursue (Katzman 1980a). Thus, from the commission's creation until the 1970s some thought that the FTC was a quintessential example of agency capture (e.g., Stone 1977). At the height of the consumer movement in 1969, however, there was a revitalization of the FTC following critical reports by Ralph Nader and the American Bar Association. President Nixon designated Caspar Weinberger as FTC chair to initiate the revitalization. Large personnel changes occurred at the agency, with "deadwood" attorneys replaced by young, enthusiastic graduates from the best law schools in the nation. FTC budgets and authority grew throughout this period by substantial amounts. The approach to regulation, however, was still case by case.

In 1975 Congress granted the FTC new authority to promulgate industrywide trade regulation rules that could have a profound impact on entire industries. Little immediate use was made of these rules, however, until the Carter administration arrived on the scene in 1977. President Carter designated Michael Pertshuk, who was passionately committed to the consumer movement, as FTC chair. He made wide use of trade regulation rules, and by 1980 the FTC had managed to alienate many groups, including automobile dealers, milk producers, the American Medical Association, the American Bar Association, the insurance industry, drug manufacturers, the television industry, funeral home directors, and broader-based organizations such as the U.S. Chamber of Commerce and the National Association of Manufacturers.

A large turnover in 1977 in the House and Senate oversight committees produced a Congress that was sympathetic to these "backlash" groups. During 1979 and 1980 Congress made several attempts to rein in the FTC; however, the Carter administration resisted these efforts. In May and June 1980 Congress twice actually allowed FTC funding to expire. In late May 1980 Congress passed and the president signed the Federal Trade Commission Improvements Act, which authorized funding through fiscal year 1982 but restricted the agency's rulemaking authority.

As a result of these changes, the Reagan administration was in a good position to influence policy at the FTC in 1981. During the campaign, candidate Reagan hardly mentioned consumer protection or antitrust. But it was clear from his regulatory relief stance that he intended to change such policies. One indication of Reagan's strong interest in the FTC was his appointment of James C. Miller III as chair in September 1981. Miller was a distinguished economist who had headed the president's Task Force on Regulatory Relief during the early months of the administration. He also played a principal role in writing Executive Order 12291, which required cost-benefit analysis for new regulatory rules, and he was the first director of the OMB office responsible for regulatory review.

Miller shared the Reagan philosophy that consumers were best served through a minimum of government interference in the market economy. This was reflected in the FTC transition team report that Miller helped author. This document showed that Miller was committed to toning down the most ambitious elements of the consumer movement. Economic regulation (i.e., antitrust) was to be eliminated for the most part because it inhibited the operation of free markets as defined by the Reagan administration. Social regulation (i.e., consumer protection), however, was acknowledged to have a legitimate role in protecting the public from negative externalities. Social regulation was to be reformed to make it less costly.

Even before Miller took over at the FTC, the Reagan administration tried to reform the agency (Harris and Milkis 1989). David Stockman, the president's budget director, proposed slashing the $73 million fiscal year 1981 FTC budget to $67.7 million, with a reduction for 1982 to $59.4 million. As proposed, the Stockman budget would have eliminated the Bureau of Competition, which was responsible for antitrust enforcement, as well as the ten FTC regional offices. These draconian measures were fought off by the FTC commissioners and Congress.

In September 1981 Miller took over the FTC. As chair, Miller was an agent of Congress and responsible for administering the activities of the commission with efficiency and effectiveness. He also was an agent of the president and was charged with promulgating his policies. Between 1981 and 1983 the FTC budget was reduced from $73 million to $63 million, with similar reductions in personnel. Miller did not try to carry through on the administration plan to eliminate the Bureau of Competition; however, he did spend much political capital in an effort to do away with the ten regional offices. After lengthy negotiations with Congress, a deal was struck to retain their organization but with only a skeleton staff.

The resource reductions and attempted reorganizations of the FTC could all be justified in the name of government efficiency. However, Miller's different enforcement pattern and his effort to clamp down on an "activist" staff could hardly be justified on these grounds. He shifted the enforcement pattern from one emphasizing trade regulation rules to one emphasizing case-by-case interventions. Much greater use was made of economic analysis in conducting both activities as well as in deciding what types of cases to pursue. An extremely important element of Miller's administration was the very demanding evidentiary standards required to pursue regulatory initiatives. With regard to rulemaking, this meant mounds of surveys and economic research to document industrywide abuses. With regard to individual cases, this meant that attorneys had to present prima facie evidence of reduced consumer welfare before pursuing a case. That is, activities that earlier had been deemed per se illegal or of questionable merit (i.e., trade restraints such as price fixing or bid rigging) were subjected to economic analysis prior to being taken up by the commission. Some observers thought that these changes were intended to slow down or halt regulation rather than make it more efficient and effective. It is obvious that the very demanding evidentiary standards and increased requirement for economic analysis, combined with reduced personnel and resources, were a surefire prescription for reduced outputs.

Nevertheless, there is considerable uncertainty in the published research over whether the FTC responded through time to political influence either during the Reagan administration or earlier. For example, Robert Katzman (1980b) considered FTC decisions for 1970–1976 on the types of cases pursued. He concluded that internal power struggles within the agency were most important in explaining the mix of cases the FTC handled. In contrast, Weingast and Moran (1983; see also Calvert, Moran, and Weingast 1987) examined annual data for 1964–1976 on FTC case selection decisions and found they varied systematically through time with congressional ideology. That is, probusiness congressional orientations meant probusiness FTC case selection. Moe (1982) used annual data for 1945–1977 to examine covariations between changing presidential administrations and the number of FTC complaints issued. He concluded that the number of complaints varied through time, but not in the manner one would intuitively predict. Republican administrations brought *larger* numbers of FTC complaints against business, an obviously counterintuitive result. In contrast, Joseph Stewart and Jane Cromartie (1982) used annual data to examine FTC deceptive trade practice cases and found they varied predictably with changing presidential administrations. However, Bruce Yandle (1985) challenged Stewart and Cromartie's finding, arguing that deceptive trade practice cases were only one dimension of FTC performance. The larger picture, he argued, revealed no presidential effects.

Previous empirical research, then, leaves unresolved the question of FTC susceptibility to political influence. It also suggests, however, some stimuli that should have changed FTC activities if political control really occurred. For one thing, there was a dramatic turnover in the membership of the congressional committees responsible for overseeing the FTC in 1977. Membership changed from a markedly proconsumer orientation before 1977 to a markedly probusiness orientation after 1977. Thus, if the agency responded to congressional influence, the vigor of FTC regulation should have declined after 1977. Qualitative evidence suggests that the Pertschuk FTC did not yield to congressional influence after 1977 since Congress continued its highly visible efforts to manipulate the agency. Between 1977 and 1980 Congress expressed disapproval of FTC policies by not approving an FTC budget and funding its activities through a series of continuing resolutions. A budget-maximizing bureaucracy would have taken these "signals" and changed direction.[6] Finally, in July 1981 the Reagan administration nominated Miller, a conservative economist, to head the FTC. The Miller administration led to budget reductions as well as administrative changes. So the vigor of FTC activities should have declined after Miller's arrival at the FTC in October 1981.

To evaluate whether these stimuli produced responses in FTC behavior, we selected data on the number of enforcements between 1977 and 1987. The enforcement measure was a monthly sum of all consent decrees obtained, final administrative orders issued, and concluding agreements reached by the FTC. The statistical results are in Table 3.3. The empirical data and model-predicted results are in the graphs of Figure 3.3.

Concerning changing congressional oversight, the budget cutoffs, and the 1980 reform legislation, the data offered no support for subsystems theory. Interest groups operating through congressional committees were unable to rein in the FTC and its activist policies. There was no statistically significant post-1977 downward trend. There was also no response to model components for budget cues or legislation. Rather, model noise terms explained fluctuations throughout this period as well as deterministic variables, so these variables were dropped from the model.

Concerning presidential influence, however, the data yielded a statistically significant finding. In the same month Miller became commission chair there was a drop of about 3.5 enforcement actions (about 50 percent) in the monthly number of actions by the agency. Visual inspection of Figure 3.3 also suggests a continued lower average level of FTC activities after Miller for the remainder of the Reagan administration. However, since the time series was drifting with no equilibrium level, we cannot confidently provide preintervention and postintervention estimates of what

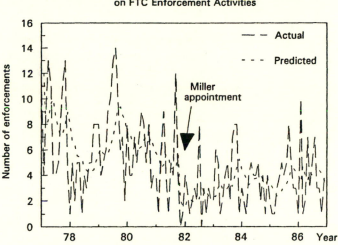

FIGURE 3.3 The Impact of the Miller Appointment
on FTC Enforcement Activities

TABLE 3.3: The Impact of the Chairman on Enforcement
Activities of the Federal Trade Commission

Variable	Parameter	Estimate	t-statistic
Miller Appointment	ω_0	-3.50	-2.17
Moving Average	θ_1	0.81	15.63
Measures of Fit			
RMS (Noise Only)		7.77	
RMS (Full Model)		7.57 Change = 2.60%	
Autocorrelation of residuals		Q = 27.26 with 23 D.F	

Note: The dependent series was differenced to achieve stationarity. The intervention series was a step input. All model parameters were significant at the 0.05 level or less.

the mean levels were. Nevertheless, the timing and magnitude of the response to the Miller appointment suggest that the administration appointee affected FTC activities.[7]

Were these changes from the Miller appointment consistent with congressional intentions or public preferences? They were clearly consistent with those of the oversight committee and some interest group intentions after 1977. However, there was also considerable scrutiny by Congress after 1981 of the declines in antitrust and consumer protection activities. Pertshuk and many other consumer advocates testified before Congress that consumers were not better protected by an FTC that no longer promoted fair competition and protected consumers from deceptive trade practices. It is also unclear whether the public at large had clear preferences on these issues. So we cannot judge whether the president and the bureaucracy were appropriately accountable to congressional or public preferences.

The Nuclear Regulatory Commission

Congress created the NRC in 1974 as a response to suspicions that the older Atomic Energy Commission (AEC) had subjugated safety concerns in promoting nuclear power. Congress passed the Energy Reorganization Act of 1974, which split the AEC into two agencies, the NRC and the Energy Research and Development Administration (ERDA). The legislation charged the ERDA with developing nuclear and other forms of energy and the NRC with regulating nuclear safety. Because of the technological risks associated with nuclear safety, Congress initially designed the NRC to emphasize technical rationality over accountability and responsiveness to political control.

The NRC was established as an independent commission headed by five commissioners serving five-year staggered terms. The president designates the chair and nominates the membership. The primary qualification for membership on the commission, however, has always been expertise, not loyalty to the administration. The president has traditionally exerted little continuing influence over NRC policy, except when crisis raised the issue to one of high salience. Although the OMB scrutinizes the NRC's budget, it does not review the NRC's legislative proposals because of the independent posture of the commissioners (Goodman and Wrightson 1987: 166–171). Moreover, prior to June 1980 the agency's internal structure insulated commissioners from routine administrative functions by separating the commission from its staff both geographically and organizationally (Waterman 1989: 147). An executive director administered the agency until that time.

During the 1976 campaign candidate Carter (who had been trained as a nuclear engineer) expressed doubts about the viability and safety of nuclear energy. President Carter, however, came to embrace nuclear power after Department of Energy (DOE) energy demand projections implied that fossil fuels would be in substantial shortfall by the year 2000. Carter's energy secretary, James Schlesinger, was a strong advocate of nuclear power and proposed liberalizing the licensing process to stimulate production of nuclear plants. The administration proposed licensing reform legislation in 1978 and 1979, but opposition by environmental groups assured that the bills never moved beyond the hearing stage. The accident at Pennsylvania's Three Mile Island (TMI) nuclear power plant on March 28, 1979, ensured that "regulatory relief" for the nuclear power industry was not soon to be forthcoming.

In the aftermath of the TMI accident, President Carter appointed a special panel to study the NRC and industry safety practices. The twelve-member panel, headed by president of Dartmouth College John Kemeny, made numerous recommendations. Among other findings, the report concluded that human error, rather than deficient equipment or engineering practices, was the root of the problem. However, the panel also found that there were serious problems with the administration of the NRC. The report concluded that NRC commissioners and the chair were unclear as to their respective responsibilities at the commission. The Kemeny panel's strongest recommendation was that the NRC be abolished and replaced with a single-headed executive-branch agency responsible directly to the president. The General Accounting Office (GAO) issued a separate report in 1980 also alleging that there was a lack of leadership and accountability at the commission (Davis and Helfand 1985).

President Carter did not take the Kemeny commission's advice about abolishing the NRC. Instead he attempted to strengthen the agency through reorganization. His reorganization plan, which went into effect in June 1980, addressed the leadership issue by increasing the authority of the chair over the agency. From that time the chair assumed full responsibility for administering the various NRC programs as well as for planning responses to nuclear emergencies. The executive director was to report directly to the chair, with operating staff accountable to both the director and chair. There still were, however, serious limitations on the chair's ability to administer the agency.

In 1983 President Reagan's *Private Sector Survey on Cost Containment* (also known as the Grace Commission) argued that the position "still lacks the executive and administrative authority provided by law to the Chairman of other Federal regulatory agencies." The report was also highly critical of restrictions on communication between the NRC commissioners and staff, concluding that "this vestige of a need to separate the promotional and regulatory functions ... impedes the Commission's ready access to the most knowledgeable sources of staff technical advice and impairs the chairman's ability to exercise effective staff oversight" (Grace Commission 1983: 55).

During the 1980 campaign candidate Reagan expressed strong support for developing the U.S. nuclear power generating capacity. He also gave strong credence to the industry view that excessive governmental regulation was at fault for the feeble state of the U.S. nuclear power program. His initial presidential policy statements gave nuclear power industry of-

ficials reason to celebrate; the administration intent was to provide regulatory relief by liberalizing the nuclear power plant licensing process
(Goodman and Wrightson 1987: 165–166). By 1982 President Reagan had
appointed three of the five NRC commissioners. He had also designated
the chair, Nunzio Palladino, a staunchly pronuclear advocate.

Evidence of chair Palladino's support for the nuclear industry came
from several articles he had written. In one, Palladino argued that the es-
calating financial crisis in the nuclear industry was largely the result of the
increased uncertainty created by antinuclear groups. He also argued that
continually changing regulatory requirements were contributing to the
industry's financial burden. Although Palladino clearly supported the industry's view, he also believed that the nuclear industry had to have a better record on safety (U.S. Senate 1981b: 10–11, 36–39). In a speech on December 1, 1981, Palladino criticized the nuclear industry's record, stating
that the industry had to do its part or no level of regulatory reform would
be sufficient to save it (cited in Lanouette 1983).

Did the Palladino appointment and the various other stimuli just discussed result in a change in NRC enforcement behavior through time?
The prior expectation is that the agency would be insensitive to political
manipulation because the NRC's organizational design emphasizes technical rationality over external control.[8] To evaluate the independence of
NRC activities from external politics, we obtained monthly data on safety
violations found by NRC field inspectors from 1978 to 1988. Preliminary
interviews with NRC officials suggested two events that may have caused
changes in NRC enforcements. First, changes may have resulted from any
increase in violations found as inspectors used their new civil penalty authority in the months following the 1980 legislation. Second, activities
may have responded to changes from the Reagan administration. During
the 1980 campaign candidate Reagan expressed the desire to reform nuclear safety regulation and promote the ailing nuclear power industry.

Between 1981 and 1987 there was a gradual reduction in the NRC's
budget of about 10 percent in current dollars. According to NRC officials,
the budget reductions were almost completely absorbed by the research
program and unlikely to have affected NRC enforcements. A more likely
event was the arrival at the commission of Palladino. Accordingly, we hypothesized a decline in NRC enforcements corresponding with the appointment of Palladino in June 1981.

Table 3.4 reports statistical results for these predictions. Figure 3.4 presents the actual data along with a graph of the model predictions from Table 3.4. Both the legislative and presidential interventions were significant. In July and August 1980, following the new legislation, there was a
substantial increase in the number of safety violations cited by NRC inspectors. The increase for July was about 155 violations above the

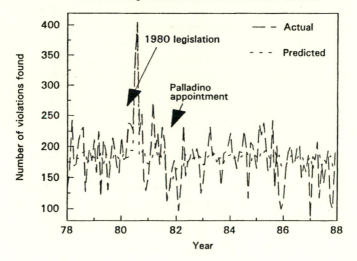

FIGURE 3.4 The Impact of the Palladino Appointment
and 1980 Legislation on NRC Enforcement Activities

TABLE 3.4: The Impact of the Chairman on Enforcement
Activities of the Nuclear Regulatory Commission

Variable	Parameter	Estimate	t-statistic
Palladino Appointment	ω_0	-68.41	-2.02
	δ_1	.76	4.24
1980 Legislation	ω_0	154.82	4.09
	ω_1	214.15	5.69
Autoregressive	ϕ_1	0.21	2.24

Measures of Fit

RMS (Noise Only)	1860.04
RMS (Full Model)	1404.15 Change = 24.51%
Autocorrelation of residuals	Q = 15.62 with 22 D.F.

Note: The Palladino intervention series was a step input. The legislation interventions were both pulse inputs. All model parameters were significant at the 0.05 level or less.

preintervention mean when the effects of autoregressive noise were controlled for. For August the increase was about 214 additional violations.

There was also a weak but statistically significant response beginning in the same month Palladino arrived at the commission. In June 1981 there was an abrupt decline of about 68 violations per month, which decayed gradually back to the preintervention level. This calculates to a total reduction in NRC-detected safety violations of about 285 fewer than would have been found absent the Reagan appointee.[9] This effect is not large, but it still demonstrates political influence in an agency that most observers consider to be independent.

These results show that the NRC adapted to both legislative and presidential stimuli. However, there are again questions of accountability and control associated with the results. NRC enforcements declined, but only temporarily, following the Palladino appointment. This decline in enforcements was deregulatory and consistent with Reagan's 1980 campaign agenda. However, it was inconsistent with past congressional and public demands for stronger nuclear safety regulation. This pattern of presidential intervention followed by return to a more pluralist equilibrium is characteristic of several other agencies examined here. However, the transitory nature of the NRC intervention makes us question whether Reagan or his appointee really intended to deregulate nuclear safety over the long term. Thus, there is ambiguity about whether the president and the bureaucracy were accountable to congressional or public preferences after the 1980 election.

The Food and Drug Administration

The FDA, unlike the ICC, EEOC, FTC, and NRC, is a semi-independent executive-branch agency in the direct chain of command of the president. Formally, the statutory authority of the FDA is granted to the secretary of health and human services, who selects the commissioner of the FDA. The president, however, exercises clearance over the leadership of the FDA. The secretary delegates authority to the commissioner, but all decisions of the commissioner are subject to the review and revision of the secretary. The commissioner is assisted by a deputy and six associate commissioners, who are each responsible for separate elements of FDA administration.

The structure and powers of the FDA have evolved slowly over time in response to various crises and executive-branch reorganizations (Quirk 1980; Bryner 1987). The origins of the FDA can be traced to the entrepreneurial efforts of Harvey W. Wiley, chief chemist of the Department of Agriculture's Bureau of Chemistry during the early twentieth century. Soon after joining the bureau in 1883, Wiley began experimenting with food and drug adulteration. His experiments on live human subjects, in which he fed them small doses of poisons commonly found in foods and drugs, increased public awareness of the hazards of contamination and led to the passage of the Food and Drug Act of 1906.

Wiley's Bureau of Chemistry began implementing the act in 1907 within the Department of Agriculture. In 1927 responsibility for implementation was transferred to the Department of Agriculture's newly created Food, Drug, and Insecticide Administration. In 1931 its name was changed to the Food and Drug Administration. Congress expanded the FDA's powers in 1938 with the passage of the Food, Drug, and Cosmetic Act, which required manufacturers to prove the safety of a new drug before it could be marketed. The act was a response to the death in 1937 of 107 persons from a seemingly harmless cure-all, elixir of sulfanilamide. In 1940 the FDA was transferred to the Federal Security Agency, a new independent agency established to protect the public health. In 1953 the Federal Security Agency was incorporated into the Department of Health, Education, and Welfare (HEW).

The regulatory authority of the FDA was substantially broadened in 1958 with the passage of the so-called Delaney Amendment to the Food, Drug, and Cosmetic Act, which required manufacturers to prove the safety of food additives and prohibited the use of food additives known to cause cancer in humans or animals. FDA authority was increased again in 1962 when Congress passed the Kefauver Amendments to the Food and Drug Act, which required drug manufacturers to prove the effectiveness as well as the safety of their products before they could be marketed. The FDA was also authorized to order the immediate removal of dangerous drugs from the market. This was at least partially in response to publicity surrounding the use of thalidomide, a tranquilizer that was linked in Europe with birth defects after the drug had been used by pregnant women. In 1979 Congress passed legislation removing education functions from HEW and renaming it the Department of Health and Human Services (HHS), which is where the FDA now resides.

Currently the FDA has primary responsibility for assuring the safety, purity, cleanliness, and effectiveness of U.S. drugs, cosmetics, medical devices, and some foods. In fulfilling such statutory duties, the FDA engages in two broad types of activities: analysis and enforcement. The analysis function involves evaluating the marketability of new products through research, testing, and examination of scientific reports. A staff of scientists and medical personnel develops standards on the composition, quality, safety, and efficacy of human and veterinary drugs. This staff also tests new products submitted by drug manufacturers for FDA approval, licenses manufacturers of old and new drugs, and develops guidelines for good food and drug manufacturing practice. Also, the staff conducts research on the health effects of both old and new biological products.

The FDA's enforcement function involves monitoring by field inspectors of manufacturing establishments to assure the purity of marketed foods and drugs. Sometimes enforcement also involves taking positive actions to protect the public when inspectors find violations of FDA rules. About one thousand FDA inspectors perform on-site inspections of the more than 90,000 plants located in the United States as well as of import entry points (Greer 1983). On finding violations, enforcement personnel have a full arsenal of administrative tools for protecting the public. They can take informal action by making office visits or phone calls. They can issue formal letters of violation, warning the manufacturer of the infraction or possible impending action. They can seek injunctions on the continued manufacture or marketing of unsafe products. They can also ask the manufacturer to voluntarily recall products already marketed. Failing this, they can sometimes seize hazardous products to protect the public health and safety. Finally, as a last resort they can file lawsuits against negligent manufacturers or even publicize violations.

The mission of the FDA—protecting the purity of the nation's foods and drugs—by its very nature engenders public support. This is not to say, however, that FDA activities have always been uncontroversial. The agency has frequently drawn fire from the businesses it regulates; however, during the 1970s it also drew fire from the public at large and consumer groups. The Delaney Amendment was a particular target of opposition, with critics claiming that the law was too rigid in not recognizing the potential benefits of suspect substances. In particular the 1977 FDA-proposed ban on Saccharin drew such a strong public outcry that Congress enacted a law imposing a moratorium on the FDA's ability to remove the food additive from the market. Controversies also arose during the 1970s over the drug Laetrile, over toxic shock syndrome, and over the FDA's proposed regulation of caffeine. Many observers also claimed that the new drug approval process took too long, denying potential health or longevity to those who might benefit from new drugs.

In 1978 the Carter administration responded to these complaints by proposing a massive drug law revision, but the bill was never reported out of committee. In September 1979 Senator Edward Kennedy (D–Mass.) steered a similar bill through the Senate, but the House did not act to approve the legislation. The 1980 election, however, opened up new possibilities for changing FDA policy.

In 1981 President Reagan's Task Force on Regulatory Relief put the FDA's new drug approval process on its hit list of the top twenty governmentwide regulatory problems. Additionally, the new FDA commissioner, Arthur Hull Hayes, appointed in April 1981 by Secretary of HHS Richard Schweiker, sought to infuse FDA rulemaking activities with the regulatory relief priorities of the president. The agency began a review of existing rules in July of that year. At the core of this effort was an open invitation to the public to identify those regulations perceived as burdensome and to suggest potential cost savings that rule changes might produce. Accordingly, in 1981 the FDA approved more new drugs than it had in any single year since the 1962 legislation requiring premarket evaluation.

The Reagan administration's regulatory relief program should have affected the FDA. However, effects should have differed between FDA functions. There was strong public and institutional support for changing analytical functions to make them faster, less rigid, and more cost-effective. However, there was no evidence of public support for changing the FDA's enforcement functions related to the inspection and sanctioning of food and drug manufacturing establishments. Thus, it is interesting to question whether such changes actually occurred in the FDA's enforcement programs after 1981.

To explore this issue, we constructed three different measures of FDA enforcement activities through time. The measures were the quarterly number of food and drug establishment inspections, product seizures, and legal actions taken (defined as the sum of all prosecutions and injunctions obtained in each quarter). The data ran quarterly from 1977 to 1990.

We began with little prior expectation about what events should have caused change in FDA enforcement activities throughout this period. Reagan's regulatory relief agenda may have been important, but food and drug enforcement issues were hardly the hot topic of the 1980 campaign. Interestingly, there was a gradual increase in the FDA's budget throughout the first term of the Reagan administration, so it was not reasonable to expect a negative response to changing fiscal conditions. Nevertheless, commissioner appointee Hayes was ideologically consistent with Reagan on deregulation, so the most likely specification was a response to the Hayes appointment.[10]

Table 3.5 reports results for all three models. The empirical data and model-predicted results are in Figures 3.5, 3.6, and 3.7. The results show a decline of 5.73 percent in the number of inspections in the first quarter after Hayes's appointment. This decline continued until a new equilibrium level was reached, which was 60.22 percent below the old level. For product seizures there was a decline in the same quarter that Commissioner Hayes arrived at the FDA of about 43.9 percent. This was an immediate decline that lasted for the duration of the series. Legal actions declined in the same quarter that Commissioner Hayes arrived at the FDA by about 49.6 percent and lasted for the duration of the series. Thus, we posit a straightforward case of top agency leadership manipulating the activities of an agency.

TABLE 3.5: The Impact of the Burford Contempt Citation and Fiscal Year 1984 Budget on Environmental Protection Agency Hazardous Waste Enforcements

Variable	Parameter	Inspections	Litigations	Penalties/ Referrals
Hayes Appointment	ω_0	-0.06 (-2.61)	-0.58 (-3.32)	-0.68 (-4.40)
	δ_1	0.94 (26.92)		
Autoregressive	ϕ_1	-0.46 (-3.86)		0.34 (3.34)
Moving Average	θ_1		0.79 (8.86)	0.90 (11.10)
Moving Average	θ_2			0.26 (1.72)

Measures of Fit

		Inspections	Litigations	Penalties/ Referrals
RMS (Noise Only)		0.07	0.09	0.24
RMS (Full Model)		0.05	0.08	0.20
RMS (Percent Change)		27.75	13.44	16.51
Autocorrelation (Q)		17.34	8.44	11.80
		D.F. = 23	D.F. = 23	D.F. = 22

Note: t-statistics are in parenthesis. All intervention parameters were significant at the 0.05 level. All interventions were step inputs. All series were logged to eliminate variance nonstationarity. The Inspections series was differenced quarterly and the Seizures and Legal Actions series were differenced regularly to achieve level stationarity.

FIGURE 3.5 The Impact of the Hayes Appointment on FDA Inspections

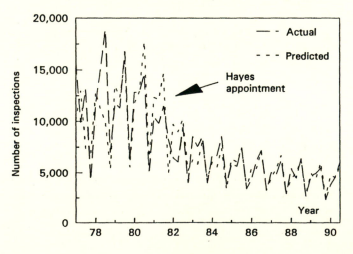

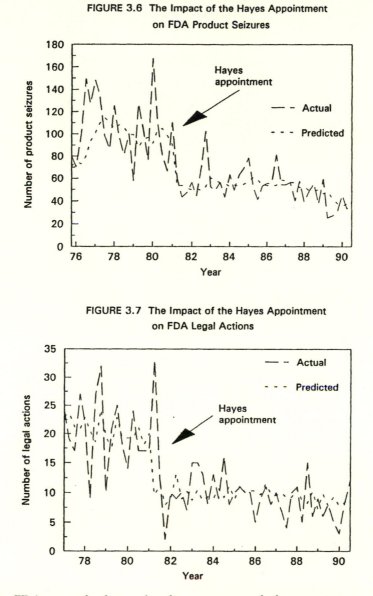

FIGURE 3.6 The Impact of the Hayes Appointment
on FDA Product Seizures

FIGURE 3.7 The Impact of the Hayes Appointment
on FDA Legal Actions

The FDA example shows the clear response of a bureaucracy to a leadership stimulus. It is also interesting, however, to again speculate as to whether the responses were consistent with public or congressional preferences. Certainly there was some public and congressional support for changing the FDA's analytical functions. It is unclear, however, whether there was any public or congressional support for relaxing the FDA's food and drug establishment enforcement functions. Bureaucratic accountability and executive accountability were missing since there was no evidence that the public or Congress was aware of these changes. The question we cannot resolve here, however, is whether the changes in the FDA's enforcement program were consistent with presidential preferences or just those of the FDA's new leadership. Was this a case of adverse selection by the secretary or a case of presidential control? In either case, it seems clear that the accountability issue extends well beyond the bureaucracy.

The National Highway Traffic Safety Administration

The NHTSA is an agency within the Department of Transportation that administers federal programs designed to increase motor vehicle safety and efficiency. An outgrowth of the consumer movement of the early 1960s, the agency was charged with establishing "reasonable, practicable, and appropriate" safety standards for automobiles and creating a system for finding and reporting safety defects. The agency is headed by an administrator nominated by the president and confirmed by the Senate. The administrator is assisted by a deputy administrator and six associate administrators, who are each responsible for various agency functions.

Prior to the mid-1960s federal regulation of the automobile industry was virtually nonexistent. The industry vigorously opposed automobile safety regulation, claiming that it made safe cars and that most traffic accidents were the fault of poor drivers, not defective engineering. The industry also claimed that the public did not want to pay for expensive safety features, preferring instead to spend money on style, power, and comfort (Gerston, Fraleigh, and Schwab 1988). The thrust for change originated in the early 1960s when automobile fatalities had climbed from about 38,000 a year to more than 50,000 by 1965 (Meier and Morgan 1981: 161).

The regulatory environment changed abruptly in 1965 with the publication of Ralph Nader's *Unsafe at Any Speed*, which focused public attention on the safety defects of the Chevrolet Corvair. Nader claimed that General Motors executives marketed the vehicle even though they knew of major safety hazards resulting from design defects. During the same year congressional hearings began on auto safety, with Senator Abraham Ribicoff's (D–Conn.) committee on government operations taking the initiative. Early in 1966 President Lyndon Johnson sent a highway safety bill to Congress that would allegedly end the carnage on U.S. highways. After several months of heated debate and testimony by auto and insurance industry representatives and consumer advocates, the National Highway Traffic Safety Act was passed.

The 1966 legislation directed the secretary of transportation to "reduce traffic accidents and deaths and injuries to persons resulting from traffic accidents" and to issue motor vehicle standards that "meet the need for motor vehicle safety, and shall be stated in objective terms." The NHTSA was given primary responsibility for developing such standards based on testing and empirical evidence. Accordingly, the NHTSA conducts its own field tests and engineering evaluations. It also provides a consumer hotline and maintains a computer tracking system for reported problems. The agency has legislative authority to fine automakers, but more often it relies on semivoluntary recalls or publicity to effect compliance. The 1975 Energy Policy and Conservation Act also gave the NHTSA responsibility for issuing automobile fuel economy standards.

During the Carter administration the NHTSA was a zealous advocate of automobile safety standards. Joan Claybrook, the Carter NHTSA administrator and a zealous consumer advocate, sponsored the adoption of various new rules for promoting automobile safety. These included the controversial passive restraints regulation issued in June 1977, which required the auto industry to begin installing passive restraints for front-seat occupants by September 1, 1981. The NHTSA was also responsible for the installation of numerous safety devices, including dual braking systems, padded instrument panels, lap and shoulder belts, shatterproof windshields, headrests, and energy-absorbing steering wheels and bumpers (Meier 1985). According to Claybrook (1984), vehicle standards lowered insurance costs for consumers by more than $3 billion annually and reduced costs from accidents due to health care, rehabilitation, unemployment, family disruption, and psychological trauma. In addition, the Department of Transportation estimated that each dollar spent by consumers on auto safety resulted in twenty-seven additional lives saved.

Before 1980 the relationship between the federal government and the auto industry was very adversarial. The industry resisted regulation vigorously through the courts and also used various delaying tactics to avoid implementation. Besides NHTSA regulation, various events and economic conditions during the 1970s led automakers to seek regulatory relief from government. The oil embargo of 1979 resulted in about a 50 percent increase in the price of fuel, which caught the auto industry by surprise. Consumers no longer preferred the large, powerful "gas-guzzlers" produced by Detroit but turned instead to smaller foreign-manufactured cars. A recession beginning in early 1980 also diminished sales of new autos, with massive layoffs of autoworkers during that year. By the end of 1980 U.S. firms had lost more than $4 billion, leading to increased concern for the strong link between the health of the auto industry and the U.S. economy.

During the 1980 presidential campaign Reagan made much of the plight of the U.S. auto industry. He claimed that it was a quintessential example of excessive government regulation, stating that "the U.S. auto industry is virtually being regulated to death" (Claybrook 1984: 173). In

April 1981 the Reagan administration announced a series of measures intended to bring relief to the auto industry, including promises to relax environmental and safety regulations through the administrative process. The fiscal year 1982 budget for NHTSA included a 15 percent reduction in current dollars for NHTSA; furthermore, the current dollar budget authorization never rose above 1981 levels for the remainder of the Reagan administration.

The Reagan appointee to head the NHTSA, Raymond Peck, was strongly committed to the Reagan deregulation strategy. In October 1981 he announced that the agency was withdrawing requirements for the installation of passive restraints such as air bags. The plan drew much criticism from Congress, former administrator Claybrook, and the insurance industry. State Farm Mutual Insurance Company sued the NHTSA and Department of Transportation under the Administrative Procedure Act, contending that the rescission had not followed proper administrative procedure and was therefore illegal. In June 1982 the U.S. Court of Appeals held that the rescission was arbitrary and illogical and reinstated the passive restraint requirement. The court further held that the NHTSA could rescind the passive restraints rule at a future date only after finding nonarbitrary reasons to support its judgment.

The preceding history suggests that outputs from the NHTSA should have increased during the Carter administration when the agency was administered by consumer advocate Claybrook. The contextual evidence also suggests that outputs should have decreased during the Reagan administration either after the confirmation of Peck or after the budget reductions. To test these hypotheses, we obtained data from the NHTSA on the number of auto safety defect engineering evaluations performed per quarter. Unlike the seven other agencies, NHTSA records go back to before the Carter administration, so we can formally test the hypothesis that the Carter administration also made a difference.

Preliminary examination of the data showed that, as predicted, Claybrook increased agency activities to levels much higher than the Nixon-Ford and Reagan administrations. However, what was more interesting was that some NHTSA activities declined even *before* the appointment of Peck or the Reagan budget reductions in fiscal year 1982 *without any apparent executive or legislative stimulus.*

Figure 3.8 graphs the data for quarterly engineering evaluations by the NHTSA from 1973 to 1988. The figure shows that the number of evaluations declined as early as the first quarter of 1980, more than a year before any possible effect from the Reagan administration. Furthermore, a search of congressional records showed no apparent inducement from Congress. Because of the timing and magnitude of this decline, we were compelled to ask why such a dramatic change occurred.

We conducted interviews with officials who were at the NHTSA

FIGURE 3.8 The Impact of Carter and Reagan Administration
Appointments on NHTSA Engineering Evaluations

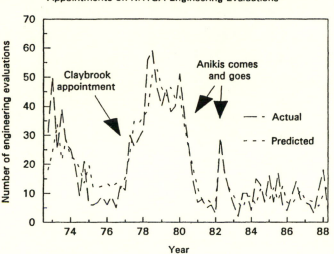

throughout this period. They directed our attention to a serious staffing error made by administrator Claybrook. The unexpected change resulted from a clear-cut case of adverse selection. As one official told us, "Claybrook thought she had quite a find." Instead her appointee, George Anikis, proved to be an individual who did not share her regulatory philosophy. Anikis, according to one respondent "never could find a good reason for conducting an engineering investigation." Thus, in explaining the premature decline, we hypothesized that engineering evaluations changed beginning with the Anikis assignment to the Office of Defect Investigations. We also expected to see an increase when he left, given his apparent unpopularity with NHTSA personnel.

Table 3.6 reports the statistical results. Figure 3.8 reports empirical data and model predictions. The results confirm statistically the strong increase in the number of auto safety defect engineering evaluations in the quarter after Claybrook arrived at the NHTSA. Also, there was a decline in evaluations corresponding perfectly with her errant designation of Anikis to head the Office of Defect Investigations. In the second quarter of 1980 there was an initial decline of around 23 evaluations. The decline continued until Anikis left in the second quarter of 1982, when the NHTSA conducted about 37 fewer quarterly reviews than the average before his assignment. Interestingly, his departure marked an apparent celebration since engineering evaluations increased sharply. For one quarter there was a rise of 21 evaluations followed by a rapid decline to the postintervention mean as the Reagan administration took charge. This level remained for the duration of the Reagan administration.

Obviously, not all of these changes were consistent with presidential

TABLE 3.6: The Impact of the Carter and Reagan Administration Appointees on Engineering Evaluations by the National Highway Traffic Safety Administration

Variable	Parameter	Estimate	t-statistic
Claybrook Appointment	ω_0	9.09	1.79
	δ_1	0.69	3.28
Anikis Appointment	ω_0	-15.79	-2.44
	δ_1	0.60	4.00
Anikis Resignation/Reagan Appointment	ω_0	23.45	3.01
	δ_1	.41	1.27
Autoregressive	ϕ_1	0.50	4.23

Measures of Fit

RMS (Noise Only)	85.16
RMS (Full Model)	58.66 Change = 64%
Autocorrelation of residuals	Q = 16.15 with 23. D.F.

Note: The Claybrook and Anikis appointment intervention series were step inputs. The Anikis resignation/Peck appointment series was a pulse input. All model parameters were significant at the 0.05 level or less.

preferences. The Anikis appointment was a mistake that led to movements inconsistent with Carter administration policy, a clear example of adverse selection. This appointment was also inconsistent with legislative and, presumably, public preferences. The inactivity of the NHTSA after the Anikis resignation suggests that the Carter administration may have provided a bonus to the incoming Reagan administration. No change was necessary to accomplish deregulation at the NHTSA. Whether this continued inactivity was consistent with legislative or public preferences after 1981 is unclear, but there is certainly reason to question whether the 1980 election mandate was a call for reduced automobile safety.

The Office of Surface Mining

Congress established the OSM within the Department of the Interior in 1977 to implement the Surface Mining Control and Reclamation Act of 1977. The OSM administrator is designated by the secretary of the interior without the advice and consent of the Senate. An outgrowth of the environmental movement, the primary mission of the agency is to protect society and the environment from the harmful effects of coal mining operations. In performing this function, the OSM establishes minimum national standards for regulating the surface effects of coal mining. Originally, the agency was responsible for implementing the law in coordination with states; however, now it primarily assists states in implementing coal mining regulatory programs. Additionally, the OSM promotes reclamation of previously mined lands.

Before the 1977 legislation regulation of strip mining was purely a state function. But state laws, regulations, and agencies were often inadequate, resulting in mine operations destructive of the environment and, in some cases, dangerous to human health. States that lacked a diversified economy, such as Kentucky and West Virginia, were particularly disinclined to regulate vigorously due to their excessive economic dependence on coal mining operations. By passing the 1977 strip mining legislation, Congress intended to change these conditions by focusing primary responsibility for regulation on the national government, but through a federal scheme.

The OSM developed rapidly during the Carter administration as an agency intent on obtaining compliance. There was a perceived mandate at the OSM for strong regulation when President Carter publicly expressed disappointment that the legislation was not as tough as he had wanted. This, along with the appointment of several persons of similar philosophy to the OSM startup task force, meant a "gung-ho" attitude among agency personnel. Many OSM officials were former state agency inspectors who, disgruntled by their inability to regulate at the state level, wanted to make a point at the federal level (Shover, Clelland, and Lynxwiler 1986). OSM officials mistrusted the coal mining industry and state agencies on the matter of strip mining regulation, and their behavior during program startup reflected this fact. In 1978 when the agency began operation standards were established in an atmosphere of forced compliance. There was also rapid growth in OSM enforcement activities throughout this period.

Enforcement personnel basically used five tools to enforce regulatory compliance: inspections, notices of violation, cessation orders, fines, and litigations. Inspections demonstrated regulatory presence. Many operations, however, especially those in eastern states, were "outlaw" operations, so establishing compliance required coercion. A mild form of coercion was the notice of violation, which warned of impending action. In extreme cases, when violations continued or there was hazard to public health, safety, or the environment, the OSM issued cessation orders to halt mining operations. During 1979 and 1980 the OSM made liberal use of cessation orders, with as many as 175 written in a single month by the seventy or so agency inspectors.

Surface mining regulation and enforcement were coercive both to mine operators and states with economies dependent on mining operations.

State regulatory officials objected strongly to the allegedly "high-handed" tactics and inflexibility of OSM managers. Industry representatives complained loudly that they had been shut out of the standard-setting process, resulting in regulations that were too detailed and burdensome. Frustrated by tough regulations and vigorous enforcement, they counterattacked with an intensive publicity and lobbying campaign in 1979 and 1980. The 1979 oil embargo also emphasized the nation's dependence on cheap coal, placing mine operators in a position of increased influence. As a result of these pressures, oversight hearings were held in 1979 and 1981 by the Senate Committee on Energy and Natural Resources and the House Subcommittee on Energy and the Environment. The industry also brought a number of lawsuits against the OSM between 1978 and 1980, some of which were also joined by individual states.

OSM personnel did not help their relations with the states and industry by the uncompromising intensity of their efforts. There was also a marked disparity in the vigor of enforcement between eastern and western OSM regions. During 1979 and 1980 OSM inspectors issued about 37 notices of violation in the East for every 1 issued in the West. Consistently, they also issued about 180 cessation orders in the East for every 1 issued in the West. The response of eastern operators and states to this apparent discrimination was predictable. An intensive lobbying effort began in Congress to gain relief from the zealots at the OSM.

Some qualitative evidence suggests that the OSM had already seen the wisdom of moderation before the Reagan election in November 1980 (Shover, Clelland, and Lynxwiler 1986; Hayes 1992). If the agency had not, however, then the early Reagan administration attack on environmental regulation surely made the point. President Reagan appointed anticonservationist James Watt to head the Department of the Interior. Watt summarily named James Harris as director of the OSM. In May 1981 Harris informed OSM regional directors that the agency was being reorganized. The reorganization plan involved structural changes to facilitate returning "primacy" to the states. It eliminated field enforcement offices. It also reduced the number of OSM personnel from about one thousand to around six hundred because, according to congressional testimony, state agencies would soon be taking over enforcement responsibilities (U.S. House 1981, 1982a; Culhane 1984). Perhaps most important, the reorganization plan stripped field personnel of discretionary authority to write notices of violation, issue cessation orders, or initiate litigation without prior approval from central offices (Shover, Clelland, and Lynxwiler 1986).

Meanwhile, not all states willingly accepted the primacy offered by the Reagan administration. In seven eastern states judges issued injunctions that prohibited state primacy applications. Two states, Tennessee and Oklahoma, refused to provide adequate resources to run their programs according to federal standards. In April 1984 the OSM reimposed federal strip mining regulation in these two states (Pasztor 1984; Derthick 1987: 70; Reagan 1987: 190). The OSM resumed its preemptive role in prodding state agencies to assume regulatory responsibility.

Several events from this historical account should have been relevant to OSM enforcement behavior. Congressional hearings conducted prior to the Reagan administration may have suspended OSM zealotry. The most dramatic stimulus, however, should have been the installation of Reagan administration appointees at the OSM early in 1981. Additionally, the reorganization of the agency and the removal of enforcement authority from field personnel should have been important. Finally, the resumption of some enforcement activities in 1984 to prod reluctant states should have produced change.

To test for these effects, we selected monthly time series from 1979 through 1988 of notices of violation and cessation orders issued by the OSM. Model results are in Table 3.7. Graphs of the data and model predictions are in Figures 3.9 and 3.10. Unexpectedly, for both series there was no response to the Reagan appointments. Rather, the decline had already occurred beginning with the Reagan election in November 1980. Follow-up interviews suggest this timing was an example of an anticipative response by self-interested bureaucrats trying to save their jobs. Agency officials, already beleaguered by external pressure from Congress, the industry, and coal mining states, moderated OSM enforcements to appease the incoming Reagan administration.

Beginning about the time of the Reagan election in November 1980, there was an immediate reduction of about 199 notices of violation per month, followed by a continuing decline to a new level, which was about 274 notices lower than prior to the intervention. For cessation orders the initial decline was by about 34 orders per month. The new equilibrium level was about 137 cessation orders lower than the peak in 1980. Thus, by the time Harris took control of the OSM, the agency was already mostly subdued.

In spite of the obvious reduction in the vigor of coal mining enforcement that had occurred prior to the start of the Reagan administration, the new OSM leadership followed through on its plans for reorganization. In August 1982 there was a second response. The reorganization produced a decline of about 68 in the number of notices of violation per month, followed by a continuing decline to a new level that was about 220 notices lower than prior to the intervention. For cessation orders there was a decline of 24 cessation orders per month. Enforcements remained at this level until April 1984. Beginning in this month the OSM resumed regulation in two reluctant states, with an increase of about 148 notices of violation and 26 cessation orders per month. This resurgence, however, was

TABLE 3.7: The Impact of the 1980 Election and Reorganization on Office of Surface Mining Enforcements

Variable	Parameter	Notices of Violation	Cessation Orders
1980 Election	ω_0	-198.87 (-7.55)	-34.20 (-5.39)
	δ_1	0.27 (2.56)	0.75 (12.50)
Reorganization	ω_0	-68.07 (-4.42)	-24.43 (-2.31)
	δ_1	0.69 (6.54)	
1984 Preemption	ω_0	148.39 (6.54)	25.78 (2.93)
	δ_1	0.89 (11.34)	0.59 (3.61)
Autoregressive	ϕ_1	0.25 (3.55)	0.23 (2.62)
Autoregressive	ϕ_2	0.49 (7.18)	
Moving Average	θ_1	0.76 (8.33)	0.56 (7.83)
Moving Average	θ_2	-0.29 (-3.24)	

Measures of Fit

RMS (Noise Only)		2240.19	231.91
RMS (Full Model)		1400.41	170.86
RMS (Percent Change)		59.97	35.73
Autocorrelation of residuals		23.37	24.58
		D.F. = 20	D.F. = 22

Note: t-statistics are in parenthesis. All intervention parameters were significant at the 0.05 level. The 1980 Election and Reorganization interventions were step inputs. The 1984 Preemption series was a pulse input. Both Series were differenced to achieve level stationarity.

only temporary. From this level there was a gradual decline in both measures to 1988.

The Environmental Protection Agency

President Nixon created the EPA in 1970 through an executive reorganization that consolidated fifteen different environmental programs under one administration. The agency implements both regulatory and distributive programs, including the Clean Air acts, Clean Water acts, sewer

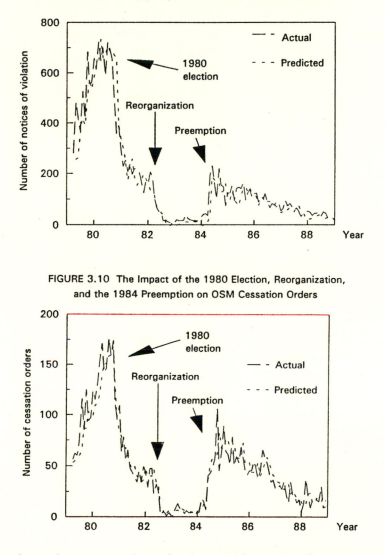

FIGURE 3.9 The Impact of the 1980 Election, Reorganization, and the 1984 Preemption on OSM Notices of Violation

FIGURE 3.10 The Impact of the 1980 Election, Reorganization, and the 1984 Preemption on OSM Cessation Orders

grants, hazardous wastes, Superfund, pesticides, toxic substances, marine protection, and noise control. The discussion here deals only with the hazardous waste program, but analyses of several other EPA programs are forthcoming in the next two chapters.

The EPA's structural arrangement relative to elected institutions is unique compared with the other seven agencies. It is an independent executive-branch agency with a single administrator located directly in the chain of command of the president. The chief executive appoints the EPA administrator with the advice and consent of the Senate. In addition, however, the president also appoints the deputy administrator as well as the heads of the various EPA divisions. Since the president has the ability to appoint and remove all top EPA officials, this provides the chief executive with the potential for extraordinary leverage over agency policy.

In spite of being created as an independent executive-branch agency, the EPA grew throughout the 1970s as an organization in substantial independence of executive authority. This independence was enhanced by a number of factors. Environmental laws had clear, goal-oriented mandates that bounded bureaucratic options. Environmental issues received the frequent attention of the media, keeping the matter salient to publics and politicians alike. Program constituencies, both groups and the diffuse public, strongly supported vigorous environmental regulation. Many of the personnel of the organization were themselves zealous supporters and highly expert in the environmental technologies that developed throughout the 1970s. Most environmental legislation allowed citizen lawsuits, ensuring the continued involvement of interest groups and federal courts in agency matters (Melnick 1983).

Congress also maintained a special relationship with the EPA throughout the 1970s since most environmental legislation originated there rather than in the executive. During these early years legislative sponsors chaired important oversight committees and held frequent hearings to assure continuing program development. Moreover, congressional attentiveness to environmental issues remained strong because of the high salience and popularity of these programs with the American people. With such a complex array of political forces, it is unclear what particular external influences should have affected EPA behavior most.

Congress, a dominant force for the EPA during the 1970s, protected and maintained the agency and its programs. Energy crises in 1974 and 1979, however, slowed the upward growth in appropriations for environmental programs. President Carter appointed individuals to lead the organization who wanted more efficiency and flexibility in accomplishing environmental goals. Nevertheless, the agency was largely stable throughout this period.

After the 1980 election these stable conditions ended abruptly. Reagan made it clear from the beginning that his administration wanted to deregulate the environment. He campaigned on a theme that decried the evils and inefficiencies of "big government," endorsing a shift in responsibility for many federal programs toward the states and localities. Regulatory relief for business and industry was a major part of the Reagan agenda, with environmental policies especially targeted because of their allegedly large impact on the economy.

The Reagan administration used the entire array of administrative tools to subdue the professional bureaucrats at the EPA. Reagan nominated and Congress approved in May 1981 a strongly antienvironmental administrator, Anne Gorsuch (later Burford), to head the agency. Before and after Gorsuch's arrival there were massive personnel shifts and reorganizations of various subunits. Many key positions within the organization were filled with administration loyalists who were antagonistic toward the agency mission. Personnel rules were used to transfer those identified as "troublemakers" into positions where they were least likely to obstruct reform. Through careful personnel manipulation, the White House created an administrative environment that should have been receptive to the relaxation of regulation. (See Chapters 4 and 5 for further discussion of Reagan administration efforts to curtail environmental regulation.)

There were also resource changes that could have affected environmental regulation. Beginning in fiscal year 1982 there were large budget and personnel reductions for virtually every program. The operating budget declined by 24 percent in fiscal year 1982. Between 1981 and 1983 the number of full-time employees was reduced by about 20 percent, with many important positions left unfilled. Thus, as we discuss in Chapter 4, political control could have come through multiple channels.

Congress was disillusioned with the new administration's policy. An aroused EPA constituency, along with the upcoming 1982 elections, probably sparked some of this disillusionment. Hearings began in October 1981 and occurred frequently until the end of July 1982. A specific focus of many hearings was the EPA's management of the hazardous waste program. There was strong evidence that administrator Burford and Hazardous Waste Division administrator Rita Lavelle knowingly allowed (even encouraged) the dumping of hazardous chemicals at illegal sites. Finally, the administration made a crucial mistake. Congress requested hazardous waste enforcement files, but the administration refused to provide them, claiming executive privilege. In December 1982 Congress cited Burford for contempt of Congress. The ensuing adverse publicity led to the firing of Lavelle in February 1983. By March 1983 Burford was seen by the White House as a reelection liability. White House staff members pressured her into resigning. President Reagan accepted her resignation, which was soon followed by the resignation of all other Reagan appointees. The president quickly nominated William Ruckelshaus to replace her.

Congress easily approved the Ruckelshaus nomination since he was widely respected as the first EPA administrator. Ruckelshaus moved swiftly to restore EPA programs by recruiting zealous personnel and providing strong leadership. In October 1983 Congress reaffirmed its commitment to environmental policy by restoring some of the funds removed in fiscal year 1982. Ruckelshaus was replaced in February 1985 by Lee Thomas, who was committed to balancing economic and environmental concerns through agency policy.

The preceding historical analysis suggests that multiple stimuli could and did affect EPA activities between 1981 and 1983. We report here an analysis of three different outputs from the EPA's hazardous waste program: the monthly number of inspections, litigations, and civil penalties/referrals from January 1981 through June 1988. Table 3.8 and Figures 3.11, 3.12, and 3.13 describe the fluctuations in these outputs.

None of the measures shows a response to any of the early Reagan administration policy interventions. Because the hazardous waste program was new, particularly in comparison to the air and water programs, hazard waste enforcement levels were still quite modest. Thus, with regard to hazardous waste enforcements, the task for the newly arrived Reagan administration in 1981 was fairly simple. Rather than having to devise means to reduce enforcement levels, as was the case in the other divisions, the administration only had to keep hazardous waste enforcements at their preexisting level.

Beginning in December 1983, the same month Congress cited Burford for contempt, there was a step increase in the number of hazardous waste litigations by regional offices. In January 1983 there was a similar increase in the number of inspections. This was two months before the resignation of Burford and the nomination of Ruckelshaus to head the EPA. Numerically, the contempt citation caused a doubling in the number of litigations per month. It also changed the number of inspections to a level 3.82 times higher than the preintervention mean (or from about 7.17 to about 27 inspections per month). Inspections, however, are a resource-intensive activity, so larger increases may not have been possible until Congress restored EPA's budget.

Beginning in fiscal year 1984 there was an immediate doubling of the number of inspections, followed by a gradual increase to a new level 5.96 times higher than the level after the Burford contempt citation (or from about 27 inspections to about 163 inspections per month). The number of civil penalties and referrals increased by 357 percent after the fiscal year 1984 budget. Thus, for the EPA policy in which Congress was most directly involved, hazardous waste, legislative influence was clearly manifested through the powers of oversight and appropriations.

After December 1982 the EPA's hazardous waste program responded to public and congressional preferences for increased enforcement vigor. However, one is led to question whether any of the early Reagan administration deregulatory stimuli should have occurred in the first place. Were presidential signals to the bureaucracy consistent with public or congressional preferences? Was Burford acting in a manner suggesting bureau-

TABLE 3.8: The Impact of the Burford Contempt Citation and Fiscal Year 1984 Budget on Environmental Protection Agency Hazardous Waste Enforcements

Variable	Parameter	Inspections	Litigations	Penalties/ Referrals
Contempt Citation	ω_0	1.34 (8.29)	2.87 (2.44)	
FY 1984 Budget	ω_0	0.71 (3.35)		1.52 (3.95)
	δ_1	0.60 (5.50)		
Autoregressive	ϕ_1	0.31 (2.86)		0.34 (3.34)
Autoregressive	ϕ_2		0.28 (2.68)	
Autoregressive	ϕ_3		0.20 (2.07)	
Autoregressive	ϕ_4		0.21 (1.98)	0.31 (3.06)
Moving Average	θ_1	0.33 (3.07)		0.61 (3.30)

Measures of Fit

RMS (Noise Only)		0.28	5.96	0.37
RMS (Full Model)		0.14	5.18	0.29
RMS (Percent Change)		50.17	13.10	21.60
Autocorrelation (Q)		18.50	13.79	25.03
		D.F. = 21	D.F. = 20	D.F. = 21

Note: t-statistics are in parenthesis. All intervention parameters were significant at the 0.05 level. All interventions were step inputs. The Inspections and Penalties/Referrals series were logged to achieve variance stationarity. The Penalties/Referrals series was differenced quarterly to achieve level stationarity..

cratic accountability? (We return to these questions in the concluding chapter.)

CONCLUSION

The case studies just detailed demonstrate causal movements in the programs of eight different federal bureaucracies from the late 1970s through most of the 1980s. When viewed in isolation, each case study contributes something to an understanding of the particular policies discussed. Con-

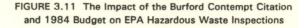

FIGURE 3.11 The Impact of the Burford Contempt Citation
and 1984 Budget on EPA Hazardous Waste Inspections

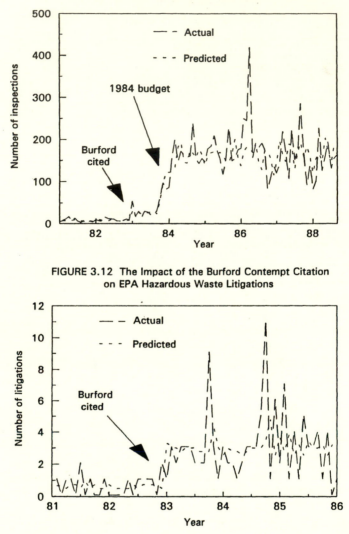

FIGURE 3.12 The Impact of the Burford Contempt Citation
on EPA Hazardous Waste Litigations

sidered as a unit, however, they offer improved understanding of the
more general dynamics of political control of the bureaucracy. This second
view merits emphasis for several reasons. First, the eight cases reveal the
scope and mechanisms of political control of the bureaucracy. Second,
they suggest some of the covariates of bureaucratic responsiveness that
may guide future research on political control. Finally, they point to a
form of policy analysis that could enhance future democratic control of
the bureaucracy.

FIGURE 3.13 The Impact of the 1984 Budget on
EPA Hazardous Waste Penalties/Referrals

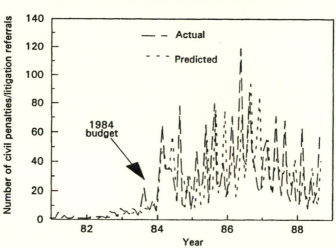

Concerning the scope of political control, the case studies show causal movements in all eight agencies. Movements occurred repeatedly through time for some agencies. Stated more generally, at certain times in the cycle of American politics, responsiveness permeates the U.S. bureaucracy. As new democratic majorities sweep newly elected officials into office, nonelective bureaucracies process demands for change from those elected officials. Of course, the election of Reagan and a Republican Senate in 1980 marked an extraordinary time in the cycles of U.S. politics, so the stimuli to bureaucracies were very strong. Nevertheless, that movement occurred in all eight cases suggests that bureaucratic responsiveness is not all that uncommon.

Concerning the specific mechanisms of political control, the case studies demonstrate that political appointments, a shared tool of the president and Congress, are very important. In six of the eight programs, agency outputs shifted immediately after a change in agency leadership. In five of these cases (the ICC, NRC, EEOC, FTC, and FDA) change followed an appointment at the beginning of a presidential administration. The direction and magnitude of these responses reflect the increased power of a chief executive in the period after a presidential election. The case of the EEOC, however, also shows change in the middle of an administration, when pluralist forces are more likely to dominate. In both cases, the responses reveal that political appointments dominate the dynamic of institutional control of the bureaucracy.

The case of the NHTSA highlights the importance of political appointments beyond the context of institutional control. The Anikis appointment at the NHTSA reflected neither congressional nor presidential influence since no Senate confirmation occurred and the change was an apparent mistake by the Carter administration. In this unusual situation, movement followed the path prescribed by the appointee, not by political institutions. This situation implies that political appointees, even absent top-down support, can have extraordinary influence over agency policy. This case also suggests the importance to elected officials of careful selection processes and diligent monitoring of agency activities.

The leadership of an agency is the most frequent mechanism for changing agency behavior, but it is not the only mechanism. Reorganizations, congressional oversight, and budgeting are also important. The OSM case illustrates the importance of agency organization to political responsiveness. When leadership at the OSM and Department of the Interior centralized control of enforcement decisions, there was an immediate reduction in enforcements by field personnel. Thus, the greater is the centralization of agency decisionmaking processes, the greater is the executive control over bureaucratic outputs.

The EPA's hazardous waste enforcement program illustrates the importance of congressional oversight and budgeting to political control. Enforcements by the EPA's Hazardous Waste Compliance Division increased sharply after intense congressional interest and the resulting Burford contempt citation. That citation, however, was largely symbolic, and the agency could not respond fully without increased enforcement capacity. It took the budget increases of fiscal year 1984 to move hazardous waste enforcements to significantly higher levels. Thus, congressional signals were important, but it was the congressional appropriations process that determined the EPA's capacity to respond to political demands.

These conclusions contain several implications for future studies. Various scholars have suggested that the stable equilibria of bureaucracies reflect passive political control by Congress and the president, who jointly create federal programs, as well as by the courts. However, the pattern of movements shown in this chapter demonstrates active political control. We believe this evidence of active political control is so strong that controversy over whether political control occurs should end. Future research should turn toward exploring the *determinants* of political control.

Several questions should be important to future studies on such determinants. Does bureaucratic responsiveness depend on bureaucratic structure, personnel attributes, mission complexity, or administrative constraints? How do constituency effects relate to political-bureaucratic equilibria? Is issue salience an important factor? Are movements in bureaucracy always consistent with electoral mandates and public preferences? Is there congruence between the signals sent to the bureaucracy by political principals and public preferences? This analysis by design, with its focus on discrete stimuli, was not equipped to answer these questions. However, comparison of movements among agencies does imply something of these relations.

Roughly, agency responsiveness and stability can be arrayed along a continuum that aligns nicely with certain bureaucratic attributes. The agencies most responsive to executive influence, as gauged by the magnitude and duration of change, were those situated in the executive departments. The FDA in the Department of Health and Human Services, the NHTSA in the Department of Transportation, and the OSM in the Department of the Interior had outputs that remained lower than their preintervention levels for the duration of their series. These agencies also implemented programs lower in issue salience, weaker in constituency support, and further from congressional attention.

The agencies with the most stable outputs were the independent regulatory commissions. The NRC reflects the extreme position since its outputs moved only briefly away from an equilibrium to return quickly without external intervention. The EEOC Office of General Counsel responded for a time to executive influence, but outputs rebounded when Congress and aroused constituencies intervened. The FTC was an exception to this rule since its outputs remained depressed throughout the Reagan administration. The FTC, however, was also exceptional in that both the president and congressional oversight committees agreed that decreased FTC activity was desirable. The ICC was also an exception with its reregulation of the trucking industry after 1981. Nevertheless, the findings suggest that structure is important but not overriding when democratic principals demand a policy outcome.

Concerning the consistency of movements in the bureaucracy with public preferences or election mandates, the analyses presented in this chapter suggest that problems may exist for bureaucracy in democracy. Ronald Reagan had no electoral mandate to reregulate the trucking industry after 1981. Rather, he ran on a platform of deregulation and moved policy in a direction different from his stated preferences and perhaps different from those of the public. Furthermore, it is unclear whether the movements at other agencies were consistent with campaign promises or public preferences. Few Americans would have favored reducing FDA scrutiny of food and drug manufacturing operations after 1981 as actually occurred. Nor were the dramatic changes that occurred at the EEOC, NHTSA, FTC, NRC, OSM, and EPA necessarily consistent with public preferences. Rather, they were responses to the particularistic demands of groups, suggesting that the presidency is plagued every bit as much with special interest influence and nonaccountability as Congress is.

The findings and methods used in this chapter show that, contrary to the past literature, bureaucracy is frequently responsive to political institutions. They also suggest, however, that movements by politicians and bureaucrats may sometimes lack accountability and consistency with public preferences. Interestingly, the findings and methods used in this chapter also suggest a form of policy analysis that could enhance future democratic control of politicians and the bureaucracy. We turn to the subject of reforming government in Chapter 6.

4

The Dynamics of Political-Bureaucratic Adaptation

Empirical political science research has demonstrated that bureaucracies do respond to external top-down and bottom-up political forces. In Chapter 3 we demonstrated the broad scope of bureaucratic responsiveness by evaluating outputs over time of eight different federal agencies. In the process we also examined some of the mechanisms of political control of the bureaucracy. The movements modeled in Chapter 3 illustrated specific political-bureaucratic adaptation processes since all bureaucracies responded in a dynamic fashion through time to discrete political stimuli. The analysis was limited, however, by its emphasis on multiple agencies and discrete stimuli. In this chapter we demonstrate the complexity and richness of bureaucratic adaptation processes by focusing on a single agency and considering multiple stimuli and stimulus types.

By looking at the programs of one agency, we answer several questions. What are the specific stimuli that drive changes in bureaucratic behavior? What is the relative importance of these various stimuli to policy movements? Do changes in the bureaucracy result from discrete events and event processes alone, as past research suggested, or do they also result from long-term forces such as the changing *tone* of political-bureaucratic relations? Do bureaucracies always respond quickly and fully to all change stimuli, as suggested by the static models of past research, or do they also respond gradually, with movements distributed through time in probabilistic fashion?

We answer these questions by developing a model of political-bureaucratic adaptation and empirically testing it on output data from four programs of the EPA. As in the previous chapter, we find that political institutions critically shape bureaucratic behavior. We also isolate many of the specific mechanisms through which political institutions operate, and we identify their relative importance. Some mechanisms involve discrete events and event processes; others evolve more gradually through time. Some responses are immediate and completed very quickly; others are delayed, gradual, and distributed through time in various causal patterns with different speeds of adjustment. The image produced is one of complex, dynamic bureaucratic adaptation, indeed much more complex and dynamic than the simple dyadic patterns depicted by past research.[1]

PAST RESEARCH

The analyses presented in Chapter 3 made simplistic assumptions about the stimuli that flow from political institutions and about responses by the bureaucracy. These analyses underemphasized the number of stimuli that may occur and did not take into account the multiple stimulus types that can arise. Most past quantitative political science research on bureaucracy made these same assumptions and also presupposed that all bureaucratic responses are complete in a single time period. In short, past studies misspecified both theoretical and statistical models by underestimating the complexity of the stimulus environment and ignoring the possibility of rich bureaucratic response dynamics.

Conceptually, past research operationalized institutions broadly, not looking at the multiple stimuli that flow from each institution. For example, most research on presidential control of the bureaucracy asked simply whether changing presidential administrations affect bureaucratic behavior (e.g., Moe 1982, 1985; Chubb 1985; Scholz and Wei 1986; Eisner and Meier 1990; Wood 1991, 1992). Typically, these studies represented the multiple stimuli emanating from the presidency but did so with a single policy intervention switching on at the first year of an administration. Obviously, with annual data such specifications leave much to the imagination regarding *how* presidential control occurs. The president can operate through multiple control mechanisms, all of which may develop in multiple months and years. So a single intervention switching on at the first year of a presidential administration is obviously inappropriate.

Likewise, studies of congressional control of the bureaucracy specified models that ignored the true stimulus process emanating from Congress. Scholars typically argued that committees or subcommittees are important but then used annual interest group support scores to measure their influence (see, e.g., Weingast and Moran 1983; Chubb 1985; Moe 1985; Scholz and Wei 1986; Eisner and Meier 1990; Wood 1992). Yet interest group support scores are only annual surrogates for multiple underlying stimulus processes. These scores are simply tallies of how members of Congress voted on key issues of concern to interest groups. Such tallies may be indicative, but they do not truly reflect stimulus-response processes.

Past models of politics and the bureaucracy ignored the multiple stimuli that can flow from political institutions and failed to reflect the different stimulus *types* that can occur. In the extreme, some studies tried to explain political-bureaucratic relations using only intervention stimuli (e.g., Moe 1982; Wood 1988, 1990; Wood and Waterman 1991). Indeed, in Chapter 3 we used this same approach in evaluating bureaucratic responses to the Carter and Reagan administrations. Such specifications contain the implicit assumption that the only stimulus type that can affect the bureaucracy is *the critical event*. Yet intuitively people know that change can result from other stimulus types as well. For example, multiple budget changes over a period of time can produce the same impact as a onetime budget change when the dollar amounts involved are equal. Similarly, to minimize resistance and avoid controversy, a shrewd politician may seek to impact the bureaucracy through multiple small policy changes rather than through a single dramatic break with the past. Thus, it is clearly erroneous to hypothesize that all responses are due to intervention stimuli.

Some studies have modeled political-bureaucratic relations using both intervention and process variables under the assumption that both events and progressions of events are important to bureaucratic behavior. However, no study has considered the possibility that events may produce no immediate response in bureaucratic behavior while having important longer-term effects. That is, the critical signals to bureaucracy may be changes in the tone of political-bureaucratic relations rather than discrete stimuli that develop instantaneously as each event occurs.

Past models of politics and the bureaucracy also ignored the complex stimulus environment of the bureaucracy and made simplistic assumptions about the nature of bureaucratic responses. Specifically, they assumed that all responses are completed in a single time period; an event at time t produces a change that occurs only at time t *or* t+n, where n is some positive number of time periods. To be sure, various studies included lagged responses, but none modeled bureaucratic responses as distributed across time so that a stimulus at time t produced a change in bureaucracy at times t+n *through* t+n+k, where n and k are the beginning and end points on some finite distributed lag of responses. Yet it is reasonable, given the common assertions in the literature about bureaucratic inertia and shirking, that both lagged and distributed effects should occur.

AN ADAPTIVE MODEL OF
POLITICS AND THE BUREAUCRACY

We have developed a theoretical model that depicts bureaucracy as an adaptive entity responding concurrently to stimuli of different types and from various sources in the policy environment. In this model bureaucracy responds to both top-down and bottom-up forces. Unlike past research, however, we operationalize institutional forces with multiple variables to reflect the multiple stimuli emanating from those institutions. The variables also implicitly recognize the shared character of power in the U.S. system. Additionally, we posit that institutional actors compete with other actors, such as interest groups, the news media, and the mass public, for control of the bureaucracy.

The model also differs from those of past research by operationalizing both the stimulus and response as dynamic. That is, both the stimulus and response can develop gradually over a period of time. The stimulus types considered include discrete events, event processes, and changes in the tone of political-bureaucratic relations. Responses considered include those that are instantaneous and completed in a single time period and those that are delayed, gradual, and distributed through time in a probabilistic fashion.

The Sources of Political Stimulus

The sources of stimulus to the bureaucracy include the president, Congress, the courts, and the larger political environment. The president as chief administrator can apply multiple inducements that affect bureaucratic behavior. He nominates top leaders for most agencies and some lower-level administrators. Once nominations are approved, the president continues to influence top leaders through personal persuasion, common ideological bonds, and periodic meetings. He also manipulates the resources available to bureaucracy through the OMB and the Office of Personnel Management (OPM). Finally, the president can issue executive orders (e.g., 12291) to centralize decisionmaking, and he can reorganize the bureaucracy to effect structural changes.

Although the Constitution invests formal administrative powers in the president, Congress as chief policymaker shares in manipulating these powers. The Senate must approve all executive nominations before leaders can assume office. Committees and subcommittees in both houses of Congress frequently call agency leadership to answer for agency performance in oversight, authorization, and appropriations hearings. Congress also has a critical say over agency resources through the budget and appropriations process. Through the GAO and the Office of Technology Assessment (OTA), Congress investigates the efficacy of bureaucratic activities. Congress can also rescind executive orders, reorganizations, or personnel shifts by enacting new legislation. Thus, virtually all executive administrative powers are also congressional administrative powers.

The courts have no power, formal or informal, to administer the bureaucracy. Nevertheless, they do shape administrative behavior in other ways. Courts impose constraints by establishing judicial precedent and potential judicial review. They also offer more direct inducements such as orders, variations in awards or penalties, and landmark judicial rulings.

Such stimuli can be reflected either as sudden changes or as gradual shifts in the tone of judicial-bureaucratic relations. In either case, the courts can also affect bureaucratic behavior through multiple channels.

The larger political environment of an agency is another important source of stimuli to the bureaucracy. For example, critical events (such as disasters or dramatic news coverage) can alter relations in a policy system to affect bureaucratic behavior directly or indirectly through democratic processes. Inducements can also work through more subtle mechanisms. For example, interest groups exert constant pressure on bureaucracies through lobbying activities, litigations, and publicity. News media coverage of agency activities can alter the visibility and perception of agency programs. The status of some policies is also determined by more diffuse factors, such as changing public opinion or national economic conditions. Thus, a wide range of diverse stimuli from the larger political environment continually impinges on the bureaucracy.

The Types of Political Stimulus

Three different stimulus types can emerge from all of these sources: discrete events, event processes, and changes in the tone of political-bureaucratic relations. Discrete events are stimuli that occur just once but are expected to have effects that last for some time. The analyses presented in Chapter 3 all utilized discrete events as the causes of changes in bureaucratic behavior. Specific examples of discrete events include the appointment of a new agency administrator, a large one-year budget change, the enactment of new legislation, a landmark judicial ruling, or a Three Mile Island–type disaster. With data of adequate time resolution, say quarterly or monthly, discrete events can be represented empirically by intervention (dummy) variables corresponding to the presence or absence of a discrete event.

Event processes are sequences of discrete event stimuli that pass through time. Examples of event processes that should affect the bureaucracy include the time-ordered set of all budgets, all congressional oversight hearings, all relevant rulings by the courts, and all news stories on a particular policy process. Event processes are just time-ordered variables containing the set of all discrete events in an episodic sequence. The multiple events of an event process variable may produce changes just as large as a single intervention variable. Changes resulting from an event process stimulus, however, may be more difficult to observe since they occur gradually rather than abruptly (as shown in the previous chapter).

Tonal stimuli are those that develop gradually over time rather than being manifested through each discrete event. They consist of accumulations of events that affect the character of relations between political actors. A more precise definition of a tonal stimulus makes use of a moving average measure. A moving average is just a window of lagged averaged observations drawn from an event process occurring through time. Each step forward in time adds a new observation but drops the initial observation from the previous window.

One way to identify a tonal process is by observing the lagged responses to the corresponding event process measure. Intuitively, one would expect the response to a discrete event to diminish as time progresses. In contrast, tonal stimuli should differ from event process stimuli in that the lagged response does not diminish as one would intuitively expect. The response remains relatively constant over time. Later, we use this characteristic to distinguish a dynamic stimulus from a dynamic response. For now, however, we simply want to observe that a tonal stimulus utilizes the same events as the event process but measures the longer-term forces operating on bureaucratic behavior.

Intuitively, a tonal stimulus says that it is not the actual events themselves that cause change in bureaucratic behavior. Rather, it is the change in the tone of relations resulting from the actual events. Change results from a gradually developing force disassociated from the actual events rather than from each event occurring discretely.[2]

The Types of Responses

In theory, each of the stimulus types just discussed can evoke responses that occur instantaneously at time t, or they can produce responses that occur some time later at time t+n. Additionally, when a response by bureaucracy does occur, it can be a zero order response (i.e., completed in a single time period), or it can be distributed across times t+n through t+n+k. At a more practical level, there is no such thing as an instantaneous or zero order response because all movements have an associated time dynamic regardless of speed. Thus, with data of adequate temporal resolution, all bureaucratic responses should be distributed through time. Social science research, however, has limited ability to measure some processes, so responses only appear to be instantaneous and/or zero order.

Beyond this theory of bureaucratic dynamics, there are also important substantive reasons to expect that bureaucratic responses should be distributed across time. For convenience of discussion, we categorize these reasons as technological factors, bounded rationality, or political interests.

Technological factors can affect the bureaucratic response dynamic through intraorganizational dependencies and/or inertial effects. Some bureaucratic activities depend on the activities of other actors or activities for completion. An agency that litigates, for example, may find it difficult to increase litigations instantly because these depend on prior activities for completion (e.g., preliminary investigations and enforcements). Referrals and evidence may have to come from field offices, making it difficult for central offices to proceed as desired. Similarly, it may also be difficult to halt litigations because cases have already been developed and referred and bureaucracies are bound by administrative rules to file litigations under these circumstances. In other words, bureaucratic inertia can make it difficult for political leaders to change agency activities. Obviously, the exact nature of the technological factor varies with the agency and process. However, technological factors generally produce a lag between the times of stimulus transmission and response initiation as well as a distribution of response movements through time.

The bounded rationality of political and bureaucratic actors is another potential source of bureaucratic response dynamics (see, e.g., Simon 1947; Lindblom 1959). On the one hand, political actors may be uncertain and ambiguous about the signals they want to send, thereby causing a delay in transmission and/or uncertain responses. Strategic politicians may seek to avoid alienating constituents by sending weak or conflicting signals (and, in the extreme, producing a tonal message). On the other hand, even if political actors do send clear signals, bureaucrats may still be uncertain about an appropriate response. In a political system emphasizing multiple competing principals and pluralist bargaining, bureaucrats may not know how to maximize their self-interest. Virtually any path will alienate someone, so it is more rational to change gradually, extending responses over a period of time, than to make drastic change under conditions of uncertainty. Incremental change allows for adjustment and lower risks and is often more consistent with the interests of the actors involved.

Bureaucratic response dynamics can also result from divergent political interests. For example, the literature on agency theory suggests that the signals sent by central institutions will often conflict with the interests of bureaucracy. When this occurs, bureaucracy is alleged to display a so-called shirking tendency. Under these conditions it is natural for bureaucracies to respond slowly; the greater the preference gap is between the principal and the agent, the more laggard should be the response. Change occurs gradually because bureaucrats want it to occur gradually. At a more general level, inducements from any source can cut across bureaucratic interests to produce a tension between intended and actual responses. The result is lagged and protracted bureaucratic response dynamics.

DATA, MEASUREMENT, AND HYPOTHESES

The dynamics of political-bureaucratic adaptation can be illustrated using output data from four different federal programs, each operated by the EPA. The programs each involve substantively important issues, namely, the EPA's regulation of air pollution, water pollution, hazardous wastes, and pesticides. Our primary purpose in choosing these programs is expository, not substantive.

The clean air program is administered through the EPA's Office for Air and Radiation. Congress passed legislation in 1963, 1967, 1970, and 1977 requiring establishment of national standards for ambient air pollution emissions from mobile and stationary air pollution sources. The legislation also established limits on hazardous air pollutant emissions such as asbestos, mercury, and vinyl chloride. Especially controversial is the 1977 legislation, which required the EPA to identify areas of good, moderate, and poor air quality and prevent significant deterioration in those areas. The EPA enforces standards through administrative procedures designed to monitor and penalize emissions violators.

Responsibility for water programs is located in the EPA's Office for Water. Primary authority from this office stems from two different legislative enactments: the 1972 Federal Water Pollution Control Act and the 1974 Safe Drinking Water Act. The 1972 legislation and amendments in 1977 made it national policy to control the discharge of pollutants into the nation's navigable waters. The 1974 enactment granted the EPA authority to protect public drinking water by establishing standards for maximum levels of contaminants that might be hazardous to human health. Accordingly, we deal with the EPA efforts to enforce standards associated with these enactments.

Hazardous waste program authority stems from the Resource Conservation and Recovery Act (RCRA) of 1976 and amendments passed in 1984. RCRA required the EPA's Office for Solid Waste and Emergency Response to maintain a tracking system that follows hazardous wastes from the time of manufacture through transportation, use, and ultimate disposal. Under the legislation, hazardous-waste-generating facilities must identify the wastes they create and report their means of disposal. Transporters of hazardous wastes are licensed and monitored. Disposal sites must be adequate to prevent the waste from moving through the soil and into water supplies. The EPA maintains an enforcement program to assure compliance through each stage of hazardous waste use and treatment.

Finally, pesticide programs are administered by the EPA's Office for Pesticides and Toxic Substances. The original legislation regulating pesticides—the Federal Insecticide, Fungicide, and Rodenticide Act of 1947—placed primary regulatory authority with the Department of Agriculture. Amendments in 1972, 1975, and 1978, however, placed the EPA in charge of pesticide regulation and granted the agency enhanced authority. Currently, the law requires that all pesticides intended for use in the United States be registered and certified as safe. Pesticide applicators must be licensed and trained in the safe use of the products. Producing establishments must register and submit to periodic inspections. The Office for

Pesticides and Toxic Substances maintains a program for enforcing these various requirements.

Litigation referrals from each of these four programs result from an enforcement process that works generally as follows. Each program implements legislation through ten regional offices located across the nation. The Office for Enforcement and Compliance Monitoring assists the regional offices by gathering and preparing evidence for civil proceedings against alleged pollution violators. Regional offices conduct inspection and surveillance activities to monitor pollution sources. Upon suspecting a violation, regional offices notify the alleged pollution source and give it a period to correct the activity. If the violation is not corrected within a prescribed period, then the agency usually enters into informal negotiations with the pollution violator. If the informal process fails, then the EPA and the alleged violator can argue the charge in formal administrative hearings. Failing to achieve resolution through formal administrative hearings, the Office for Enforcement and Compliance Monitoring may refer a case for litigation in civil court. These referrals for litigation are the dependent variable for the analysis presented in this chapter.

Referrals are common to all four programs. The number of referrals is only one dimension of an enforcement process that differs among programs. However, this dimension of program activity reflects the willingness of program offices to pursue implementation through to final conclusion. Practical considerations also drove our decision to limit the analysis in this chapter to referrals. There were slight differences in how the enforcement process works among offices as well as in how different enforcement actions are reported into the EPA's Compliance Data System. We have greater confidence in the reliability of this measure since the data on referrals come from one central computer rather than from the computers of four different program offices.

The data on referrals extend from the first quarter of 1979 through the second quarter of 1988 and are organized into a pooled-time-series cross-section to facilitate efficient statistical estimation. The data are time-series, rather than cross-section, dominant, which has important implications for estimation.[3] Pooling also enables us to compare programs for differences in responsiveness to political stimuli. Because there may be inherent differences in the number of referrals among programs as a result of differences in the enforcement process among offices, pooling allows us to test for such differences, and, if necessary, control for them through covariance specification (Hsiao 1986).

The number of referrals is a surrogate for the number of enforcements in each EPA program. The strongest predictor of enforcements should be the budget allocation since each program office requires personnel and equipment to operate. The budget is an event process variable reflecting the joint preferences of the president and Congress for a particular program. Variations in the annual budget should explain variations through time in program activities and variations among programs in enforcement outputs.

With the resources available for policy implementation held constant, enforcements should also change as a function of manipulation by political actors of other control mechanisms. For example, the president has the initiative in nominating political appointees, but the Senate must approve nominations before leaders can take office. Both the president and Congress are constrained by their respective constituencies on the range of acceptable nominees. Thus, political appointment is a shared tool of multiple institutions operating in a pluralist context. EPA appointments throughout the period of analysis should illustrate this point well.

Before 1981 a fairly consensual nominee, Douglas Costle, led the EPA. This Carter appointee was sympathetic to environmental programs and therefore met with little resistance from the Democratic Senate and others influential in the nomination process. In contrast, between 1981 and 1983 the controversial Burford headed the EPA. Burford was blatantly antienvironmental and was strongly opposed by environmental interest groups. Nevertheless, her nomination met with little resistance in a Republican Senate. Her stay at the EPA, however, was so problematic that she was forced to resign under pressure in March 1983. The Reagan administration, reeling from the strong reaction to its environmental policy, nominated Ruckelshaus, who satisfied most critics. Ruckelshaus served from 1983 to 1985, when he was replaced by Thomas. Thomas, like Ruckelshaus, was a consensus nominee who satisfied most observers.

If the leadership provided by these appointees made a difference to bureaucratic behavior, then there should be changes in agency outputs beginning at the start of each appointee's term. To capture this notion, we include a set of discrete event variables coded 0 for the time period prior to an appointee and 1 for time periods thereafter. Outputs from all four programs should have declined during the Burford tenure because of her strong antienvironmental stance. Outputs should have increased during Ruckelshaus's term because of his strong support of the environment. There was no discernible difference between the Thomas stance and that of Ruckelshaus, so there should be no change after Thomas assumed leadership of the EPA.

Changes in the budget and administrative leadership should affect enforcements in a manner consistent with the changing preferences of the president and Congress. Some have argued, however, that the president exerts control through means other than direct administrative channels (e.g., Nathan 1983; Waterman 1989). That is, deference to the chief executive and/or personal persuasion may extract additional loyalty and responsiveness from the bureaucracy. To capture this notion, we include a measure of presidential preferences on the environment. We did a content analysis of all presidential statements on the environment reported in *Public Papers of the Presidents of the United States* for the years 1979–1988. Each presidential statement was coded on a five-point scale ranging from antienvironmental to proenvironmental. An event process variable was created as the product of the number of presidential statements per quarterly period and the average of this index of presidential statements for each quarter. If the president also affected policy through less formal channels, then the scale of presidential environmentalism should be positively related to activities in each of the four programs.

EPA implementation should have responded to presidential leadership and persuasion and to the less formal control mechanisms of Congress. The oversight committees are especially important in this regard because they are in the most intimate contact with the bureaucracy. The four programs under investigation, however, have much different oversight constituencies. For example, the primary oversight committees for clean air are the Senate Committee on the Environment and Public Works and the House Energy and Commerce Subcommittee on Energy and the Environment. These committees have a history of strong support for environmental programs. In contrast, EPA's pesticide program has a much less supportive congressional constituency. Pesticides fall under the jurisdiction of the Senate Agriculture, Nutrition, and Forestry Committee and the House Agriculture Subcommittee on Department Operations, Research, and Foreign Agriculture. Both agriculture committees are dominated by representatives from farm states, where pesticides may benefit farmers. Naturally, there is less support for strong pesticide regulation on the agriculture committees than there would be on the environmental committees. Thus, we expect a difference in implementation among offices and through time relating to the varying environmental activism of congressional committees.

To measure the committee environmentalism concept, we created an event process variable consisting of both the frequency and substance of congressional hearings. We measured the frequency of congressional hearings as the number of hearing days on each program during each quarterly time period by the primary oversight committees. We measured the substance of those hearings as the average score for each committee in each year on the League of Conservation Voters (LCV) rating. The LCV scores were then standardized to the center rating (50) to form a scale, with positive numbers indicating above-average LCV ratings, zero indicating indeterminate ratings, and negative numbers indicating below-average LCV ratings.[4] Committee environmentalism was then measured as the product of the number of days of oversight hearings per quarter and the standardized LCV score for each committee. This measure consisted of actual events (hearings) that should have covaried positively with bureaucratic outputs across both programs and time.

The courts have no formal administrative authority over the federal bureaucracy, but they do send signals that reflect their support or nonsupport for agency outputs. We measured judicial support as an event process variable: the total quarterly penalties in millions of dollars levied against pollution violators for each of the four programs. This measure depended both on cases won (events) and on the size of the penalties in each case. We expected these differences in judicial supportiveness to relate positively to litigation referrals by the four program offices.

Beyond signals emanating from the three major U.S. political institutions, various other forces from the larger political environment should have affected movements by the bureaucracy. As discussed earlier, interest groups attempt to influence policy through publicity, litigations, and lobbying activities. We recorded the number of news stories per quarter in the *New York Times* that mentioned environmental interest groups (and dealt with one of the four issue areas) as the measure of interest group activities.[5] Because stimuli from the larger political environment may also arise from more diffuse sources, we included two additional measures to reflect the larger political environment. The number of news stories per quarter on each of the four issues reported by the *Reader's Guide to Periodical Literature* reflected general media interest in the issues.[6] We measured national economic conditions as the change in the U.S. unemployment rate during each quarter. Group activities and diffuse public attention should have covaried positively with program outputs. Change in unemployment should have covaried negatively.

All of the preceding measures were constructed to represent discrete events and event processes. However, a complementary conception of some variables would include a tonal stimulus. For example, it might seem implausible that news stories reported, say, a year earlier would determine current decisions to refer cases for litigation. Or it might seem very plausible that accumulations of news stories over the previous year could affect current decisions. Likewise, presidential and congressional environmental activism, groups, and economic effects could also register influence through tonal, rather than event process, channels. Thus, we also evaluated a model that included tonal stimuli for some variables.

FOUR MODELS OF POLITICAL-BUREAUCRATIC ADAPTATION

We devised four different empirical models of political-bureaucratic adaptation, each reflecting different assumptions about possible stimulus types and bureaucratic response dynamics. The first two models are for expository purposes only; they represent the two extremes of theoretical constraint. The first model is the most constrained, allowing no distribution of either the stimulus or the response over time. The second model is the least constrained, positing bureaucratic responses as distributed across time but assuming a common response dynamic for most variables. The third model alters the second model by eliminating nonrelevant variables and assuming that lagged responses can differ between variables. However, it does not consider possible tonal effects. The fourth model revises the third model by including tonal stimuli for some variables in place of distributed lags of event processes.

Model 1: A Static Specification

The first model is static, showing the result when making assumptions similar to those of past empirical research. Here all bureaucratic responses are instantaneous and completed in a single time period (one fiscal quarter), and the only stimuli to the bureaucracy are discrete events and event processes.[7] For purposes of analysis the dependent variable is logged to minimize heteroscedasticity in the time dimension.[8]

Table 4.1 reports estimates of how the various factors discussed previously affected program enforcements.[9] The model shows that the budget, political appointments, and news media all produced differences in the number of litigation referrals from each program through time. Subject to certain restrictions, estimates in the natural log metric when multiplied by 100 can be interpreted as a percentage change for each unit change in the independent variable.[10] Thus, each $1 million change in the program budget changed the number of litigation referrals by about 0.5 percent. The Burford appointment decreased the number of referrals from program offices by about 41 percent. The Ruckelshaus appointment, which followed large budget decreases and the Burford era, increased referrals by about 199 percent. Each additional news story per quarter on program issues increased litigation referrals by about 2.8 percent. However, no other variables were statistically significant, and the regression diagnostics suggest a model that is underspecified. The explained variance (R squared in Table 4.1) is low by time-series standards. There is also evidence of different responses among programs (the significant F statistic in Table 4.1), suggesting either the need for covariance specification or an omitted variables problem.

Model 2: A Least-Constrained Dynamic Response Specification

The static model can be marginally improved by lagging some right-side variables, as has been done in past empirical research. However, the ques-

TABLE 4.1: Static Specification for Determinants of Outputs from
Four EPA Divisions (1979-88)

Variable	Percent Change	Standardized Coefficient	t-statistic
Budgets	0.49	0.59	8.12*
Burford	-40.60	-0.18	-2.36**
Ruckelshaus	198.89	0.51	5.03*
Thomas	4.90	0.02	0.28
House Committee	0.70	0.01	0.28
Senate Committee	1.09	0.03	0.58
Courts	10.43	0.23	-1.12
News Media	2.79	0.18	3.56*
Presidential Statement	-0.48	-0.06	-1.12
Groups	3.28	0.08	1.44
Economy	16.68	0.07	1.12

Pooled Q=26.64* with 5 d.f. LM_{BP}=18.54** with 11 d.f LM_{sigma}=25.04* with 6 d.f

(Ljung-Box test for autocorrelation)	(Breusch-Pagan test for heteroskedasticity).	(Lagrange Multiplier test for mutual unit correlation)

Buse R^2 = 0.63*   Intercept = 0.20 $F_{3,121}$ = 12.87*
n = 152   (0.79)   (Wald test for different
                                                                      intercepts)

Note: * indicates significance at the 0.01 level. ** indicates significance at
the 0.05 level. The Pooled Q and Lagrange Multipler statistics are Chi
Squared distributed.

tion of the number of lags to apply and to what variables typically involves some relatively ad hoc considerations. Moreover, such an approach is fundamentally flawed in that it imposes unrealistic theoretical
constraints. All movements through time take time to complete. And
there are technological, rational, and political factors that can cause response dynamics in bureaucracy. The statistical model should reflect this
fact.

Thus, the remaining three models estimate bureaucratic responses as a
finite distributed lag using the methodology developed by Shirley Almon
(1965).[11] A common problem with the distributed lag approach is inefficient estimation resulting from collinear lags and lost degrees of freedom.
Extreme collinearity can also produce unstable and meaningless esti-

mates. The Almon approach ameliorates these problems by restricting the lag response to lie on a polynomial of degree less than the total number of lags. The researcher must select the appropriate polynomial degree as well as an upper lag length based on theoretical, empirical, or statistical criteria.

We use theoretical and empirical criteria to choose the upper lag length for the political appointment and budget variables. Theory would predict that responses to these variables should be faster than responses to the other variables because political appointments and budgets operate more *directly* on bureaucratic behavior. Appointees can issue orders and apply various formal powers to immediately change the number of litigation referrals. Likewise, budget changes also affect litigation referrals directly by altering the resources available for implementation.[12] In the case of large budget cuts, as occurred at the EPA in fiscal years 1982–1983, budgets may also send strong signals to the bureaucracy that activities should be curtailed, or further reductions might follow. Moreover, political appointments and changing budgets produce less uncertainty within the bureaucracy about the intended direction of a response, so there is less reason or opportunity for ambiguity or shirking.

Beyond these theoretical reasons for positing quicker responses to political appointments and the budget than for the other variables, we also have past empirical research to guide us. B. Dan Wood (1988) used monthly data to show that the EPA's clean air program had responded fully to changes in the budget and political leadership about one month after such stimuli occurred. In Chapter 3 we confirmed this quick response to budget changes for the EPA's hazardous waste program. The data used here are quarterly, so we constrain the budget and political appointment variables to an unlagged zero order specification. We reemphasize that the unlagged zero order specification does not mean that we believe the response to these stimuli is instantaneous. Rather, all movements have an associated dynamic regardless of speed. However, it is impossible to show this dynamic because of measurement limitations.

In contrast, the other variables of this analysis are more *inducements* to bureaucratic behavior than direct controls. Accordingly, we predict that the responses to congressional hearings, presidential statements, news stories, group preferences, and economic performance should be gradual, distributed across time in probabilistic fashion. However, theory offers no guidance about the specific amount of time required for such stimuli to produce a response. Thus, absent prior empirical evidence, we use statistical criteria to determine the appropriate lag length and polynomial degree for these variables.[13]

Results from this least-restricted model are reported in Table 4.2. After the additional lags are included, there are no longer any differences in responsiveness among the four programs (as shown by the F test for different program intercepts).[14] These estimates confirm again that the budget, political appointments, and news media are good predictors of program outputs. The coefficients for the budget and Ruckelshaus and Thomas appointments remain almost unchanged from those specified previously. However, the response to Burford was somewhat larger, and the news media variable showed effects distributed across time. The total effect from a distributed lag variable is measured by the sum of the lag coefficients. Thus, each additional news story on program issues resulted in 6 percent more referrals over a five-quarter period, more than twice the effect registered by the zero order response reported in Table 4.1. Individual lag coefficients and sums of lag coefficients for several other variables are now statistically significant.[15] The diagnostics show that the second model performs considerably better than the first, explaining about 30 percent more residual variance (R squared in Table 4.2). The Wald test for the joint significance of the additional lags is also highly significant, suggesting that the additional lags are relevant. Nevertheless, the large number of nonsignificant coefficients and sums of lag coefficients imply a model that is overparameterized (i.e., has too many variables or lags of variables).

Model 3: A More Parsimonious Dynamic Response Specification

Nonrelevant variables and lags in a statistical model impair the precision of estimates for individual coefficients as well as reduce the power of hypothesis tests.[16] Also, if the nonrelevant variables cause excessive collinearity, then unstable estimates can result. Therefore, it is desirable to have a model containing only relevant variables. The third model constrains the second model by eliminating all nonrelevant variables and lags.[17] The resulting model, reported in Table 4.3, performs as well statistically as the unconstrained version, but with a substantial reduction in model complexity. The Wald F test for the joint significance of the omitted variables and lags is nonsignificant, and SC is considerably lower for this version.

Statistically, the total magnitude of the response to each variable reported in Table 4.3 is contained in the sum of the lag coefficients. The relative magnitude of response is in the sum of the standardized lag coefficients. The relative speed of response is in the mean lag estimate.[18] The response dynamic is in the impulse response weights. The impulse response weights, reported in Figure 4.1, are just the conditional probability of a response to a variable at a particular lag.[19] Coefficient estimates for each lag reported in Table 4.3 are a product of these conditional probabilities and the sum of the lag coefficients. Substantively, each of these statistics provides a different indication of bureaucratic responsiveness. The magnitude measure shows "how much" bureaucracy responds; the mean

TABLE 4.2   Polynomial Distributed Lag Model for Determinants of Outputs from Four EPA Divisions (1979-1988)

Lag	Budgets	Burford	Ruckels-haus	Thomas	House Committee	Senate Committee	Courts	News Media	Presidential Statements	Groups	Economy
0	0.53 (9.18)a	-75.36 (-4.87)a	193.23 (3.93)a	-12.34 (-0.94)	-3.68 (-1.50)	-0.68 (-0.47)	8.03 (4.59)a	1.83 (2.72)a	-1.08 (-2.51)a	1.08 (0.60)	3.15 (0.23)
1					3.81 (2.76)a	0.10 (0.11)	4.38 (3.12)a	1.09 (2.76)a	-0.78 (-2.48)a	1.52 (1.46)	8.43 (0.88)
2					6.53 (4.15)a	1.08 (1.00)	0.97 (0.60)	0.77 (1.79)	-0.67 (-2.20)b	0.92 (0.75)	9.85 (0.91)
3					4.48 (3.34)a	2.27 (2.42)a	-2.20 (-1.56)	0.89 (2.56)a	-0.75 (-2.85)a	-0.72 (-0.70)	7.42 (1.00)
4					-2.35 (-1.17)	3.65* (2.54)a	-5.11 (-2.41)a	1.44 (2.21)b	-1.01 (-2.70)a	-3.40 (-1.99)	1.14 (0.09)
Sum of lag coefficents	0.53 (9.18)a	-75.36 (-4.87)a	193.23 (3.93)a	-12.34 (-0.94)	8.80 (1.75)	6.42 (1.85)	6.06 (1.20)	6.01 (5.31)a	-4.30 (-3.81)a	-0.60 (-0.17)	29.98 (1.02)

Pooled Q = 58.02a with 5 D.F. (Ljung-Box test for autocorrelation)
LM_{BP} = 41.38 with 39 D.F. (Breusch-Pagan heteroscedasticity test)
LM_{sigma} = 6.97 with 6 D.F. (Lagrange Multiplier test for mutual unit correlation)
$F_{3,107}$ = 1.74 (Wald test for different intercepts)
$F_{28,96}$ = 3.40a (Wald test for joint significance of added lags) SC = 0.94
Buse R^2 = 0.81a N = 136
Intercept = 1.22 (3.08)a

a Indicates significance at the 0.01 level.
b Indicates significance at the 0.05 level.
Note: The numbers in parentheses are t statistics. The Pooled Q and Lagrange Multiplier statistics are Chi Squared distributed.

TABLE 4.3 Dynamic Response Model for Determinants of Outputs from Four EPA Divisions (1979–1988)

Lag	Budgets	Burford	Ruckelshaus	House Committee	Senate Committee	Courts	News Media	Presidential Statements
0	0.52 (10.99)[a]	-68.98 (-4.67)[a]	90.14 (5.28)[a]			7.49 (4.12)[a]	2.02 (3.12)[a]	-0.86 (-2.13)[b]
1				3.33 (1.52)		2.29 (1.07)	0.84 (2.34)[b]	-0.72 (-2.77)[a]
2				7.71 (3.78)[a]	1.63 (1.01)	2.06 (0.99)	0.31 (0.73)	-0.72 (-3.07)[a]
3				1.13 (0.56)	5.30 (3.09)[a]		0.44 (1.27)	-0.85 (-4.64)[a]
4					1.37 (0.84)		1.23 (1.91)	-1.12 (-3.69)[a]
Sum of lag coefficients	0.52 (10.99)[a]	-68.98 (-4.67)[a]	90.14 (5.28)[a]	12.18 (3.08)[a]	8.30 (3.51)[a]	11.85 (3.12)	4.83 (5.28)[a]	-4.27 (-4.59)[a]
Sum of lag beta weights	0.54	-0.39	0.30	0.25	0.21	0.25	0.32	-0.57
Mean lag	0	0	0	1.82	2.97	0.54	1.59	2.15

Pooled Q = 30.79[a] with 5 D.F. (Ljung-Box test for autocorrelation)
LM_{BP} = 45.89[a] with 22 D.F. (Breusch-Pagan heteroscedasticity test)
LM_{sigma} = 9.97 with D.F. Lagrange Multiplier test for mutual unit correlation)
$F_{3,114}$ = 1.47 (Wald test for different intercepts)
$F_{16,96}$ = 0.53 (Wald test for joint significance of omitted variables) SC = 0.69
Buse R^2 = 0.60[a] N = 136
Intercept = 1.38 (4.06)[a]

[a] Indicates significance at the 0.01 level.
[b] Indicates significance at the 0.05 level.
Note: The numbers in parentheses are t statistics. The Pooled Q and Lagrange Multiplier statistics are Chi Squared distributed.

FIGURE 4.1 Dynamic Response Model Impulse Response Weights

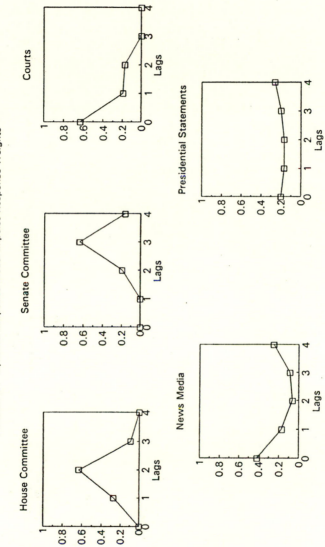

lag measure shows "how fast" it responds; and the response dynamic measure shows "how long and how" it responds.

Again, the estimates show that the most important determinants of EPA program behavior are the shared administrative tools of the president and Congress (i.e., the budget and political appointments). Each $1 million increase in the budget produced a 0.5 percent increase in the number of litigation referrals. The Burford tenure produced a decline in referrals of about 69 percent, whereas the Ruckelshaus term increased them by about 90 percent, only about half the estimate of the previous models. These were all zero order responses and were consistent in direction with the previous model.

Responses to the other variables were distributed through time in probabilistic fashion. The bureaucratic response to House hearings was larger than the response to Senate hearings. A one unit increase in House activism produced 12.2 percent more referrals over a twelve-month span; Senate activism resulted in 8.3 percent more litigation referrals over a fifteen-month span. The response to House hearings was also faster than the response to Senate hearings. The mean lag for a response to the House was about 1.82 quarters (5.5 months), whereas the mean lag for a response to the Senate was about 2.97 quarters (8.9 months). Figure 4.1 reports the impulse response weights associated with hearings by the House and Senate committees. The graph for the House committee is interpreted as follows. Given a response to House hearings, there was a 0.28 probability of occurrence in the first quarter after the hearings. The conditional probabilities of a response in the second and third quarters after House hearings were 0.65 and 0.10, respectively. Analogous interpretations can also be made for the graph of the response to Senate hearings.

The response dynamics for the House and Senate committees are similar in shape but have different magnitudes and timing. This difference may offer some insight into how multiple principals affect bureaucratic behavior in a democratic system. Throughout most of the period of this study, EPA preferences were closer to those of the House committee than to those of the Senate committee. The Senate committee was controlled by Republicans who were less environmentally oriented than members of the House committee. EPA careerists responded with greater magnitude and speed to principals in the House than to principals in the Senate. Therefore, a rule for predicting relative bureaucratic responsiveness in a multiple principal system might be the following: All other factors being equal, the bureaucracy always responds with greater magnitude and alacrity to the principal whose preferences are closest to those of the bureaucracy.

The relative response to the courts was of about the same magnitude as the relative response to the House hearings; however, it was only about half the response to the House and Senate combined. In unstandardized units, each increment of increase in the judicial penalties index produced an additional 11.85 percent litigation referrals over a nine-month span. Interestingly, however, the response to the courts was much faster than to either congressional committee. The mean lag for responses to the courts was about 0.54 quarters (1.6 months). This evidence of faster responses to the courts is bolstered by an examination of the impulse response weights shown in Figure 4.1. The figure shows a pattern of immediate exponential decay following increased penalties by the courts. This suggests an image of rational bureaucrats ever mindful of litigation awards, indeed much more so than of legislative inducements. As the particular dependent variable of this study highlights judicial influence, the results may not be generalizable across different measures or agencies.

The bureaucratic response to news stories is in the predicted direction, but the response dynamic is counterintuitive. Each additional news story per quarter produced an additional 4.83 percent litigation referrals over a five-quarter period, with an average response speed of about 1.59 quarters (4.77 months). The response dynamic, however, for the news media, shown in Figure 4.1, does not decay as one would expect if the true response was to an event process. The response that occurred four time periods after an increase in news stories was actually larger than it had been one time period after. Moreover, the lagged response dynamic was relatively flat.[20]

The response to presidential statements on the environment is substantively counterintuitive. Substantively, the direction of the response is negative, which says that antienvironmental statements by the president produced *stronger*, not weaker, EPA enforcement. This result can be understood by recognizing that most of the period under study was the Reagan presidency, a time of great tension between the White House and EPA loyalists. Thus, in this case the evidence shows that EPA officials did not respond to executive leadership or personal persuasion as theory would predict. They reacted to it in a manner suggesting a dearth of executive influence.[21]

The impulse response function for presidential statements is also statistically counterintuitive because it fails to decay in a fashion similar to the news media variable. Substantively, it is hard to understand how presidential statements made over a year earlier could make any difference at all to EPA enforcements unless they were critical events. Yet the bureaucratic response to presidential statements some fifteen months after they had occurred was larger than the zero order response. The solution to this apparent anomaly lies in proper identification of the stimulus process.

Model 4: A Dynamic
Stimulus-Response Specification

The models just presented depict dynamic response processes, but they do not consider possible dynamic stimulus processes. We should also test the notion that stimuli develop slowly over time, as do responses. Now the bureaucratic response to events should decay with time as the events become more remote and the reasons for the distributed lag work their way through the system. If, however, the events themselves are not the actual cause of response movements, except to the extent that they contribute to the changing tone of political-bureaucratic relations, then a distributed lag of responses to events will produce anomalous results.

As discussed earlier, the response to a tonal stimulus should be distributed more or less evenly through time because all events, regardless of timing, contribute the same to the true stimulus.[22] It follows that a tool for identifying a tonal stimulus is a distributed lag of responses to an event process variable. The distributed lags of responses to presidential statements and news stories, reported in Table 4.3 and Figure 4.1, show impulse response weights that are almost equal across multiple lags. Therefore, tonal specifications could be appropriate for these variables. We should also, however, do statistical tests to confirm this.

We began by expanding the dynamic response model to include tonal effects for all variables. The optimal span of the moving average measures was determined to be five lags.[23] We estimated all possible versions of this model, sequentially eliminating nonrelevant variables as before.[24] Interestingly, we found significant tonal effects for the news stories and presidential statements variables but none for the other variables.

The final model, reported in Table 4.4 and Figure 4.2, is more parsimonious than the dynamic response model, but with no statistical difference in explained variance.[25] The dynamic stimulus-response model also produced no meaningful change in parameter estimates from those just reported. Indeed, there was not even a change in the magnitude of estimates for the tonal variables. The effect of presidential statements on litigation referrals (-4.35 percent) were about the same as the sum of the lag coefficients for presidential statements in the dynamic response model reported in Table 4.3 (-4.27 percent). The estimates for the zero order and tonal responses to the news media ($1.59 + 3.12 = 4.71$ percent) were about the same as the sum of the lag coefficients from the news media variable reported in Table 4.3 (4.83 percent).[26]

There is no difference in explained variance or the magnitude of estimates between the dynamic response model and the dynamic stimulus-response model. Theory, however, offers an important reason to prefer the latter model over the former. The dynamic response model posits a re-

TABLE 4.4   Dynamic Stimulus-Response Model for Determinants of Outputs from Four EPA Divisions (1979-1988)

Lag	Budgets	Burford	Ruckelshaus	House Committee	Senate Committee	Courts	News Media	News Media Tone	Presidential Tone
0	0.52 (10.59)[a]	-70.29 (-5.69)[a]	91.38 (5.27)[a]			7.60 (4.19)[a]	1.59 (1.94)	3.12 (2.55)[b]	-04.35 (-5.15)[a]
1				4.00 (1.92)		2.28 (1.08)			
2				8.04 (4.01)[a]	2.13 (1.37)	2.15 (1.07)			
3				1.62 (0.82)	5.37 (3.18)[a]				
4					1.48 (0.93)				
Sum of lag coefficients	0.52 (10.59)[a]	-70.29 (-5.69)[a]	91.38 (5.27)[a]	13.66 (3.56)[a]	8.98 (3.95)[a]	12.03 (3.20)[a]	1.59 (1.94)	3.12 (2.55)[b]	-4.35 (-5.15)[a]
Sum of lag beta weights	0.54	-0.41	0.30	0.28	0.21	0.26	0.10	0.16	-0.38
Mean lag	0	0	0	1.83	2.93	0.55	0	0	0

Pooled Q = 19.94[a] with 5 D.F. (Ljung-Box test for autocorrelation)
LM_{BP} = 29.67[a] with 15 D.F. (Breusch-Pagan heteroscedasticity test)
LM_{sigma} = 9.78 with 6 D.F. (Lagrange Multiplier test for mutual unit correlation)
$F_{3,117}$ = 1.42 (Wald test for different intercepts)
$F_{7,113}$ = 0.56 (Wald test for joint significance of omitted variables) SC = 0.58
Buse R^2 = 0.79[a] N = 136
Intercept = 1.43 (4.71)[a]

[a] Indicates significance at the 0.01 level.
[b] Indicates significance at the 0.05 level.
Note: The numbers in parentheses are t statistics. The Pooled Q and Lagrange Multiplier statistics are Chi Squared distributed.

100

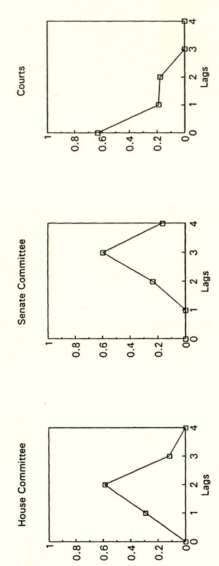

FIGURE 4.2 Dynamic Stimulus-Response Model Impulse Response Weights

sponse to news stories and presidential statements that is larger in the four quarters after the stimulus occurred than in the first quarter after the stimulus occurred. In contrast, the dynamic stimulus-response model posits a bureaucracy responding to a stimulus developing slowly over time. News stories and presidential statements over a fifteen-month period accumulated to produce changes in bureaucratic behavior. We view this latter interpretation as a more reasonable approximation of reality. Thus, we favor the dynamic stimulus-response model over the dynamic response model for both theoretical and statistical reasons.

CONCLUSION

The empirical results presented in this chapter complement those of Chapter 3 by demonstrating the relative richness of bureaucratic adaptation processes. The simple dyadic images depicted by past research should now give way to an image of bureaucracies as continually adapting to multiple, concurrent, and diverse stimuli. Some stimuli are discrete events, some are discrete event processes, and still others are tonal. Responses may be quick, delayed, or distributed through time in probabilistic fashion. Also, the pattern of bureaucratic response movements offers insight as to the technological, rational, and political factors throttling bureaucratic responses.

Beyond enhancing appreciation for the richness of bureaucratic adaptation processes, we wanted to highlight some of the specific mechanisms of political control of the bureaucracy and provide a measure of their relative importance. In Chapter 3 we identified several specific mechanisms of political control of the bureaucracy by performing time-series quasi-experiments across multiple agencies. Here we model movements in the programs of one agency in response to multiple stimuli. The findings bolster those from the previous chapter by showing that certain stimuli are important even after other possible factors are controlled for. Of more importance, however, is that *a focus on one agency allows the relative importance of various tools of political control to be discerned.*

The "best" model, reported in Table 4.4 and Figure 4.2, shows that the most important tools of political control are the shared tools of the president and Congress. The budget and political appointment variables explain most of the variation in EPA enforcements; they also produce the fastest responses. This is plausible since one would intuitively expect control over agency resources and leadership to be more effective than mere incentive stimuli. Yet this primal insight has not been incorporated into any previous research.

Administrative resources and leadership are the most important determinants of adaptive movements by the bureaucracy. We have also shown, however, that bureaucracy responds to various other, less formal incentives. Presidential statements alter the tone of executive-bureaucratic relations to produce movements suggesting a reaction against, rather than a response to, presidential influence. This finding runs counter to existing theory on informal presidential influence (Nathan 1983). It also supports the notion that some stimuli unfold gradually over time rather than occurring instantaneously with each event.

Congressional hearings and judicial decisions affect bureaucratic behavior by evoking gradual changes that are distributed probabilistically through time. The shape of the lagged response structures for Congress and the courts (shown in Figure 4.2) suggests the relative character of these responses. The quickest response was to the courts; the largest was to congressional committees, with magnitude about twice that of the response to the courts. Between the two congressional committees, the larger and quicker response was to the House, the actor whose preferences were closest to those of the bureaucracy. It is also clear as a result of this analysis that actual events, and not just ideologies or philosophies (as suggested by past research), were the specific stimuli affecting bureaucratic behavior.

We have shown the relative importance of various tools for democratic control of the bureaucracy. But our analysis also reveals a more direct channel of political influence through the news media. The final model shows that news stories make up two stimulus types, one short term and the other long term. Together both produce effects about equal in magnitude to those resulting from congressional hearings and judicial decisions. The relative quickness of these responses is also enlightening. The response to the short-term news media stimulus was faster than the response to most other stimuli, suggesting that bureaucracy is very sensitive to media perceptions. Indeed, the relative speed of these responses shows that bureaucracy is more sensitive to media perceptions than to perceptions by elected officials on congressional committees. The normative implication of this finding makes future investigation of the media-bureaucracy relation especially important. On the one hand, the response to the media may be considered just another form of democratic control. On the other hand, the efficacy of responsiveness to actors that are not accountable to the electorate may be questioned.

Dynamic methods such as those used in this chapter increase understanding of the richness of political-bureaucratic adaptation processes. They also allow researchers to determine the specific mechanisms of political control of the bureaucracy and their relative importance. Future research in these and other areas should use such methods and also adopt more creative causal theories.

5

A Bottom-Up Perspective on Political-Bureaucratic Adaptation

The last two chapters demonstrated empirically that administrative behavior often varies systematically with stimuli emanating from U.S. political institutions. This means that democratically elected officials can and sometimes do control the behavior of nonelected bureaucracies. Furthermore, it means that bureaucracies are indeed sometimes responsive to their elected principals. Both findings contradict many of the basic assumptions, delineated in Chapter 2, upon which scholars have traditionally based their descriptions and evaluations of the bureaucratic process. The empirical data provide a definitive answer to the question of whether hierarchical control of the bureaucracy is possible. The answer is an unambiguous yes! Other questions remain unanswered, however.

Because elected institutions do sometimes affect the behavior of nonelected bureaucracies, should the earlier literature that argued that bureaucracies dominate the principal-agent relationship be completely cast aside? Are bureaucracies merely limp receptacles of democratic power responding in any direction political principals want them to go? Or do public bureaucracies also have power of their own (as suggested by the earlier literature), sometimes using that power to alter outcomes in their relations with other actors? If so, then what are the sources of bureaucratic power? This chapter answers these questions by presenting two quantitative case studies. The first evaluates the NRC's civil penalty policy during the late 1970s following the Three Mile Island disaster. The second examines the EPA's clean air program during the early 1980s as that agency responded to Reagan administration initiatives to halt regulatory programs.

Both analyses emphasize the underemphasized element of agency theory as applied to the bureaucracy. Public bureaucracies have interests of their own that often cut across the interests of elected institutions. Bureaucracies sometimes shirk efforts at political control, and they employ their own political resources to alter system outcomes. Moreover, because of the circular nature of U.S. politics, bureaucracies may even alter the behavior of political principals and the stimuli they send. Stimuli for policy change can emanate from the bottom up as well as from the top down, and signals for policy change move in multiple directions, often simultaneously. In other words, relations in a principal-agent system are dynamic and nonrecursive, not just one way, as depicted by much recent empirical analysis, including that of the previous two chapters.

THE SOURCES OF BUREAUCRATIC POWER

In his classic 1949 article on power and administration, Norton Long (p. 250) argued that "the lifeblood of administration is power." We agree with Long's argument. Bureaucracies require power to effectively perform their assigned functions and maintain their position within policy systems relative to other actors. Variations in bureaucratic power are manifested through the design and operating characteristics of particular bureaucracies and determine an agency's ability to affect efforts by external actors to alter administrative processes.

Rourke (1984; see also Meier 1993) observed the sources of bureaucratic power as consisting of four factors: expertise, vitality, leadership, and constituency. Expertise confers bureaucratic power through superior knowledge of a problem or policy. An expert bureaucracy in possession of a complex problem is often in a position of overpowering authority relative to other actors. Outside actors lack the bureaucracy's understanding of the policy problem. They lack information on critical organizational functions and competence in implementation technologies. Furthermore, they do not have the time, training, education, or interest to become expert participants in the policy process that governs particular agencies. Therefore, the standard argument is that bureaucracies can dominate policy systems requiring expertise and involving complex implementation technologies.

Vitality refers to the commitment of bureaucratic personnel to job, program, or organization. Meier (1993) called this attribute cohesion. Some bureaucracies are careful to recruit only those personnel with a strong prior commitment to the goals of an organization (Kaufman 1960). This initial commitment, whatever its level, is reinforced by continuing service with the bureaucracy. Personnel develop a deeper commitment to the bureaucracy through experience and exposure to programs. They also become dependent on the organization as their income and personal rewards increase. With the development of a strong committed cadre of personnel, bureaucracies are better able to resist efforts at change that runs counter to bureaucratic interests. Thus, some bureaucratic power stems from the personnel of an organization.

Rourke also argued that leadership in an organization can enhance these first two attributes. A strong leader possesses both expertise and vitality, thereby amplifying the organizational position relative to other actors. Such an individual augments the resources of an organization through effective interactions with outside actors. This results in larger budgets and greater authority for the organization, which can in turn attract more expert and committed personnel. Furthermore, effective leadership can itself generate excitement about an organization, which attracts better personnel with expertise and vitality. This excitement also brings out the best in the personnel who are already there. Thus, the multiple dimensions of leadership enhance bureaucratic power both directly and indirectly.

Constituency heightens bureaucratic power through the ability of a bureaucracy to mobilize external support or curb political opposition. Bureaucratic constituents consist of all institutions, individuals, or groups that are served in any way by an agency's programs. This includes institutional actors such as the president, Congress, and the courts. It also includes interest groups and the mass public. All bureaucracies have constituencies, or they would not have become bureaucracies in the first place; nor could they exist for very long without these constituencies. However, some bureaucracies have stronger constituencies than others. As Marver Bernstein (1955; see also Downs 1967) observed, the constituencies present at the time of policy legitimation may change from those present during the time of policy implementation. Congress or the president may become less concerned with the policy after it is established. Interest groups and the mass public may consider their mission accomplished when laws are passed and bureaucracies are created. Such attitudes may lead to program perversion (i.e., capture) as a bureaucracy with loose administrative discretion reaches out for other sources of political support. These attitudes may also lead to program decline as the bureaucracy loses the resources and authority necessary to accomplish policy goals.

A lack of constituency may also result in excessive responsiveness by the bureaucracy to institutional forces. Under such conditions, the bureaucracy can become slave to actors that may or may not be bound by public preferences. Conversely, strong constituency support can also enable the bureaucracy to resist efforts at political control. Bureaucracies may even possess the ability to alter the behavior of other institutional actors. The opportunity for bureaucracies to maintain strong external support is enhanced by various attributes of the policy and policy environment.

The policy itself is important in this regard. Those policies that appeal to large numbers of citizens, evoke broadly based coalitions, arouse economic interests, have benefits dispersed across the country, and elicit strong commitment from citizens and groups are likely to result in increased bureaucratic outputs, along with increased bureaucratic power.

Citizens and groups enjoy receiving the benefits that bureaucracies provide. They become dependent on these benefits and are reluctant to give them up. Thus, when external actors threaten these benefits, other constituents of the bureaucracy become aroused.

A slightly different perspective on constituency is that support for a bureaucracy's policy varies because of the relative salience of the policy, which is a function of its intrinsic features as well as of exogenous events that occur in the policy environment. For example, it is easy to see that citizens are more interested in the Environmental Protection Agency than they are in the Federal Maritime Commission because they are more affected by environmental issues than by maritime ones. Everyone breathes air, drinks water, swims, or has some potential exposure to toxic substances. However, few people perceive themselves as significantly affected by the operations of oceangoing common carriers. Even if they were, it is still sexier to support environmental protection than maritime regulation. There is something intrinsic to the policy that makes it more appealing.

All policies can be characterized as having a degree of innate and continuing public interest. However, this continuing public interest varies across political actors and through time. Citizens tend to be less interested than politicians and bureaucrats who are continually exposed to policy problems; however, sometimes the reverse is true.[1] Interest groups tend to be more interested in particular policies than citizens are generally. At some times the president is more interested than Congress in a particular policy; at other times the reverse is true. The bureaucracy tends to be continually interested in the policy that concerns it; however, the constituencies of the bureaucracy do not always share this same degree of interest. Issue salience along the participant dimension is dynamic and continually changing.

Issue salience changes across participants and through time as a function of both long-term and short-term forces. Some analysts have argued that public mood, a very gradually changing stimulus, is important to the attention focused on particular issues (see, e.g., Stimson 1991). That is, public attention and attitudes toward particular issues change at an almost imperceptible pace, but such changes do affect democratic institutions and policy outcomes in a consistent fashion. Others have argued for the relative importance of focusing events in determining issue salience and policy outcomes (Kingdon 1983; Baumgartner and Jones 1993). That is, occasionally critical events occur that are related to the policy and that generate intense public attention. Salience is also tied to matters such as the relative severity of a problem, the number of people affected, elite leadership, news media coverage, and related dramatic events. In any case, a flow of exogenous stimuli continually impinges on policy systems to affect the interest of citizens, groups, elected officials, and bureaucracies alike.

This confluence of forces *from both inside and outside of the bureaucracy* can be viewed as producing a sort of equilibrium in bureaucratic outputs. Shocks may occur from one segment of the policy system to move outputs away from this equilibrium. However, another sector of the policy system may provide energy to attract the policy back to a stable condition located at the same or a different point. The results presented in the last few chapters suggested that shocks may cause movement to an entirely new position. However, policy always returns to a stable condition somewhere, at least temporarily.

EXPERTISE, EXOGENOUS EVENTS, ISSUE SALIENCE, AND NONRECURSIVE POLITICAL-BUREAUCRATIC ADAPTATION

The case studies presented in Chapters 3 and 4, along with various other empirical works, focused on whether and how political control of the bureaucracy exists. Although some of these studies were dynamic in the sense that they modeled the evolution of policy through time, they did not consider the simultaneous nature of interactions between political institutions and the bureaucracy. That is, these studies considered stimuli for policy change as flowing in only one direction, from external actors (mostly top down) to the bureaucracy. Such a perspective views the bureaucracy as essentially passive, able to shirk, but unable to do much else. However, the preceding discussion suggests that the true relationship is nonrecursive: Feedback exists and stimuli flow in both directions. Bureaucracies have power independent of other political institutions and compete with these other institutions for legitimacy and policy outcomes. But is this characterization true? And how and when does the exercise of bureaucratic power make a difference in political-bureaucratic relations?

The NRC: Historical Background

The forerunner of the NRC, the AEC, was established on January 1, 1947. Yet it took another two and a half decades before generalizable standards were established for the regulation of the nuclear power industry. Prior to 1970 there were less than one dozen generic rules on the books (Freudenburg and Baxter 1985: 99), and the licensing process was consistently biased in favor of the development of the nuclear power industry (Ebbin and Kaspar 1974). Furthermore, no major contested rulemaking proceeding was conducted prior to 1972 (Chubb 1983: 95).

Although the AEC was ostensibly created to regulate nonmilitary uses of nuclear power, its primary goal throughout the 1950s and 1960s was promoting the development of the nuclear industry. This goal required streamlining regulations and licensing procedures. Few critics voiced concern over the AEC's policy bias during an era in which nuclear power held out the promise of safe, reliable, and efficient energy. As public concern over nuclear safety increased during the late 1960s and early 1970s, however, the AEC's regulatory practices came under increased congressional scrutiny (Patterson 1983).

This increasing political pressure had two primary effects. First, the number of regulations increased from less than a dozen prior to 1970, to several dozen in 1974, and to several hundred by 1977 (Freudenburg and Baxter 1985: 99). Second, and of greater importance, Congress, through the 1974 Energy Reorganization Act, replaced the AEC with a new regulatory agency. Congress clearly intended that the NRC be dedicated to one goal: vigorous regulation of the nuclear power industry. Meanwhile, the AEC's promotional goal was assigned to another new agency, the ERDA, which was later incorporated in the new Department of Energy.

To ensure that the NRC would vigorously promote nuclear safety, Congress granted this commission-type agency an unambiguous regulatory mandate and emphasized this point by designing a unique administrative structure. To limit the possibility that political officials might attempt to influence the agency's professional staff, Congress divided the NRC's internal organization between a five-member commission appointed by, but not subject to removal by, the president and a professional staff composed almost exclusively of civil servants. Congress also delegated limited power to the commission to influence the activities of its own professional staff and located the commission and its staff in different buildings in diverse geographical locations, thus further underscoring the intent to establish an independent professional staff (Waterman 1989).

With this emphasis on impeding political control from the top, Congress also attempted to ensure that bureaucrats were held strictly accountable. The agency's enforcement manual is a testament to Lowi's (1979) call for limiting bureaucratic discretion by providing clear and unambiguous direction to the bureaucracy. The NRC's *Rules of Practice for Domestic Licensing Proceedings* (NRC 1986) explicitly addressed this latter point. The policy statement acknowledged that some measure of discretion is required but also delineated specific criteria for assessing a particular penalty and clear parameters for defining each type of penalty (of which five severity levels exist at present), the circumstances under which penalties can be assessed, the size of the appropriate penalty for each severity level, the conditions under which discretionary authority can be employed, and the identity of the superiors with whom inspectors must consult when discretionary authority is required. What these clear procedures suggest is that the NRC hierarchy is imposed by clear procedures rather than by a top-down organizational structure. Therefore, even though the potential exists for the NRC to change the pattern of regulatory enforcement, the agency is greatly constrained by the detailed procedures that it must follow. As the civil penalty case shortly demonstrates, these constraints on top-down and bottom-up effects have played an important role in the development of NRC enforcement policy.

In summary, because of its unique organizational structure, the NRC is a regulatory agency in which top-down political effects should be strictly limited. Although the analysis in Chapter 3 did identify a modest top-down effect associated with Reagan's 1981 appointment of Palladino as NRC chair, Congress's clear intent in establishing the NRC was to limit the role of politics and allow its professional staff to make decisions on the basis of scientific evidence and other technical criteria (Goodman and Wrightson 1987; Waterman 1989: Chap. 6). As a result of this organizational structure, agency personnel possess a great deal of technical expertise but do not have the power to make "policy without law." At the same time, political principals at the commission level are greatly dependent on their agents for policy expertise. Under these circumstances, the political environment is ripe for policy signals to flow from the bottom up, as agents attempt to inform their principals about needed policy change.

NRC Safety Policy

The 1970s witnessed a veritable revolution in the regulation of the nuclear power industry. The old AEC was abolished, the newly established NRC was given a clear and consistent regulatory mandate, and the number of regulations increased exponentially. Given this changing political environment, it is not surprising that the NRC's staff felt committed to a goal of vigorous regulatory enforcement of the nuclear power industry. Given the relative newness of the regulatory process, it is also not surprising that dysfunctions were soon identified. NRC enforcement personnel quickly discovered that the regulatory tools at their disposal were not sufficient to induce safety violators to comply with the two laws that defined the NRC's regulatory role: the 1954 Atomic Energy Act and the 1974 Energy Reorganization Act.

Internal studies conducted by NRC staff during 1977 and 1978 concluded that the maximum civil penalty that the NRC could assess was insufficient to induce compliance from industrial actors reaping huge annual profits. The maximum amount had originally been set at $5,000 in 1969, when the civil penalty procedures were put in place, and had not been changed since. In addition, the maximum amount that could be assessed against any violator during a consecutive thirty-day period had been set at only $25,000.

Since the financial effects of the current NRC penalties were "negligible," the NRC staff considered an increase in the maximum civil penalty size to be critical to nuclear safety because civil penalties provided "flexible sanctions to enforce regulations that otherwise could be enforced only by the extreme measure of license revocation" (U.S. House 1979: 477). According to one NRC report, the agency "would have imposed higher penalties on these licensees had the authority been available. ... The present $5,000/$25,000 limits define too narrow a spectrum to accommodate a scale of penalties commensurate with many types of licensees and the varying seriousness of violations" (U.S. House 1979: 480–481). The NRC staff concluded that an increase in the maximum penalty level to $100,000 would force the nuclear industry to pay closer attention to the NRC's standards (Baumgartner and Jones 1993).

The problem that the NRC staff confronted was that neither it nor the commission had the authority to unilaterally increase the maximum penalty size. The commission could, on a case-by-case basis, agree to the assessment of a higher penalty level, and NRC enforcement personnel could assess multiple penalties against a single violator. Even under these lugubrious procedures, however, the maximum amount that could be assessed against any violator during a thirty-day period was still only $25,000.

Given the perceived need for increased authority and the commission's inability to satisfy this need, the only option available to NRC personnel was to request additional enforcement authority from Congress. The NRC did just that. During authorization hearings before the House Subcommittee on Energy and the Environment on February 22 and March 2, 1979,[2] NRC chair Joseph Hendrie proposed that Section 234 of the 1954 Atomic Energy Act be amended to increase the maximum fine level to $100,000. Furthermore, he recommended that there be no ceiling on the total penalty that could be assessed. In a letter to the subcommittee's chair, Representative Morris Udall (D–Ariz.), Hendrie wrote:

> The Commission has been concerned for some time about the usefulness of the present statutory scheme of civil penalties. After reviewing eight years of experience with the civil penalty sanction, we believe that the limits on civil penalties needs to be increased substantially and that a change to the system of administrative imposition is desirable. The Commission has concluded that the maximum penalty for a single violation should be increased to $100,000. (U.S. Government 1967: 479)

Thus, a stimulus for policy change commenced with the NRC enforce ment staff, moved next to the commission level, and then progressed the House Subcommittee on Energy and Environment—a clear bottom-ι process. The commission's initial formal proposal was made as early as

February 21, 1979. Note that this proposal was not a reaction to the Three Mile Island nuclear accident since the proposal occurred before that accident. Moreover, the internal debate and studies occurred long before that catastrophe.

At 4 A.M. on March 28, 1979, the accident at Three Mile Island occurred, providing an additional stimulus for change that had an impact on the NRC enforcement staff, the commission, and all other institutional actors. The TMI accident had the immediate effect of mobilizing media attention and altering public attitudes. Largely as a result, President Carter removed Hendrie as the NRC's chair, though the president did not have the authority to remove Hendrie from his seat on the commission. The president further underscored his interest by making a highly publicized visit to the TMI nuclear site. Shortly thereafter a presidential commission was formed to investigate the causes of the accident. The findings from the president's commission proved highly critical of the NRC's organizational structure. They recommended that the commission be abolished and that it be replaced by a single administrator to be appointed and directly subject to removal by the president (President's Commission 1979). The NRC's own reports also were critical of the agency's regulatory conduct (NRC 1979, 1980). Thus, following TMI both the NRC's principals and their bureaucratic agents were subject to intense external pressure to change the agency's enforcement policy.

How then did the NRC enforcement staff respond to the crisis at Three Mile Island? Our interviews with NRC enforcement personnel suggested that they did not immediately respond, largely because the limitations inherent in Section 234 of the Atomic Energy Act prevented them from assessing individual fines larger than $5,000. However, our quantitative analysis of the actual civil penalty data provides a different interpretation.

As shown in the graph presented in Figure 5.1 and the intervention analysis provided in Table 5.1, in the quarter following the TMI nuclear accident there was a sudden increase of about 34 percent (or about 2.74 civil penalties) in the number of civil penalties levied by the NRC. Furthermore, in each succeeding quarter there was a gradual increase in the number of penalties assessed. The pre-TMI equilibrium was 2.05 penalties per quarter, whereas the final equilibrium level was 12.58 penalties per quarter. Thus, the eventual equilibrium level was 613 percent greater than the preintervention level. This sharply increased activity represents clear evidence of a response by NRC enforcement personnel to the TMI accident and contradicts the interpretation of NRC staff that they did not immediately respond to the crisis.

In addition to the number of penalties assessed, we also analyzed the size of the penalties for each quarter from 1972 to 1990. With regard to the size of the penalty, NRC personnel also responded to the Three Mile Island accident. As the graph in Figure 5.2 and the analysis in column 2 of

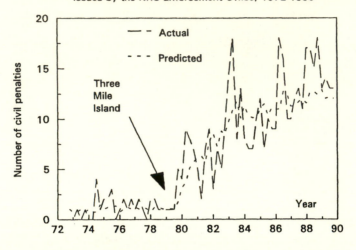

FIGURE 5.1 The Number of Civil Penalties
Issued by the NRC Enforcement Office, 1972-1990

TABLE 5.1: Three Mile Island, Increased Civil Penalty Authority, and NRC Enforcement

Variable	Parameter	Number of Civil Penalties	Size of Civil Penalties
Three Mile Island	ω_0	0.29 (3.78)	3.92 (4.49)
	δ_1	0.84 (18.61)	0.59 (4.75)
New Legislation	ω_0		3.02 (13.29)
Autoregressive	ϕ_1	0.21 (1.72)	
Measures of Fit			
RMS (Noise Only)		0.24	1.29
RMS (Full Model)		0.17	0.83
RMS (Percent Change)		41.37	55.59
Autocorrelation (Q)		21.60	16.33
		D.F. = 22	D.F. = 23

Note: t-statistics are in parenthesis. All intervention parameters were significant at the 0.05 level. All interventions were steps, except the Three Mile Island intervention for size of civil penalties. The dependent series were logged to attain variance stationarity.

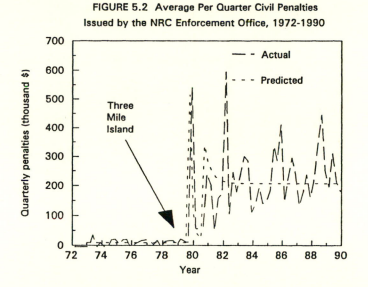

FIGURE 5.2 Average Per Quarter Civil Penalties
Issued by the NRC Enforcement Office, 1972-1990

Table 5.1 show, one quarter after the TMI accident there was an abrupt increase in the average penalty amount assessed—from a mean of $10,176 prior to the accident to $512,860 afterward. In this case, however, the increased level of penalties could not be sustained over time because of the limited civil penalty authority provided in the statutes authorizing NRC operations.

Ironically, then, the NRC's response to the TMI accident is evidence supporting the suppositions of the staff's earlier request for increased authority. Even when the commission and its personnel were subject to intense political pressure as well as increased oversight from elected leaders, they were not capable of implementing a larger penalty over time. They did issue more penalties, but given the legal limit of $5,000 per violation, this activity still did not represent an effective regulatory response.

Thus, our findings are consistent, at least to an extent, with the remembrances of NRC personnel. They did not respond by assessing higher penalties over time because legally they could not. If the NRC was to have the necessary resources to intensify its regulatory oversight of the nuclear power industry, and therefore prevent another TMI-like accident from occurring, then its enforcement personnel would need a grant of additional authority from Congress. Consequently, TMI underscored the limitations of the NRC's enforcement capabilities, thus placing additional pressure on Congress and the president to amend Section 234 of the Atomic Energy Act.

Congress ultimately responded to this combined pressure in June 1980 by granting additional authority to the commission and its enforcement staff. The commission in turn issued a new policy statement in October 1980 setting the new maximum penalty level at $100,000, with no maximum on the total number of penalties that could be assessed. What was the aftermath of this increased authority? Figure 5.1 and column 1 of Table 5.1 show no response in the number of penalties assessed by NRC enforcement personnel. The TMI incident totally dominated this series. However, Figure 5.2 and column 2 of Table 5.1 show that there was an immediate and continuing response in the average size of civil penalties assessed. After the policy statement was issued in October 1980, the average quarterly civil penalty levied jumped to $208 million, an increase of more than 2,000 percent from the pre-TMI penalty level.[3] Implicitly, the combination of a crisis event, increased civil penalty authority, and agency disposition resulted in a dramatic shift in NRC safety enforcement behavior.

Implications of the NRC Case

What are the implications deriving from this case study of NRC enforcement policy? This analysis illustrates the importance of bureaucratic expertise, exogenous events, and issue salience to political-bureaucratic adaptation. It also shows that bottom-up influence can sometimes be important to political-bureaucratic relations.

The initial stimulus for increased nuclear safety originated from within the bureaucracy. With its greater expertise and knowledge of the NRC enforcement process, the commission identified a dysfunction that limited its ability to force the regulated industry to comply with the 1954 Atomic Energy Act. Evidence of this dysfunction was first produced in internal studies at the staff level and was then presented to the commission. Next the studies were supported by a majority of the commissioners. Finally, they were recommended to the agency's House oversight committee. All of this occurred before the Three Mile Island accident, manifesting a stimulus clearly emanating from the bottom, rather than the top, of a political-bureaucratic hierarchy.

Bureaucratic expertise was at work in affecting the nuclear safety process. However, it was an exogenous event, the TMI disaster, that provided most of the energy for moving policy to a new equilibrium. The TMI accident dramatically increased the salience of nuclear safety policy, which altered the behavior of all actors in the policymaking system. Ironically, this increased salience became an instrument of power for the NRC, even though the commission itself came under fierce attack by the media, some groups, and the public. This salience presented an opportunity for the commission to showcase the limitations of the existing nuclear safety policy. Although NRC personnel attempted to respond to the accident by increasing the number of civil penalties assessed, they were unable to sustain an increase in the average penalty size through time. Once the accident occurred, as one would anticipate, political pressure was exerted on the commission and its staff. Statutory limitations, however, prevented their responding fully to the crisis.

The Three Mile Island incident placed great pressure on the commission and its nuclear safety program. However, the increased visibility of nuclear safety after TMI placed even greater pressure on the politicians responsible for oversight of the bureaucracy. Congress and the president found themselves relatively powerless to pursue their own interests under a popular mandate to do something about the safety of the nuclear power industry. Implicitly, both politicians and the bureaucracy were carried along on a wave of public sentiment for resolving the nuclear safety problem.

That the NRC staff had already identified a dysfunction with the regulatory process and proposed a solution allowed politicians to act quickly in adopting a publicly desired policy change. Interestingly, under these conditions the enhanced civil penalty authority requested by the NRC was not even a matter for congressional debate. No witnesses were ever called to testify on the matter, and there was no discussion of the future economic implications for the U.S. nuclear industry in published hearings. The amended authority requested by the NRC sped through the process hardly noticed by the media or nuclear industry participants. The result was an enhanced safety regulation capacity and an exercise of that capacity in a manner consistent with the revealed preferences of the bureaucracy and mass public.

The end result, however, also proved beneficial to the commission, the president, and Congress. The new authority and increased regulatory vigor removed much of the negative public and media attention from the commission, which had been subject to intense scrutiny immediately following the TMI accident. In addition, the agency's increased regulatory vigor worked to the advantage of both congressional committee members and the president by demonstrating their clear concern for nuclear safety.

CONSTITUENCY, VITALITY, AND LEADERSHIP IN POLITICAL-BUREAUCRATIC ADAPTATION

The NRC case study demonstrates how bureaucratic power can be enhanced through dramatic events and the increased issue salience associated with those events. It also highlights the importance of bureaucratic expertise and bottom-up initiatives to final policy outcomes. However, there is little evidence from the NRC case study to demonstrate how leadership, vitality, constituency, or other organizational attributes affect political-bureaucratic adaptation.

An analysis of EPA's clean air program as it responded to Reagan administration initiatives for bringing regulatory relief to industry can bring a focus on these other attributes. Chapter 3 looked at some of these same initiatives in regard to the EPA's hazardous waste program after December 1982. Chapter 4 contained an evaluation of four EPA programs generally, but from a purely top-down perspective. However, the focus here is on the most controversial and salient EPA program, clean air, and whether the top-down perspective offers a completely accurate picture of principal-agent relations.

There are some other parallels between the NRC and clean air cases. Issue salience was high for clean air, just as it was for nuclear safety following the TMI accident. Additionally, there is some anecdotal evidence that EPA personnel were responsible for stirring up public and congressional discontent with the Reagan administration initiatives. So the clean air case may also represent a case of bottom-up initiatives altering the behavior of key political institutions.

The EPA's Clean Air Program: Historical Background

Comprehensive clean air regulation was initiated in 1970 with the passage of the Clean Air Act Amendments. The 1970 legislation (and amendments in 1974 and 1977) assigned responsibility for clean air to the EPA and its counterparts at the state and local levels. The EPA was created by an executive reorganization under an order that consolidated fifteen different environmental programs into one agency to deal with the environment as a "single interrelated system." The structure of the organization broke from the previous trend of placing new regulatory functions in an independent multiheaded commission situated outside of the executive branch. The EPA was established as an executive agency with a single administrator appointed by the president. The agency was subdivided into areas such as enforcement, planning, research and development, hazardous material, and management. Within these divisions were offices that dealt with the major programs to be administered by the EPA. In 1980, clean air implementation was handled specifically by the Office of Air, Noise, and Radiation, with some tasks delegated to other functional areas. Most regulation was performed by the ten regional EPA offices. These offices contained technical specialists who performed the actual work of air pollution regulation as well as administrators who oversaw state clean air programs.

In spite of the EPA's status as an executive agency, during the 1970s it became substantially independent of executive control. This independence was enabled by a number of factors. Environmental laws had clear, goal-oriented legal mandates that bounded bureaucratic options. Environmental issues received the frequent attention of the media, keeping the matter salient to publics and politicians alike. Program constituencies, both aggregate and diffuse, prodded the agency to maintain vigorous environmental outputs. Many of the personnel of the organization were themselves zealous supporters and highly expert in the environmental technologies developing throughout the 1970s. The agency was closely watched by several different congressional committees that viewed environmental programs as their special bailiwick, facilitating a more vigorous enforcement of the law. The enabling statute also provided citizens with standing to sue, resulting in citizen lawsuits, which meant that courts also prodded the agency to maintain outputs. Because of these powerful supports, a tradition had even emerged whereby presidents selected EPA administrators to assuage environmental group interests rather than to exercise effective executive administration. By 1980 the EPA had grown into an organization that literally represented the environment.

These supports were manifested through the provision of copious funding for maintaining clean air enforcement outputs. At the time of the 1980 election, the EPA operating budget was at an all-time high of $1.35 billion (excluding sewer grants and Superfund), with clean air being the largest environmental program (Office of Management and Budget 1981). In 1980 about a fourth of the total budget, $326 million, was spent directly on clean air, with additional provisions coming from functionally supportive offices. A clean air staff of about 1,875 persons was maintained in central and regional offices for performing inspections, air quality testing, surveillance, litigation development, adjudication, and administration. At the time of the 1980 election, these personnel performed about 6,300 clean air enforcement actions annually and monitored state agencies that performed about 21,600 clean air enforcements annually (Wood 1987).

These national investments in clean air had impacts in the nation that were not viewed favorably from all quarters. In the 1970s industry spent more than $80 billion on air pollution control technology (Council on Environmental Quality [CEQ] 1984: Table A-19), but some estimated the cost to the economy to be much higher (Weidenbaum 1979; Arthur Anderson and Co. 1979). By 1980 the EPA and the states had gained substantial regulatory compliance from the more than 200,000 air pollution sources in the United States. The Council on Environmental Quality (1981) estimated that only 2,700 sources nationwide were not being adequately controlled. The Clean Air Acts and the EPA had changed the environmental landscape but had generated considerable political opposition in the process.

The Reagan Policy Initiatives

Ronald Reagan made it clear from the beginning that his administration would not favor vigorous environmental regulation. Generally he campaigned in 1980 on a theme that decried the evils and inefficiencies of big government, endorsing a shift in responsibility for many federal programs to the states and localities. Regulatory relief for business and industry was a major part of the Reagan agenda, with environmental policies especially targeted because of their alleged large impact on the economy.

More specific to Reagan's intentions for the EPA, his campaign rhetoric betrayed an insensitivity to the need for strong environmental regulation. Early in the campaign, he stated that air pollution in the United States had been "substantially controlled." In another speech he claimed that trees and plants were responsible for more air pollution than all of U.S. industry and went on to call for reform of the Clean Air Acts to aid the steel industry. On another occasion he said that if the EPA had its way, "you and I would have to live in rabbit holes." However, the most publicized of these gaffes was the Mount St. Helens statement in which Reagan claimed that the volcano eruption emitted more sulfur dioxide than had come from all the automobiles in the previous ten years.[4]

Between the election and the inauguration, extensive plans were laid down for reforming the EPA and its programs. That the actual administration objective was to reduce the enforcement effort was later a subject of considerable heated debate, with the administration stating that it simply wanted to bring greater efficiency to the regulatory process. But this claim was hard to maintain after congressional staffers produced documents demonstrating that in more than seventy instances Reagan's EPA administrators told OMB in plain English that they were reducing the effort to stop pollution (U.S. House 1982a: 26; see also U.S. Senate 1981a: 59). Whatever the administration's intentions, several events early in the Reagan presidency ought to have initiated change in EPA outputs.

The Reagan inauguration itself was a symbolic event that signaled to both the EPA and pollution sources that change was imminent. It was followed immediately with decisive applications of administrative tools for bringing regulatory relief to industry. Antienvironmentalist attorney Gorsuch was nominated as EPA administrator. At the Division of Air, Noise, and Radiation, Kathleen Bennett, a former paper industry lobbyist, was given responsibility for clean air. Many other key positions within the organization were filled with administration loyalists who were antagonistic toward the agency mission. A policy analyst who worked for the Reagan transition team admitted later that "hit lists" of EPA personnel had been developed to identify those most likely to resist the changes at the EPA. Personnel rules were used to place those so identified in positions where they were least likely to impede reform (Kirschten 1983; see also U.S. Senate 1981a: 10). Through careful personnel manipulations, the White House created an administrative structure that should have been more receptive to relaxation of environmental regulation.

These early personnel initiatives were augmented by reorganizations that also aimed at changing environmental regulation. Decisionmaking was centralized from the regional offices, giving the Reagan appointees more control over enforcement activities. Additionally, the enforcement division was kept in a constant state of disarray, being reorganized every eleven weeks after the Gorsuch confirmation (Gottron 1982). Previously, referrals of environmental cases to the Justice Department had averaged about two hundred annually. During the first nine months of 1981, only fifty cases were referred by the EPA for prosecution, with only twelve of these coming after the Gorsuch confirmation (U.S. Senate 1981a; see also Wenner 1984). The message was clear that the administration did not favor and would not support strong pollution control regulation.

All of these initiatives brought some striking changes in the EPA's organizational character. There were drops in personnel morale and an exodus of program zealots and professionals. Even before the confirmation of administration appointees in May 1981, the total EPA staff had been reduced by 11 percent. Much larger reductions were planned for the future (Andrews 1984). It was estimated that the turnover rate at the EPA during these times was about 2.7 percent per month, leaving a staff of conservers to run the organization (Gottron 1982). One observer remarked, "What was once a robust, dynamic entity was shriveled to a gray shadow of its former self, wracked by internal dissension, run by people with little expertise in environmental issues, and dogged by a paranoia that virtually brought it to a standstill" (cited in Crandall 1982: 29).

If the EPA bureaucracy was an agent responding passively to initiatives promulgated singularly by an executive principal, then enforcement activity should have dropped following the Reagan inauguration and definitive applications of administration power. The president removed all vestiges of executive constituency for EPA programs, making it clear that he wanted them subdued. He used his formidable personnel powers to install an administrative hierarchy responsive to his wishes. He reorganized agency decisionmaking to facilitate cooperation with his plans for regulatory relief. And all of these initiatives resulted in an organization less able to maintain the posture of bureaucratic autonomy. However, these were not the end of the EPA's woes.

A second related set of initiatives should also have caused retrenchment in EPA environmental outputs. Nine months after the Reagan inauguration, large budget reductions became effective for environmental programs. Congress, at the president's urging, consented to much-reduced fiscal supports for both the EPA and the states. At EPA the operating budget was reduced by 24 percent for fiscal year 1982 (U.S. House 1982a). These cuts had results that were specific to clean air. Between 1980 and 1983 constant dollar expenditures for air pollution regulation declined by 42.3 percent (CEQ 1984: Table A-19). The number of personnel authorized for clean air activities declined by 31 percent (U.S. House

1982a). Cuts were spread throughout the agency, decreasing EPA's ability to engage in all regulatory functions as well as provide ancillary program support services.

If the EPA bureaucracy was an agent responding passively to multiple political principals, Congress, and the president, then there should have been a permanent response to the lower budget allocations beginning with fiscal year 1982. This response should have occurred for two reasons. The first and most obvious reason was that the EPA no longer had the resources for conducting a vigorous environmental program. For clean air in particular, it took money to provide personnel and equipment necessary for air pollution monitoring and abatement activities. A second equally important reason that there should have been a decline was that the self-interested bureaucrats at the EPA wanted to preserve the organization and its programs. Continued vigorous environmental regulation could only result in additional future budget reductions and further cripple the agency. A reduction in enforcement vigor was therefore a predictable response.

From the election and throughout the first twenty-six months of the Reagan administration, an outright assault was made on environmental programs. Congress, although not antienvironmental, was more Republican than at any time since the 1950s. Additionally, it was a weak check on executive power because of the perceived mandate associated with the 1980 Reagan victory. This early reticence declined with time. A core of EPA activists remained at the agency, conducting a rearguard action through leaks to the press and contacts with friendly forces in Congress and elsewhere.

The assault on the environment had the unexpected effect of greatly increasing the salience of environmental issues. The press focused intently on the changes occurring at the EPA, often obtaining information from insiders at the agency. Public support for environmental programs grew as a result of this increased attention. By March 1982 a Harris Poll indicated that a full 83 percent of all Americans favored "strict environmental regulation" and would not vote for a candidate who opposed environmental protection (Mitchell 1984). Pollster Lou Harris told Congress during subsequent testimony that those representatives who opposed environmental protection were in peril of losing their seats. Throughout this same period membership in environmental organizations increased sharply, and groups became much more active in election campaigns (Rosenbaum 1985: 73–74). Constituents of EPA programs had most certainly been aroused.

As a result of these forces, Congress became more concerned about environmental protection. Between October 1981 and July 1982, EPA officials were called to testify before congressional committees more than seventy times to explain why they were not implementing the law (Gottron 1982). EPA administrator Burford was called on at least fifteen of these occasions. Matters came to a head with the toxic waste scandal when it was alleged that she was not only failing to execute the law but may also have been encouraging pollution sources to violate the law. As discussed in Chapter 3, Burford was cited for contempt of Congress in December 1982, resulting in some immediate changes in hazardous waste implementation. The turmoil surrounding these matters resulted in the resignation of Burford and the nomination of Ruckelshaus as the new administrator in March 1983. The Reagan administration's outright assault on environmental programs had ended.

The Burford resignation (and nearly simultaneous nomination of Ruckelshaus as a replacement) should have resulted in a positive response in the vigor of the EPA's implementation efforts. The resignation was a symbolic event that signaled administration acquiescence to public and congressional demands for renewed environmental policy. Equally important, many of the obstacles that had confronted effective regulatory administration were removed by the changes that followed. There was a housecleaning at the EPA, with most of the Reagan appointees dismissed and replaced with environmental professionals. Within a short time Ruckelshaus's leadership improved morale and renewed the spirit of the remaining EPA personnel. He even convinced Congress to restore some of the agency's budget. These reinstallations of bureaucratic supports should have resulted in a gradual return of EPA to its former position in promoting clean air.

Did the Reagan inauguration and subsequent initiatives evoke a change in clean air enforcement in the predicted manner? Or is there evidence of bureaucratic resistance to the Reagan initiatives? Did the Reagan administration budget initiatives have the hypothesized effect, as already indicated by the analysis in Chapter 3? How did the Burford contempt citation by Congress affect clean air outputs? Did Burford's resignation and Ruckelshaus's appointment affect enforcements in the predicted manner?

To answer these questions, two measures were created to aggregate different types of clean air enforcements through time. The resulting two time series, called the clear air monitoring and abatement activities series, consisted of monthly data running from 1977 to 1985. The monitoring activities series consisted of the sum of all monthly inspections, compliance tests, and routine surveillance actions conducted nationally. The abatement activities series consisted of the sum of all monthly notices of violation, administrative orders, consent orders, consent decrees, case development inspections, cases referred for litigation, and meetings for informal negotiations. The same methods described in Chapter 3 were then applied to answer the preceding questions. Results from the analysis are presented in Figures 5.3 and 5.4 and Table 5.2.

For both series, there was a response to three of the hypothesized interventions: the Reagan inauguration, the fiscal year 1982 budget reduction, and the Burford resignation/Ruckelshaus appointment. There was no response to the Burford appointment or to the congressional contempt citation. Interestingly, however, not all responses were in the predicted direction.

The response to the Reagan inauguration was in the opposite direction from what was expected, which suggests bureaucratic resistance. There was an increase in both monitoring and abatement activities between February and October 1981. For monitoring activities, there was a rise of about 105 actions per month, which constituted a change of about 30 percent over the average monthly number of monitoring actions characterizing the previous Democratic administration. For abatement activities, the EPA conducted about 85 more abatement activities per month, an increase of about 76 percent over the average number during the previous Democratic administration. These increases occurred with no change in financial resources and in the face of hostile political leadership. The direction and magnitude of the changes suggest that the EPA bureaucracy bucked the administration and used its slack resources to substantially increase the vigor of clean air implementation.

Following the fiscal year 1982 budget, the EPA was no longer able to maintain these increased levels of monitoring and abatement activities. The number of monthly monitoring actions dropped by about 185, a decline of 41 percent from the increased level and 23 percent below the average number of actions conducted during the Carter administration. Abatement actions decreased by about 105 actions per month, a reduction of 69 percent from the existing numbers and 56 percent below the average level of the Carter administration. Thus, the agency responded to dual political principals, Congress and the president, as implementation resources were dramatically reduced.

Following the Burford resignation/Ruckelshaus appointment, there was a jump in both monitoring and abatement activities. Monitoring activities increased by about 138, or about 50 percent, to equilibrate at a level 16 percent above the average numbers of the Carter administration. Abatement activities increased abruptly by about 64 actions per month to rise 52 percent above the existing level and 58 percent above the level characterizing the Carter administration. These changes occurred long before any budget restorations to the clean air program. This implies that the committed bureaucrats at the EPA somehow found the slack resources to restore activities—and to levels higher than at any other time in the agency's history!

TABLE 5.2: The Impact of the Reagan Inauguration, Fiscal Year 1982 Budget, and Burford Resignation on EPA Clean Air Enforcements

Variable	Parameter	Monitoring Actions	Abatement Actions
Reagan Inauguration	ω_0	105.47 (2.62)	84.83 (3.47)
	δ_1		0.93 (14.00)
FY 1982 Budget	ω_0	-185.45 (-4.17)	-104.80 (-3.70)
	δ_1		.87 (10.64)
Buford Resigns/Ruckelshaus Appt.	ω_0	137.87 (3.95)	63.83 (3.50)
	δ_1		0.99 (60.26)
Autoregressive	ϕ_1	0.48 (5.35)	0.25 (2.41)

Measures of Fit

RMS (Noise Only)		5068.10	1257.09
RMS (Full Model)		4223.39	914.23
RMS (Percent Change)		20.00	37.50
Autocorrelation (Q)		18.06	17.05
		D.F. = 22	D.F. = 22

Note: t-statistics are in parenthesis. All intervention parameters were significant at the 0.05 level. The interventions for the monitoring activities model were step inputs. The interventions for the abatement activities model were pulse inputs. The FY 1982 interventon for abatements was lagged 1 time period.

Implications of the Clean Air Case

A top-down model cannot explain the increase in EPA enforcements in the months following the Reagan inauguration. It cannot explain why Congress and the president changed their minds on the reduced efficacy of vigorous clean air regulation during the first twenty-six months of the Reagan presidency. Nor can it explain the level of the eventual equilibrium for EPA clean air outputs. More diverse explanations are required.

On the increase in EPA enforcements following the Reagan inauguration, it is clear that early executive leadership was ineffective. The person-

FIGURE 5.3 EPA Clean Air Act Monitoring Activities

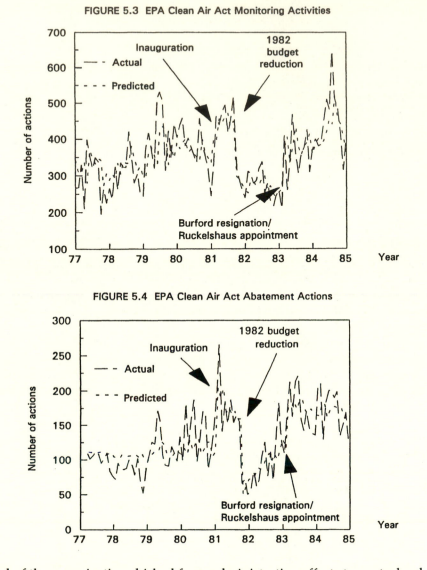

FIGURE 5.4 EPA Clean Air Act Abatement Actions

nel of the organization shirked from administration efforts to control policy. In spite of the considerable administration effort to reduce clean air outputs, alleged bureaucratic agents acted alone, contrary to administration wishes, to increase enforcements well above the numbers that had existed during the previous Democratic administration. There is no evidence that Reagan loyalists were aware of these changes or even that Congress or the public was aware. Superior information enabled EPA bureaucrats to deceive the administration and shirk from the attempted policy changes for a time. Nevertheless, the recipients of the increased enforcements were certainly aware of the expanded activity.

As to the reasons for the increases, it may be that committed EPA bureaucrats, aware of the deleterious signals from the 1980 campaign rhetoric, wanted to send a signal to business and industry that the organization was still in operation. Or there may have been a race to complete initiated enforcement actions prior to fiscal year 1982 because there was a sense that future enforcements would be curtailed. Whatever the reason, the evidence is clear that EPA bureaucrats were more than passive actors barely responding to top-down stimuli.

The fiscal year 1982 budget reduction brought to an abrupt halt the enforcement rebellion at the EPA. However, it did not end covert efforts to stifle administration policy. Some weak evidence of this covert movement could be discerned in the steady increase in the number of abatements after the 1982 budget. Abatements recovered gradually until the Burford resignation, at which time they were actually as high as during the Carter administration. However, as previously discussed, even stronger evidence of this continuing rebellion could be seen in leaks to the press and Congress on the problems at the EPA. Numerous confidential documents ended up in the hands of environmental defenders outside the organization. The zealous cadre of environmentalists remaining within the EPA made a conscious effort to mobilize their external constituencies in Congress and elsewhere.

These efforts were successful, as evidenced by the number of hearings conducted by Congress and the resulting resignation of the EPA administrator. Additional evidence is provided by the growth in public and interest group support for environmental programs through this period. This bottom-up stimulus had the eventual effect of ending the cooperation of Congress with administration policy; ultimately it reversed (at least partially) the administration environmental policy.

It is also interesting to observe the final level of the new enforcement equilibrium after March 1983 as shown in Figures 5.3 and 5.4. Clean air outputs moved to levels higher than at any other time in agency history! Why? It is only possible to speculate as to the reason, but it may be that the stronger political energy supplied by renewed program constituencies resulted in this higher equilibrium. Levels were higher because the preferences of the public, interest groups, Congress, and the bureaucracy for environmental policies were stronger. It may also be that the leadership supplied by Ruckelshaus was effective. Certainly there was a loud celebration at the EPA following the Burford resignation. Personnel at the EPA were also strongly supportive of the Ruckelshaus appointment. However, the victory over the administration may also have boosted the morale, cohesion, and vitality of the organization toward its assigned mission. Whatever the reason, it is clear that there are limits to political control. Unitary actors face constraints from bureaucratic power in their ability to manipulate agency programs. The EPA case presents an example in which manipulation not only failed but also backfired, resulting in a policy equilibrium more adverse to administration interests than in the beginning.

CONCLUSION

In this chapter we have presented two case studies for the purpose of highlighting the role of public bureaucracies in political-bureaucratic adaptation processes. We have shown that bureaucracies are more than vacuous receptacles of democratic power responding in any direction political principals want them to go. Rather, bureaucracies also have power in their own right and sometimes use that power to alter outcomes in their relations with other actors. Bureaucratic power derives from the expertise, leadership, vitality, and constituency of an organization. It may also result from exogenous events and the high salience of the policy and tasks.

These conclusions also imply that, contrary to the impressions given in past empirical studies, including those we presented in Chapters 3 and 4, relations between politicians and the bureaucracy are bidirectional, with politicians sending signals and bureaucracies responding at some times and with bureaucracies sending signals and politicians responding at other times. The centrifugal influence of bureaucracy and the centralizing influence of democratic hierarchies are both important, requiring consideration in any comprehensive theory of political control.

Some would argue that such two-way power relations are evidence of political dysfunction, given that bureaucracies are nonelected institutions. However, we suggest that the opposite is true. It is healthy for bureaucracy to use its information advantages to better inform principals on either policy matters or the nature of the bureaucratic process, as occurred at the NRC. Furthermore, as the clean air case demonstrates, bureaucratic resistance to duly elected politicians may actually sometimes be more consistent with democracy and public preferences than bureaucratic responsiveness may be. Citizens and many groups strongly opposed the deregulation of the environment advocated by the Reagan administration, and the bureaucracy served as a check on presidential power.

One might argue from the standpoint of normative theory that it is wrong for nonelected officials to exercise such power. Bureaucracies should always be accountable to elected officials, and power should always flow from elected institutions downward rather than from bureaucratic institutions upward. However, this is a fairly narrow view of the nature of U.S. democracy and representation. Theories of democracy should encompass the dual capacity in which U.S. administrative institutions operate. Bureaucracies translate current events and ideologies into change, making government more responsive to popular preferences. However, they also manifest past events and ideologies, thereby insulating government from the continual progression of external stimuli. Bureaucracies are reflections of both policy in the present and policy in the past. In this dual role they operate as *agents of the law*, which by virtue of their delegated authority are transformed into representatives in their own right. Consequently, they can themselves be an important source of the variation and substance of policy outputs through time.

This does not mean that democracy has failed. Public bureaucracies are legitimate democratic institutions charged with the obligations of both responsiveness and stability. Like elected institutions of government, they have representational tasks. They represent all those static coalitions of the past that successfully had their policy ambitions transformed into law. Bureaucracy derives its legitimate claim to representation from the laws and regulations that flowed from past coalitions. It often has inherent interests in faithfully preserving the law. Radical changes in direction should not come unless new laws are passed. At all times responsiveness should depend on bidirectional interactions that may or may not demonstrate a hierarchical aspect. Bureaucratic principals may even compete at times with elected principals for control of policy to move outputs in unanticipated directions. Put simply, bureaucracies are subject to manipulation by elected institutions under some circumstances, but their responsiveness is bounded by a legitimate representational task. And they do some manipulating of their own.

6

Promoting Bureaucratic Accountability: A Two-Way Street

As we discussed in the first two chapters, many citizens and scholars contend that bureaucracies are unresponsive to the policy objectives of elected officials. They likewise contend that elected officials are disinterested observers who seldom attempt to influence or control the administrative process. However, the analysis in the last three chapters provided a stark contrast with these widely promulgated views. For example, the empirical results presented in Chapters 3 and 4 demonstrated that bureaucracies are indeed responsive to a variety of elected officials and that elected officials actively pursue their policy goals at the administrative level. Furthermore, Chapter 5 demonstrated that bureaucracies also attempt to influence public policy outcomes. These combined findings have important implications for a theory of bureaucratic adaptation. They demonstrate that the bureaucratic process evolves in response to a highly competitive, political, and pluralist environment that shares many of the characteristic virtues and limitations of the larger American governmental system.

Beyond the more dynamic and more optimistic conceptualization of the bureaucratic process that emerged in the last three chapters, we share with many other scholars a concern for promoting the goal of bureaucratic accountability. Most past commentary, however, approached this issue from only one direction: How can bureaucrats be held accountable? Even though we share this traditional concern, in this chapter we expand the definition of bureaucratic accountability to include a second question: How can elected officials be held accountable in their attempts to influence the bureaucracy? In advancing this broader notion of bureaucratic accountability, our reasoning is as follows. The influence that political principals exert over the bureaucracy often falls outside of the realm of public disclosure. As a result, the probability that the electorate is capable of holding elected officials accountable for their actions at the bureaucratic level is greatly diminished. Consequently, true accountability can be achieved only if sufficient information is provided on the activities of both elected principals and their bureaucratic agents. In other words, account-ability should be a two-way street.

To accomplish this broader goal, we suggest in this chapter a policy an-alytic technique that we call policy monitoring (Waterman and Wood 1992, 1993). Policy monitoring is designed to promote accountability from both principals and their agents by providing an objective, systematic, and continual mechanism for analyzing bureaucratic activity over time. It allows elected principals to keep a watchful eye on their agents, thus pro-moting greater bureaucratic accountability from the top down. By identi-fying how and when elected principals attempt to influence bureaucratic outputs, policy monitoring also provides a mechanism capable of holding principals accountable for their actions. Before we turn to a presentation of policy monitoring, we first examine the theoretical link among informa-tion, monitoring, and accountability.

INFORMATION AND OVERSIGHT

In their classic book on Congress and the administrative state, Dodd and Schott (1979: 179–180) wrote:

> Information is the lifeblood of the congressional process. Congress has a constitutional responsibility to determine what the nation's policy problems are, to make a reasonable judgment about solving those problems, and to en-sure that the executive branch is adequately implementing policy. If Con-gress is to fulfill this responsibility in a reasoned, deliberative fashion, it must possess information that is reliable and sufficiently detailed to allow a balanced, independent analysis.

Dodd and Schott suggested in this passage that in the competitive world of bureaucratic politics, information is a critically important variable. Those who have access to it are at a distinct political advantage. Those who do not often become dependent on those who do.

For example, in recent years both congressional and presidential schol-ars have commented on the fact that the president has greater access to in-formation on national security matters than Congress does. As a result, most scholars agree that Congress has less influence over national secu-rity affairs than the president does. Likewise, as we discussed in Chapter 2, bureaucratic scholars have argued that agents possess greater informa-tion on the nature of the administrative process than their political princi-pals. As a result, bureaucrats have a distinct advantage over their princi-pals. To offset this information asymmetry, bureaucratic scholars have argued that political principals, such as Congress, must develop more ef-fective monitoring capabilities. Unfortunately, as Ripley and Franklin

(1986: 179–180) contended, access to reliable information has been a major problem for Congress:

> In large part most congressional committees and subcommittees either avoid asking serious evaluative questions about what ... programs [have] achieved or, if the questions are asked, are usually satisfied with a few anecdotes. And, for the most part, bureaucrats are content to present primarily anecdotes to Congress. The bureaucrats only rarely attempt to present more rigorous evaluation, even if such evaluation has been conducted. Congress rarely uses program evaluation as a basis for adjusting and reshaping agency implementation routines.

As Ripley and Franklin suggested, Congress needs greater and more reliable information to offset existing information asymmetries. It also needs to adopt a greater propensity to use such information in its analysis of bureaucratic behavior. Even though our analysis in the past three chapters demonstrated that Congress has exerted considerable influence over the bureaucracy, through its congressional committees and various other mechanisms (e.g., the budget, legislation), Ripley and Franklin's basic point is still valid. Congressional hearings do not provide a sound basis for collecting and analyzing objective and systematically derived information on the nature of bureaucratic activities over time. Nor for that matter are congressional committees, as they are presently structured, capable of providing continual and regular oversight of the bureaucracy over time. These are serious limitations that greatly impede the flow of useful information to the legislative branch.

In an attempt to compensate for these limitations, Congress has established other oversight mechanisms. For examples, the GAO provides members with a valuable tool for analyzing the efficiency of governmental operations, and the Congressional Budget Office (CBO) provides an independent mechanism for analyzing budgetary allocations. In addition, Congress has established such innovative techniques as sunshine laws, which afford members of Congress and "journalists [with] more frequent glimpses of the decision making process of powerful commissions" and "offer valuable insights to attentive publics." Thus, sunshine laws "help to equalize informational resources when participation occurs, as at public hearings" (Gormley 1989: 74). Although these institutional mechanisms have helped provide Congress with greater information, the legislative branch is still at a decided information disadvantage not only in relation to the bureaucracy but also in relation to the president. This is the case because in recent decades presidents have established new mechanisms in an attempt to increase their influence over the bureaucracy (Nathan 1983; Waterman 1989). For example, the OMB has employed cost-benefit analysis and administrative central clearance as a means of acquiring additional information on bureaucratic policy initiatives. Thus, as Meier (1993: 234) wrote, "Congress needs to continue its efforts to acquire policy information equal to that of the president."

For these reasons, we believe that Congress must have access to an objective, continual, and systematically derived source of information on bureaucratic activity. Since we have also demonstrated that other political principals (i.e., the president and the courts) exert considerable control over the bureaucracy, we also recommend that Congress have greater access to information on the activities of other political principals. Policy monitoring is designed to provide the legislative branch and other policy actors with information on the activities of the bureaucracy and its various political principals over time. Before we discuss how policy monitoring would work, we first briefly analyze the technique's underlying theoretical basis.

AGENCY THEORY

Our proposal for policy monitoring derives from agency theory. According to economists John Pratt and Richard Zeckhauser (1985: 2–3), "The challenge in the agency relationship arises whenever—which is almost always—the principal cannot perfectly and costlessly monitor the agent's actions and information." The goal, then, is to derive more effective and less costly monitoring capabilities to offset the information asymmetries that naturally exist between principals and their agents. In their analysis of agency theory, Pratt and Zeckhauser (p. 5) discussed several features that monitoring performs in the marketplace. Although our concern is with bureaucratic politics, many of these features are also relevant to the bureaucratic setting and thus warrant examination. Pratt and Zeckhauser (pp. 5–6) provided seven distinctive features related to monitoring.

1. There is usually less monitoring, or monitoring of poorer quality, when monitoring is expensive and/or substitutes for monitoring are cheap.
2. The agency loss is the most severe when the interests or values of the principal and agent diverge substantially and information monitoring is costly.
3. Ideally the agent's information and action would both be monitored. However, in a range of real-world situations, much more limited monitoring—say, of an indicator or output—is relatively or fully successful.
4. A large stock of value that could be lost through bad behavior, such as a reputation or assets subject to suit, is a strong incentive for good behavior.

5. Long-term relationships, among other benefits, develop the stocks of value needed for "enforcement" and make limited monitoring more effective.
6. The benefits of any reduction in agency loss will be shared between principal and agent in most market situations, including competition and monopoly.
7. Therefore, the principal and agent have a common interest in defining a monitoring-and-incentive structure that produces outcomes as close as possible to ones that would be produced if information monitoring was costless.

Bureaucratic scholars have long contended that existing monitoring capabilities, such as congressional hearings, are largely ineffective, primarily because existing monitoring capabilities involve a considerable political cost. For example, members of Congress get a much bigger political payoff if they participate in other activities, such as campaigning, raising funds, making speeches, or meeting with constituents. Therefore, members are generally less willing to invest their scarce political resources in monitoring unless there is a strong probability of a political payoff (e.g., increased likelihood of reelection, high levels of publicity).

Therefore, in light of the logic of Pratt and Zeckhauser's first point, if the political costs of congressional oversight can be reduced, then effective oversight of the bureaucracy is more likely to occur. The idea is to develop an oversight mechanism that is both effective and reduces political costs. This means that oversight should provide members with a greater source of information at a lower political cost—a seemingly difficult task. As Pratt and Zeckhauser noted in their second point, costs or "agency loss is most severe" when the interests of principals and agents diverge.[1] Since one of the primary assumptions of the principal-agent model is that divergences between principals and agents occur routinely, the goal is to establish an effective but low-cost monitoring capability.[2] Since political cost is a critical variable in devising an effective monitoring capability, the obvious question is, How can costs be reduced?

Pratt and Zeckhauser's third point provides an answer. Since it is too costly to keep a watchful eye on everything the bureaucracy does, the focus should be on a particular output, a series of outputs, or, in the bureaucratic setting, a series of outcomes. In this manner the political costs associated with monitoring can be reduced. Policy monitoring focuses specifically on an analysis of bureaucratic outputs and outcomes. As a result, it provides objective and systematically derived information on the nature of the bureaucratic process at a low political cost.

Pratt and Zeckhauser's fourth point suggests that even in lieu of existing monitoring capabilities, there are some natural constraints on the behavior of bureaucratic agents. Agents are aware that their reputations can be severely damaged if it is found that they have presented misleading information to Congress or other political principals. Agents must be concerned with their reputations in terms of the budgetary process, where an offending agency can be severely disciplined. A damaged reputation can also be particularly harmful to bureaucratic agents who are known primarily for their expertise and professionalism, such as scientists within the NRC or lawyers at the FTC. Thus, even though there may be a natural tendency toward shirking, the possible short-term gains from providing misleading information to a principal must be weighed against the possibility of long-term damage to an agent's reputation.

Pratt and Zeckhauser examined reputation as a factor that obviates the need for monitoring. We believe that a monitoring system capable of providing objective information on a particular agency's activities can actually enhance that agency's reputation, thus providing evidence for additional regulatory authority or increased appropriations. For example, our analysis of the NRC and the EPA Clean Air Division in Chapter 5 demonstrated that agency personnel were more committed to the goals of nuclear safety and environmental protection, respectively, than were their political principals. The dissemination of this information underscores the commitment of these agencies, and their personnel, to their mandated regulatory tasks. A broad dissemination of this information would likely have enhanced the reputations of the agencies and their personnel.

Pratt and Zeckhauser's fifth point provides another feature that obviates the need for continual monitoring: the long-term relationships between principals and their agents. In the bureaucratic world, the work life of an agent often far surpasses that of a principal. As Heclo (1977), Kaufman (1981), and G. Calvin Mackenzie (1987) noted, principals come and go, but bureaucrats remain in Washington for decades. As a result, principals have less information about the nature of the bureaucratic process, and agents can wait for the term of a principal who seeks unwanted policy change to expire. For this reason, there is an increased need to institutionalize an ongoing monitoring system so that continuity in evaluating the bureaucracy can be maintained even as various political principals come and go. A continual monitoring capability can also provide a sense of institutional memory for political principals that would otherwise be lacking.

At first glance Pratt and Zeckhauser's sixth and seventh points would seem to have a lesser application to the bureaucratic realm than they do to the marketplace. It is not immediately evident that any reduction in agency loss will be shared by principals and agents in the bureaucratic setting. Likewise, the assumptions of the principal-agent model suggest that bureaucratic agents will seldom have a "common interest in defining a monitoring-and-incentive structure that produces outcomes as close as possible to ones that would be produced if information monitoring were costless." In fact, the incentive toward shirking suggests precisely the opposite conclusion.

We contend, however, that a common interest between principals and agents can be derived if the goal of oversight is not one-sided—that is, if the focus of monitoring is not solely on the bureaucratic agent. As we noted, most scholars consider monitoring simply as a means of holding bureaucratic agents accountable for their actions. The principal monitors the agent to ensure that the agent's actions are in accord with the principal's expressed preferences. Yet if one expands the notion of monitoring to a two-way street and examines the principal's actions as well, then a common interest is more likely to be achieved. Under these circumstances, principals and agents may very well benefit from monitoring. For example, in the cases of the EPA Clean Air Division and the NRC, we provided evidence that could have enhanced the reputations of these agencies and their personnel. A monitoring system capable of providing similar information during the 1980s could have greatly facilitated agency dealings with Congress and justified even higher budgets. Likewise, principals can gain valuable information on the activities of their bureaucratic agents. Through a two-way process of accountability, both principals and agents can perceive potential benefits and costs from monitoring, thus increasing the likelihood of effective monitoring.

In summary, agency theory provides several features that provide a basis for designing a more effective monitoring capability. First, any new monitoring mechanism should reduce agency loss or the political costs associated with oversight. This will encourage greater scrutiny of the bureaucracy by Congress and other political principals. Second, this can be accomplished by focusing on a series of bureaucratic outputs and outcomes rather than the entire range of bureaucratic activity. Third, the monitoring system should provide objective analysis and information as a means of bolstering an agency's reputation or, for that matter, the reputation of a political principal, such as the president or Congress. Presidents can use such evidence to demonstrate that they have satisfied campaign promises, whereas Congress can cite similar results to demonstrate that it is active in meeting constituency needs. Fourth, oversight should be continual over time, thus providing a sense of institutional memory in a town where in-and-out government is often the rule. Finally, monitoring can be made more effective if the benefits of any reduction in agency loss are shared between principals and agents. The benefits can be shared if both principals and agents see potential political benefits (e.g., enhanced reputations) as well as costs in any monitoring system. This goal can be achieved by making sure that the activities of both principals and agents are objectively monitored—that is, by extending the logic of monitoring to a two-way street.

POLICY MONITORING

Although the concept of policy monitoring derives from theory, its primary goal is to provide actual decisionmakers (both elected principals and bureaucratic agents) in real-world situations with direct, systematically derived, and unbiased information on the level and nature of a particular policy output on a continual basis over time. As in the theoretical world, this information provides the link between effective oversight and actual control. When elected officials have an objective source of information, they are less reliant on the bureaucracy and better able to hold bureaucrats accountable for their actions. When bureaucracies have greater information on the goals and activities of elected officials, they are less likely to be the subject of blatant attempts to politicize the bureaucracy.

We propose policy monitoring to meet these diverse goals. What, then, is policy monitoring? It is an iterative policy analytic technique involving four basic steps. First, policy analysts examine qualitative evidence to determine the substantive issues involved in a particular policy-related question. This involves an analysis of existing academic literature, government documents, the historical record, interviews with various policy actors, and a variety of other source materials. It is during this first stage that the policy analyst identifies the relevant facts of a particular case such as who the relevant policy actors are, what their goals are, which stimuli they have applied in their attempts to control the bureaucracy, and what types of change they anticipate over time.

In Chapter 3, we presented eight examples of how the first stage of policy monitoring could be accomplished. Prior to our quantitative analyses, we examined each agency's history, organizational structure, task assignment, enforcement procedures, rules, regulations, and standards. We did this through an evaluation of various governmental records, including congressional hearings, legislation, legislative histories, and interviews with agency personnel. We also reviewed various secondary sources to obtain additional information. Then we used these same sources to obtain information on the possible political stimuli and/or external events that could account for variations in bureaucratic behavior over time. From this analysis we generated hypotheses for the subsequent quantitative analysis.

Once facts have been aggregated and hypotheses generated, the second stage of policy monitoring calls for the collection and management of a data base on agency outputs and outcomes. As Pratt and Zeckhauser noted, this is an effective means of reducing the costs of monitoring. It is also an effective means of gaining reliable data on how an agency performs its core functions over time. We recommend that time-series data be provided by bureaucracies at finely divided time intervals, preferably on a quarterly, monthly, or even weekly basis. This stipulation is extremely important because such data allow policy analysts to establish a close correspondence between the actual timing of a particular hypothesized event and a subsequent response. Again, as our analysis in the past three chapters demonstrated, a focus on annual data alone, which is the general practice in policy studies, obfuscates much of what analysts want to see. Meaningful change does not occur only on a year-to-year basis. Important policy changes frequently occur within each year. In addition, countervailing changes occurring within the same year can be lost in an analysis of annual data alone. By analyzing data at more finely divided time intervals, analysts gain greater insight into how, when, and why policy changes occur.

In addition to compiling data at finely divided time intervals, we also recommend that data represent a wide variety of diverse factors related to the policy in question rather than focusing on one narrowly defined policy output. Agencies perform many functions. Policy monitoring analysts should study as many of these relevant functions as possible. First, they should present as reliable a picture of an agency's activity as possible. Analysis of one or two outputs may not be sufficient to provide an accurate picture of an agency's overall activities. Second, agencies are not always homogeneous institutional entities. Important variations can exist across functional units. By using multiple indicators, analysts can examine variations across organizational space as well as across time. Third, a focus on only one or two outputs leaves the analysis vulnerable to beancounting and other threats to validity. As Gormley noted (1989: 204, 205):

> By demanding instant results, congressional investigators often demonstrate a "beancounting" mentality that encourages bureaucrats to play a "statistical numbers game" in order to appease congressional watchdogs. ...
> Ironically, this [has] resulted in less emphasis on "big cases" and more emphasis on "small cases" than Congress would have preferred. If statistics must be generated, small cases offer richer, quicker rewards to bureaucrats under the gun.

We can reduce such threats to validity as beancounting by employing multiple indicators of an agency's activities. For example, enforcement often involves a variety of diverse methods and techniques. In their study of the EPA Water Office, Hunter and Waterman (1992) found that enforcement personnel employed such widely accepted enforcement actions as inspections, notices of violation, administrative orders, fines, penalties, and referrals. In addition, EPA water personnel employed a wide variety of lower-profile but equally important enforcement mechanisms, such as telephone calls, letters to violators, and meetings with permittees. In fact, as Hunter and Waterman concluded, some 70 percent of enforcement actions carried out by the EPA Water Office were implemented at this low level. As their analysis suggests, by examining a wide variety of enforcement mechanisms, or multiple indicators, analysts can derive a more reliable and detailed analysis of an agency's activities.

Where can such diverse data on policy outputs be acquired? In the analysis presented in this book, we analyzed data acquired directly from each agency through requests made under the provisions of the Freedom of Information Act. This process was adequate for our needs but would not be adequate for a governmentwide monitoring system. We therefore recommend that data be regularly provided (monthly or even weekly) to a central data bank located in an existing nonpartisan agency, such as the General Accounting Office. Qualified personnel assigned to this office would then be responsible for managing and analyzing the data and for promulgating the results of the analysis to members of Congress, the president, and the relevant bureaucracy. In addition, upon request journalists, interest groups, and the public should also have direct access to the results. Through such an institutionalized system the process of data collection, management, and analysis could be routinized over time and institutional memory preserved. Likewise, placing these functions in a nonpartisan agency, such as the GAO, could insulate the analysis from politicization by both politicians and bureaucrats.

Depoliticization and objective analysis are also goals of the third stage of policy monitoring. This stage involves the statistical analysis of agency outputs using dynamic quantitative methods. In this process, analysts employ objective evaluation criteria (such as the ARIMA models and pooled regression techniques we used in the last three chapters) to determine the effect of a particular stimulus on a specific policy output or outcome. A variety of statistical techniques are presently available to policy analysts, each of which can ensure greater objectivity.

Analysts should also interpret statistical results as well as merely presenting the analysis. In so doing, however, analysts should reduce speculation as much as possible and instead rely on statistically derived and defensible conclusions. Since a variety of policymakers will inevitably review the results, objectivity should be a primary goal. The actual task of promoting one policy option over another should be left to policymakers, not policy analysts.

The fourth stage of policy monitoring occurs after statistical models have been analyzed and results have been derived. These results provide the basis for more informed analysis of the policy output or outcome under investigation, but they can also provide misleading information if other rival explanations are not examined and eliminated. Thus, the fourth stage involves a reexamination of government records and other qualitative sources, including follow-up interviews with relevant policy participants. These steps are taken to eliminate other rival explanations for previously identified interventions. This stage is particularly important when an analysis of a policy indicates that some response occurred but that it was not related to previously hypothesized political stimuli. For example, in our analysis in Chapter 3 of the National Highway Traffic Safety Administration we identified an obvious bureaucratic response that did not correspond to any of our hypothesized political stimuli. Follow-up interviews with agency personnel suggested that the stimulus causing the response was a lower-level political appointee who did not share the president's or the agency director's regulatory philosophy. By reexamining qualitative sources and comparing them with the results of our statistical analysis, we reliably explained an identified intervention in NHTSA enforcement practices.

The process of policy monitoring does not end with a single analysis. Policy monitoring is an iterative technique, meaning that one keeps on collecting data and analyzing it on a continual basis over time, thus providing a systematic and ongoing oversight mechanism.

Our model for policy monitoring is comprehensive and meets each of our established goals. It provides systematically derived information on agency outputs and outcomes. The analysis is conducted continually over time. The nonpartisan institutional framework of the central clearing house agency provides both a mechanism for promoting institutional memory and a means of promoting objectivity. The technique's reliance on dynamic quantitative methods also promotes objectivity. By focusing on agency outputs and outcomes, policy monitoring also concomitantly reduces the political costs—agency loss—associated with the monitoring function. Finally, policy monitoring provides useful information on the activities of both principals and their agents. It provides information on the nature of bureaucratic activity across multiple indicators over time, which in turn provides information on agency initiatives for policy change and on agency responsiveness to various principal-induced stimuli. Likewise, policy monitoring provides information on the nature of principal attempts to control the bureaucracy. Through this two-way accountability process the potential costs and benefits of monitoring are shared by both principals and agents. Thus, each can gain such benefits as an enhanced reputation or suffer such costs as public exposure of unwarranted or unpopular activities.

Even though policy monitoring is comprehensive and satisfies each of our basic goals, can it work? The analysis that we presented in the last three chapters suggested that it can. With the limited resources that were available to two university professors, we were able to analyze in detail the outputs of eight different federal agencies. We were able to determine the precise mechanisms employed by various political principals in their attempts to influence the bureaucracy. In addition, we were able to determine the precise nature of bureaucratic responses to specific principal stimuli as well as various agency attempts to set the political agenda and to resist hierarchical control efforts. We believe the results of our own statistical analysis demonstrate how a more comprehensive government system could be employed. In this system, information would be acquired by a nonpartisan government agency, stored in a central data bank, managed and evaluated by skilled analysts, and promulgated widely to various principals, agents, journalists, interest groups, and the public.

Through this process policy monitoring would not replace existing oversight systems but rather would serve as an important supplement. The objective information derived from this process could then be used in more traditional oversight hearings as well as in other government forums. Together with existing oversight capabilities, policy monitoring would greatly increase the level of bureaucratic accountability, both for agents and their political principals.

CONCLUSION

In this chapter we have suggested that bureaucratic accountability is a two-way street. By this we mean that bureaucracies should be held accountable for their actions to elected officials and the public, as much existing literature suggests, and that elected officials should be held accountable for their direction of the bureaucracy. A particular policy choice is not justifiable simply because an elected official desires it. Furthermore, if the less visible nature of the bureaucratic process means that elected officials can shift the policymaking forum from the more visible legislative stage to the less visible bureaucratic stage, then elected officials increase the likelihood that they will avoid accountability for their actions. To prevent such a palpable threat to the democratic process, bureaucratic accountability should involve both principals and their agents. As Rourke (1984: 131) wrote, "Not all the consequences of hierarchy contribute to rational calculation in policy deliberations. The inequality of power inherent in hierarchy means that the views of highly placed individuals carry immense weight, not because of the persuasiveness of their arguments but simply because of the exalted status from which they speak." Policy monitoring is designed to ameliorate such concerns about the role principals play in the bureaucratic process as well as hold bureaucrats accountable for their actions.

7

Bureaucratic Democracy
and Its Dysfunctions

In the first few chapters of this book we examined popular and scholarly perceptions of the bureaucracy and their implications for democracy in the United States. We argued that most of what government does is done by public bureaucracies that consist entirely of nonelected personnel. Popular perceptions are that bureaucracies are slow, lumbering entities, accomplishing little, and usually resistant to change. Citizens believe that bureaucracies manifest particularistic, rather than public, interests and are unresponsive through time to changing public preferences. The media and politicians perpetuate this view by their derisive editorializing and campaign rhetoric. Likewise, scholars have cultivated this view by contending that bureaucracies respond primarily to elite influence through iron triangle, subsystem, or capture politics. Elected officials are depicted as outside the policymaking loop and as unwilling or unable to make bureaucracies respond to public preferences. Such views diminish the legitimacy of U.S. institutions and also raise serious questions about the continued viability of the Constitution. As a result, the prevalent view is that democracy in the United States is not working.

In Chapters 3 through 5 we dispelled some of these popular myths by presenting empirical evidence that bureaucracy is indeed an adaptive institution that responds to democratic influences. The evidence presented in Chapter 3 showed that bureaucracies respond to elected institutions, including the president and Congress. Moreover, because we demonstrated responsiveness in all eight of the agencies examined, the implication was that bureaucratic responsiveness is not all that uncommon. In Chapter 4 we examined the particular forces that drive bureaucratic adaptation, showing that the most important stimuli to change in the bureaucracy are the shared tools of Congress and the president: political appointment and the budget. Bureaucracies also respond directly to the courts, the media, and issue salience, which is a manifestation of public attention. In Chapter 5 we presented evidence to show that bureaucracies also play an independent role in the policy process by sharing their expertise with elected officials and by representing the law and past democratic coalitions.

The image of bureaucracy in democracy that emerges from these empirical results is therefore more positive than that depicted by the popular pundits. However, we should also advise caution since the image remains incomplete without a clear exposition of how bureaucratic democracy should actually work. In this chapter we attempt to complete this image by describing how a massive nonelective bureaucracy can be reconciled with democracy and the U.S. Constitution. We discuss the roles of bureaucracy and elected officials in bureaucratic democracy. We then offer a commentary on how well bureaucratic democracy is working in the United States and make some suggestions for improvement.

ON THE LEGITIMACY OF
BUREAUCRACY IN A DEMOCRACY

As a starting point, it is important for scholars and citizens to recognize that modern bureaucracy is a response to public demands and changing economic and social conditions. The Constitution did not provide for big bureaucracy, and therefore the authors of that document did not effectively design American government for administering such a development. However, the reality is that such bureaucratic and administrative institutions have evolved through time and now exist. Furthermore, citizens want big bureaucracy to stay in spite of the disparate attitudes discussed in the Chapter 1.

If citizens were asked which particular bureaucracy they would want to do away with, their responses would likely be different from those they express on the bureaucracy generally. No doubt, individual citizens would want to do away with those bureaucracies that had little benefit for themselves but involved substantial costs. However, across all citizens as a group, this benefit-cost calculation is difficult to make. Citizens do not agree on what programs are most beneficial and too costly. Their preferences are diverse. Thus, they want to keep government services, but they do not want to pay for those services through taxes.

The adaptive processes that produced big bureaucracy unfolded slowly through time, indeed much more slowly than the processes described in Chapters 3 through 5. Growth in government occurred incrementally, with change happening mostly at the margins. Pressure for change resulted from the slow, secular accumulation of slack resources that accompany a developing nation. New social and economic demands resulted from the increased complexity and interdependence of the system. Of course, the rate of incremental change was greater in some periods than in others. Spurts of growth occurred in the New Deal and

Great Society eras. However, big bureaucracy was nevertheless an adaptive response to public demands and needs.

That modern bureaucracies are manifestations of public demands is a starting point for establishing the legitimacy of bureaucracy in the modern bureaucratic state. However, if those bureaucracies are out of control, or manifest elite influence, then there is little solace to be taken from this fact. Are U.S. bureaucracies out of control? Do U.S. bureaucracies manifest elite influence rather than popular preferences? The analyses presented in Chapters 3 through 5 of this book suggested that bureaucracies are not out of control. Elected officials send signals to the bureaucracy based on electoral incentives, and bureaucracies respond to these signals by actuating change. The analyses presented in Chapter 4 also showed more direct responsiveness to the media and to the public. However, the evidence is less clear on the question of elite influence. We found no suggestion that bureaucracies are captured or that policymaking occurs in closed subsystems, as suggested by the earlier literature. The president, Congress, and the courts are definitely in the policymaking loop with bureaucracies. However, it may well be that the president and Congress themselves manifest elite influence, which is the recent popular view on these institutions. So the answer to the second question must remain unclear.

Another question concerning the legitimacy of the modern administrative state concerns how one can reconcile a nonelective bureaucracy with popular democracy and the Constitution. That this nonelective bureaucracy executes, legislates, and adjudicates raises questions of excessive power and accountability. However, it must be recognized, and well understood, that the U.S. bureaucracy itself has evolved through time as a representative institution. In the responsible party systems of Europe and elsewhere, citizens recognize that bureaucracy is representative because it changes dramatically every time there is a new government. However, no such dramatic personnel changes occur in the United States. Nevertheless, agency theory can assist in understanding how bureaucracies are representative institutions.

Who or what does bureaucracy represent? It represents past majority coalitions and the law in a struggle with current majority coalitions for policy primacy. When democratic principals create a bureaucracy to implement a legitimated public policy, they establish a contract between a current democratic principal and the new bureaucracy. The terms of this contract are contained in the legal authority, mission statement, constraints, and design of the new agency. As the new agency develops through time, the terms of the original contract are altered through changing law and new legal interpretations. However, these are often only marginal adjustments to the original contract between past democratic principals and the bureaucracy. Bureaucracy remains bounded by law, administrative constraints, and structural incentives.

However, future majorities are not always consistent in their preferences with past majorities. Economic and social conditions change, resulting in different incentives to the policy process. Resources may become more or less constrained because of competition with more or fewer policies or because of changing economic times. Slow secular changes occur in public mood and affect institutional incentives and popular attitudes. Dramatic events may bring about a sharp realignment of public priorities. Witness, for example, the change in emphasis on environmental issues that occurred after the 1973 Arab oil embargo. Or observe the changes in presidential and congressional priorities for nuclear power following the Three Mile Island incident. Thus, current majorities often find themselves at odds over policy with past majorities. The bureaucracy, however, is bound by contract to represent these past majorities.

For whatever reason, current democratic principals attempt to change policies instituted by past principals. However, to do this they must achieve power relative to the bureaucracy. In this regard, the bureaucracy can be viewed as a democratic actor in its own right competing for power with other institutional actors. Or, alternatively, it can be viewed as an interest group vying for influence in a pluralist bargaining system. In addition to representing past democratic coalitions, bureaucracy represents itself in this process because jobs, rewards, and programs are at stake. However, bureaucratic representation in the policy process also has a public benefit since the personnel of most bureaucracies have greater expertise and experience than the generalists in Congress or the White House. As the NRC case presented in Chapter 5 demonstrated, this expertise can be a corrective that produces policy more consistent with the public good.

Given the function of representing past democratic coalitions and the law, bureaucracy also has an obligation to resist some efforts at change. Efforts by elected officials that are clearly against the bureaucracy's legal mandate should be resisted with vigor. In this regard, the bureaucracy stands as a check on the abuse of power by politicians. The bureaucracy should stand its ground until the legal mandate is altered through normal policymaking channels. However, given the vague statutory mandate of some agencies, this may leave a wide zone of acceptance for the bureaucracy. In some instances, politicians seek change that is consistent with a vague legal mandate but contrary to the public interest. What is less clear from a normative viewpoint is whether the bureaucracy has an obligation to resist efforts at change under these circumstances.

Empirically, however, there is no doubt that they do sometimes resist change under these circumstances. In Chapter 5 we observed that EPA administrator Burford was involved in illegal activities by actually encouraging hazardous waste operators to violate the Resource Conservation and Recovery Act of 1976. However, the EPA's resistance to the Reagan administration started much earlier than the alleged legal violations. Thus, as a matter of fact bureaucracies resist change that runs counter to public or organizational interests whether it contradicts the legal mandate or not. How can this be reconciled with a theory of bureaucracy in democracy?

Bureaucratic representation has both a historical and contemporaneous component. That is, bureaucracies represent past democratic coalitions against current majorities and/or elected officials, the historical component. They also represent current democratic coalitions (which include themselves) by responding to popularly generated stimuli, the contemporaneous component. Thus, bureaucracies perform an integrative function for U.S. democracy. They blend demands from past democratic coalitions with those from current democratic coalitions to produce a policy output at a consistent level.

In performing this integrative function, bureaucracies contribute to the incremental nature of public policy in the United States by acting as a stabilizer on excessive change. Not all stimuli from the external environment are translated into change. Some are totally ignored; some are only partially translated; some are fully translated. Greater weight is usually given to past conditions than to present conditions, but sometimes the force for change is too great to resist. Bureaucracies try to ensure that change is limited to the amount consistent with the legal mandate so that shifts will not be so dramatic as to reverse or halt a policy.

In summary, the ongoing struggle for control of public policy can be viewed as a process occurring through time and between actors. Bureaucracies manifest public preferences from past democratic coalitions in the ongoing policy process. They also translate current public preferences into policy changes. Thus, they are agents of the law as well as of past and current democratic coalitions in this process. As such, they perform an integrative function. In performing this function, they are not merely passive actors responding automatically to stimuli from current democratic principals; bureaucracies possess power themselves and apply it to alter policy outcomes. They may respond to current democratic principals, but they may also send some stimuli of their own as the process moves to an eventual equilibrium.

ON THE ROLES OF POLITICAL PRINCIPALS

Political principals share responsibility with the bureaucracy for assuring that the bureaucratic state is consistent with democracy and constitutional principles. In this regard, political principals have multiple roles to play. Elected actors must be accurate translators of public preferences for the bureaucracy and must send signals to the bureaucracy that reflect these preferences. When such preferences mandate a new policy, political principals must act as policymakers to alter the established course for the bureaucracy. In making policy, they should process signals coming up from the bureaucracy to assure that the process makes full use of organizational intelligence. They should also process signals from other sources to assure that policy does not reflect only bureaucratic interests. Finally, political principals must act as policy administrators to assure implementation consistent with past and present democratic preferences.

Accurately translating public preferences for the bureaucracy involves political institutions sensing the demands, needs, or interests of the citizenry. But there is a problem. On the vast majority of issues dealt with by the bureaucracy, citizens have no specific demands or needs; they operate in a vague, impressionistic world, which leaves politicians with a wide zone of acceptance. Under these circumstances, should politicians be free to respond to particularistic or elite interests? Such responses, when obvious, question the legitimacy of democratic institutions. Thus, a considerable amount of political intuition and discretion is required for elected institutions to be successful in this task. Elections and party platforms are one guide to accurately discerning public preferences. However, public preferences are more diverse than is reflected in the onetime act of voting; citizens are also relatively oblivious to the actual content of party platforms. So continuing contacts with constituents, public opinion polls, the media, and other politicians are also important aids. Whatever the means of accurate translation, administration consistent with democracy requires perceptions by elected institutions that are consistent with public preferences.

This task also implies a particular normative view of democracy, namely, that politicians should act according to a referee notion of representation. That is, elected institutions are to act as neutral arbiters of a process occurring largely external to these institutions. They are bound by public preferences, and they should not send signals to the bureaucracy based on their own preferences when these are obviously inconsistent with public preferences. Of course, gauging what public preferences are and whether the principal's preferences are consistent is a daunting task. So there is still wide latitude for politicians to differ on the signals sent to the bureaucracy.

Part of the task of sending signals to the bureaucracy involves legislative or executive policymaking. By this we do not mean to imply that all policies are to be made by elected institutions but simply that elected institutions should set directions and establish boundaries on the administrative policy process. When large corrections are necessary, elected institutions should make or amend law. Lesser corrections can be made by manipulation of administrative tools such as the budget, political appointment, reorganizational authority, oversight hearings, or personnel powers.

The bureaucracy makes most public policy in the United States, but within guidelines established by law and current institutions. And this is for good reason. The bureaucracy is often better informed, has more time, and is less susceptible to particularistic influence than elected institutions. Moreover, good public policy that addresses and solves problems is not necessarily consistent with democratic decisionmaking. However, directions and boundaries should be placed on bureaucracies to balance good policy against democratic legitimacy.

Who should establish these policymaking directions and boundaries on the bureaucracy? Should the legislative branch establish all directions and boundaries? Should the chief executive also be a policymaking institution? As we discussed in Chapter 2 and observed in Chapters 3 through 5, it is now an empirical reality that both the presidency and Congress are firmly established as policymaking institutions. The roots of congressional policymaking are in the Constitution; the roots of executive policymaking are in the vagueness of congressional statutes and in delegations of authority by Congress to the bureaucracy and chief executive. That two political principals now make policy for execution by the bureaucracy has some troubling implications.

The presence of multiple democratic principals violates the administrative precepts of hierarchy and unity of command. Competition between the president and Congress for power over the bureaucracy means that signals to the bureaucracy are often ambiguous. Communications are garbled, and the bureaucracy does not know which manifestation of democratic influence to respond to. As discussed in Chapter 4, this uncertainty can lead to delayed responses and protracted response dynamics. Multiple principals and uncertainty also increase the probability of shirking. Uncertainty about the advisability of different responses may even mean no response. Furthermore, faced with competing signals, the bureaucracy can often choose which principal to respond to, and the choice is usually the one closest to bureaucratic preferences. The problems associated with having multiple principals are accentuated during periods of divided government but are less serious during times of single-party control.

The Constitution did not establish a system with multiple principals. As originally designed there was a two-tiered hierarchy of principals and agents, with a clear division of responsibilities between institutional actors. The principle of legislative supremacy, as manifested in Article I of the Constitution, made Congress the chief policymaker and the president the chief administrator. Thus, Congress (a principal) made policy for execution by the president (an agent), and the president (a principal) was to execute the law through the bureaucracy (an agent). The constitutional charge to "take care" that the laws are faithfully executed in theory made the president an agent of the law, just as we argued for the bureaucracy. However, the institutional evolution of the presidency has also seen the chief executive become much more than an agent of the law. The presidency is now a policymaking institution that operates in relative independence of Congress.

In practice, then, there are now separate and competing principal-agent hierarchies involving the president, Congress, and the bureaucracy. In one hierarchy Congress is a democratic principal over the bureaucracy (an agent); in the other the president is a democratic principal over the bureaucracy (the same agent). Both principals compete for control of policy outputs from the bureaucracy. This is obvious from a reexamination of some of the case studies presented in Chapters 3 through 5. For example, in the EPA clean air case the president pushed policy in one direction, with Congress eventually pushing it in the other. Ultimately, Congress, which was seemingly a better reflection of mass preferences, won out, but it was inefficient for the struggle to have occurred in the first place. Similarly, there were struggles between Congress and the president over policy at other agencies, such as the EEOC, the ICC, the FTC (during the Carter era), and many other agencies that were not in our sample. In each of these other cases, it is unclear whether democratic preferences won out in the eventual equilibria of these agencies.

Competition for control of the bureaucracy between two different institutions both reflecting different constituencies is confusing for the bureaucracy. However, this competition could also be considered healthy in one respect. Competition means that both the president and Congress have reason to be more vigilant in monitoring the bureaucracy and obtaining information on policy outputs. Oversight hearings occur more frequently, and communications are more direct between elected institutions and the bureaucracy. The media scrutinize government more carefully during controversial periods of divided government. Increased monitoring activities by elected institutions and the media also suggest a more interested and concerned citizenry, all of which imply that the bureaucracy is held more accountable.

However, the existence of multiple competing principals also has another related undesirable effect. The desire for power leads to a greater incidence of information suppression and cheating on the part of one principal toward the other. In recent years the president has had a strong incentive to hide from Congress any changes that occur in bureaucratic activities resulting from executive policymaking. For example, reconsider for a moment the ICC case reported in Chapter 3.

In 1980 Congress and the Carter administration deregulated the trucking industry by passing the Motor Carrier Act and administering it in a manner consistent with legislative intent. The number of operating certificates increased dramatically between the time of the legislation and sometime early in the Reagan administration. However, the Teamsters Union had been a major supporter of Ronald Reagan during the 1980 campaign and wanted the trucking industry reregulated. The 1980 Motor Carrier Act was sufficiently ambiguous to allow the president to do so, but this was not the intent of Congress in 1980 or later. Reagan administration appointees testified before Congress that it was market forces that caused the reregulation of the trucking industry. However, we showed in Chapter 3 that reregulation occurred one month after the Reagan appointee took charge at the ICC, a result more consistent with political reregulation. This was information that Congress could have used in its competition with the Reagan administration for control of the bureaucracy. However, it is also information that was suppressed and unavailable to Congress. Deception enabled the president to move policy in a direction that was clearly inconsistent with congressional and public preferences. Additional evidence on executive suppression of information and cheating can be found in the various other case studies reported in Chapters 3 through 5 (e.g., the EPA hazardous waste and clean air cases, the OSM case, and the EEOC case).

Another role for political principals in assuring that the administrative state is consistent with democracy is administering the bureaucracy in a manner consistent with the law and public preferences. Effective political administration should ensure bureaucratic accountability. As we observed in Chapter 1, the Constitution provided for a system of separate powers and checks and balances that restrict abuse of power by any one branch. However, Congress has delegated all three powers to the bureaucracy so that now some administrative agencies execute, legislate, and adjudicate. This violates some of the fundamental premises underlying the Constitution. Because of this development, it is important that overhead institutions retain the ability to check abuses of administrative power.

However, the presence of multiple competing principals is problematic for purposes of holding the bureaucracy accountable. The president has traditionally been held responsible by Congress and citizens for scandals and abuses that occur during policy administration. However, the emergence of the presidency as a policymaking institution has blurred the distinction between what is considered abuse of discretion and what is considered executive policymaking. For example, reconsider for a moment the case of the EEOC general counsel reported in Chapter 3.

In 1981 the Reagan administration nominated and Congress confirmed Connolly to be general counsel of the EEOC. Shortly after arriving at the commission, Connolly announced that he would no longer be pressing sexual harassment, age discrimination, equal pay, and class action suits. The vague statutory mandates of the EEOC permitted him to establish such a policy, even though it was clearly inconsistent with legislative intent. But it was consistent with presidential policy, which was to return the United States to a "free-market"–oriented system. To what extent should this be considered an abuse of administrative discretion? Under the current dual principal system, for the bureaucracy to be held accountable, either of two conditions must exist. First, the abuse must be so clearly a legal violation that one principal is on a very firm footing to pursue the matter (e.g., the EPA hazardous waste controversy, the HUD scandal, Iran-contra). Or second, both principals must agree on what constitutes an abuse of discretion. This second condition is unlikely to exist when there is controversy between principals over what constitutes acceptable policy.

In summary, responsibility for assuring that the administrative state is consistent with democracy and the Constitution rests with both elected institutions and the bureaucracy. Past campaign rhetoric and finger pointing at the bureaucracy have not been useful in this regard. To establish the nexus between popular preferences and bureaucratic outputs, elected institutions must perform three functions. They must accurately translate current public preferences for the bureaucracy. They must send signals to the bureaucracy that reflect these current preferences. And they must administer and oversee the bureaucracy to assure that implementation remains consistent with democratic values and the Constitution. These tasks are made more difficult because multiple principals perform these functions in the U.S. system.

HOW WELL IS BUREAUCRATIC
DEMOCRACY WORKING?

This study offers some reason for optimism about the prospects for bureaucratic democracy. American public bureaucracies are not slow, omnipotent, or unresponsive to public preferences. Furthermore, they are not out of control, as most citizens and some scholarly literature have suggested. Politicians regularly control bureaucratic outputs using various instruments provided for under the current government framework.

Moreover, the empirical analyses presented in Chapters 3 through 5 showed that American bureaucracies are highly adaptive entities that continually respond to a flow of diverse stimuli and stimulus types. Some stimuli are discrete events, some are event processes, and others are tonal in nature. Some bureaucratic responses are immediate, some are delayed, and others are distributed through time in probabilistic fashion. The most important stimuli to the bureaucracy are top-down, which is consistent with the concept of overhead democracy. However, agencies also respond to some bottom-up influences, bypassing elected institutions. This process is also sometimes nonrecursive, with bureaucracy sending stimuli of its own to affect other actors. Thus, bureaucracies provide multidimensional representation. They integrate past and current democratic preferences and also make representation more effective by providing a rational dimension.

There is reason for optimism about bureaucratic democracy because public organizations are eminently moldable by U.S. political institutions. Agencies respond systematically to changes in political leadership, as manifested through appointments, changing budgets, reorganizations, and various other tools of administrative control. Yet ironically this same feature also gives reason for skepticism. U.S. political institutions must accurately translate public preferences and send consistent signals to the bureaucracy for bureaucratic democracy to work. However, there is strong evidence from our study that some signals to and responses from the bureaucracy were inconsistent with public preferences.

Consider, for example, the early Reagan administration effort to curtail environmental protection outputs. Were the early Reagan administration signals to the EPA true manifestations of public preferences? Or were they just manifestations of chief executive and/or elite influence? Or consider the case of the ICC and the reregulation of the trucking industry in early 1981. Were the Reagan administration appointment of Taylor to head the ICC and the subsequent reregulation of the trucking industry consistent with public preferences? Or did they simply reflect the preferences of the Reagan administration and the Teamsters Union? Consider also the Reagan administration curtailment of the FDA's food and drug safety enforcement program. Was the reduction in enforcement for food and drug safety really consistent with public preferences on this issue? Or was it more favorable to the regulated industries? All of the case studies in this book raise similar questions.

We cannot answer these questions definitively because our empirical analyses were not designed for this purpose. However, we suspect on intuitive grounds that few of these changes were consistent with public preferences. Future quantitative work should evaluate the congruence among public opinion on specific policies, policy signals sent to the bureaucracy, and policy implementation by the bureaucracy. We are dubious about whether there would be much congruence on the policies we examined if such an analysis covered the same period as our analyses.

Bureaucracies are eminently moldable instruments of policy implementation. However, the prospects for bureaucratic democracy are grim if political institutions are free to shape bureaucracies in a manner inconsistent with public preferences. This brings us back once again to the questions we asked in the previous section about who should establish policymaking directions and boundaries for the bureaucracy. We believe that the answer to this question is the same as it was more than two hundred years ago when the Constitution was ratified.

There should be a return to the two-tiered principal-agent hierarchy established by the Constitution. Congress should assume primary responsibility for policymaking, and the president should assume primary responsibility for administration. Dual competing principal-agent hierarchies lead to all of the anomalies discussed previously. They also lead to a lack of congruence between public preferences and bureaucratic performance. Without some means of assuring executive accountability, the emergence of the presidency as a strong, independent policymaking institution is dysfunctional for bureaucratic democracy. The president should be accountable to Congress in directing the bureaucracy.

We do not mean to imply by this normative assertion that there should be a politics-administration dichotomy. Administration *is* politics in that it determines who gets what, when, and where; no amount of institutional redesign can change that. Moreover, efficient administration requires taking into account political factors, such as how and whose constituencies are affected. The presidency is and should remain a political institution; nothing we could say will change that either. We also do not argue against the delegation by Congress of policymaking authority to the bureaucracy. Congress obviously has insufficient time, expertise, and incentive to effectively address many public problems. There is also great benefit to be gained from decisionmaking in the less politically charged environment of the bureaucracy.

However, we do argue for Congress to reestablish control over the president and the bureaucracy in the policymaking arena. Past congressional delegations of authority and abdications of responsibility are what enable presidential control of policymaking. The Constitution makes no such grant of policymaking authority to the president. These congressional delegations of authority can be altered or rescinded, and Congress can begin exercising its responsibilities in a manner that ensures administration consistent with public preferences.

Several specific changes flow directly from agency theory and the analyses presented in this book that could help reestablish Congress as the preeminent U.S. policymaking institution. We showed that political appointment and the budget are the two most important tools for controlling the bureaucracy. Accordingly, we propose changing the appointment and budget processes to restore a two-tiered principal-agent hierarchy. The Senate norm of approving nominations based mostly on qualifications for office, rather than on policy considerations, should be changed. In recent years, policy considerations have become more important for Senate approval of nominations. Witness, for example, the recent Robert Bork and Clarence Thomas nominations to the Supreme Court. However, we are suggesting that policy should be the primary consideration for the approval of all nominations.

Taking the initiative in the nomination approval process requires that the Senate explicitly recognize the nature of the game. Congress is a principal that faces a serious potential adverse selection problem because it does not choose the president. There is little or no guarantee that presidential preferences will be consistent with congressional preferences on specific issues. So caution should be exercised in the nomination approval process to assure that what is being purchased is really what is desired. Presidential nominees whose policy preferences diverge substantially from congressional preferences have every reason to practice deception during the nomination process. They will evade, or even lie, on policy-related questions, and great uncertainty will exist about the future direction of the bureaucracy. Congress should no longer defer to the presidency on political appointments. For Congress to be restored as the primary policy-making institution for the bureaucracy, it must regain control of agency leadership.

Additionally, the federal budget process should be altered to establish a congressional budget as the primary working document. Accordingly, the Congressional Budget Office should be expanded in its capabilities for doing policy analysis and efficiency studies. The CBO should also be concerned with policy congruence. Bureaucracies should submit their budget requests directly to the CBO, rather than to the OMB, where they are scrutinized for consistency with the president's program. The executive budget should become a token document reflecting only the expenditures required to keep services at current levels. Major policy changes through fiscal means should originate with Congress, not with the president.

Another change that would help in restoring Congress as the primary policymaking institution relates to the contract with the bureaucracy. Congress should critically evaluate past legislative enactments that leave sufficient interpretive flexibility for the president to alter established policy. Reducing administrative discretion through more specific legislation is one way to constrain executive efforts to control policy. However, this is also a two-edged sword in that more specific legislation could hamper congressional efforts to redirect policy. Caution should therefore be exercised in altering the contract with the bureaucracy to the extent that flexibility is required for future democratic control.

Most important, Congress should strengthen its capabilities for monitoring the chief executive and the bureaucracy. The detailed recommendation of the last chapter, which we dubbed policy monitoring, would go a long way toward assuring executive and bureaucratic accountability. Tracing movements in bureaucratic outputs of various types would minimize cheating and deception on the part of the president and political appointees. It would also apprise citizens of the implications of congressional policymaking. The GAO's investigatory capabilities should be strengthened so that it could seek out, rather than respond to, the emergence of administrative inefficiency and corruption. Congressional staff should be increased to better prepare members of Congress for oversight hearings. A Congress that is carefully monitoring the chief executive and the bureaucracy is more likely to achieve administration consistent with legislative policy.

CONCLUSION

In this book we used empirical evidence to dispel popular myths about the bureaucracy. Based on this evidence, we came to the conclusion that bureaucracies are competitive, adaptive, and dynamic entities. They are also representative institutions that can be made to function effectively within a democratic system. We found no evidence that bureaucracies are direct instruments of elite influence, but elite influence may be manifested through stimuli emanating from executive and legislative institutions. We made recommendations intended to improve the functioning of bureaucratic democracy that would fundamentally alter relations between the legislative and executive branches of government as well as between these institutions and the bureaucracy.

We recognize that few, if any, of these recommendations will probably ever be implemented for practical reasons. Congress may be unwilling to assume policymaking responsibility. The president may be unwilling to give up policymaking power. Neither Congress nor the president may really want the light on the policymaking process that would be shed by policy monitoring. Citizens may also question the ability of Congress to be the primary policymaking institution. However, our obligation as political scientists is to call it like we see it.

We offer one further word of caution for future students of the bureaucracy. The time will come again when there will be little movement in the bureaucracy. Undoubtedly, a reason for many of the myths of the past was an absence of movement. However, we advise future scholars against drawing conclusions similar to those of past scholars. If bureaucracies are not adapting, then the reason is not because bureaucracies are nonadaptive entities. It is because there is nothing to adapt to.

Appendix

This appendix explains the methodology of the studies reported in Chapters 3 and 5. The goal of the research was to find the "best" model for explaining political control at each agency we studied. This involved hypothesis testing, but not in the traditional one-shot deductive sense. Rather, it involved dynamic iterative procedures that integrated both qualitative and quantitative methods.

We did an initial case study of each agency to develop working hypotheses. The purpose was to determine what particular stimuli could possibly have caused political control at an agency. After all, it made little sense to hypothesize that political appointments caused change when an appointment was nonideological. Likewise, we could hardly assert that budgets, reorganizations, congressional oversight, or other political tools changed bureaucratic outputs when these stimuli were not present. Thus, we searched archives for contextual evidence on possible causes of changed bureaucratic outputs.

This qualitative research supplied us with initial expectations about what particular stimuli could possibly have caused change at the various agencies. It also told us of the timing, magnitude, and duration of potential changes. With this information, we formulated hypotheses for time-series analysis of monthly or quarterly data. The independent series were dummy variables designed to operationalize predictions from the case studies.

We modeled several dependent series for most agencies. Each reflected a different dimension of the agency's "core technology" output as defined by Thompson (1967). However, we reported only one measure for each agency because of space limitations. We selected models to report based on clarity of presentation and robustness of results.

We used Box-Jenkins (1976; Box and Tiao 1975) methods to do the time-series modeling. These methods were well suited to the task because of their unique ability to establish causal relations with finely divided data. Box-Jenkins methods establish causal sequence through empirical evidence (i.e, the cross-correlation function and hypothesis tests), not just through a priori theorizing. Another strength of these methods is their overriding concern with controlling extraneous historical effects. They require the user to develop dynamic forecasts of current observations based on past observations (i.e., ARIMA models). These dynamic forecasts are then included in final models to control for background noise before hypothesis testing.

Another reason we chose Box-Jenkins techniques was their consistency with our research strategy. We viewed modeling as a *process*, not just a one-shot hypothesis-testing procedure. Some conflict was anticipated between case study results and statistical analysis. Consistently, Box-Jenkins methods portray modeling as an iterative process that continues until a best model results (Box and Jenkins 1976: 17–19; McCleary and Hay 1980: 141–145). The researcher uses empirical tools to define and redefine model specifications until satisfying some objective statistical criterion.

The objective statistical criterion we used in this study was the minimum of Akaike's Information Criterion (AIC). We chose AIC because it is "a mathematical formulation of the principle of parsimony in model building" (Akaike 1974: 719). It measures the goodness of fit while imposing a penalty for overspecification (Sawa 1978). The statistic is computed

$$AIC = -2\ln(L) + 2k$$

where L is the likelihood function and k is the number of free parameters. We emphasize that AIC will never minimize where a model retains extraneous information, so the final models reported herein contain only relevant variables.

In some instances, the model-building process involved iteration between qualitative and statistical methods because some of the initial hypotheses from case studies were rejected by the statistical analysis. In these instances, we did follow-up research by reexamining archival sources and conducting interviews with officials. Based on new information, we developed second-iteration hypotheses. We began statistical analysis again and continued the process until we obtained a best-fitting model for each series.

This research design provided two different types of control for alternative explanations. First, it provided statistical control by modeling the history of each time series as an ARIMA process. This assured that random chance, seasonal fluctuations, and omitted process variables did not cause the findings. Second, it provided quasiexperimental control by integrating case study materials with time-series analysis. Campbell and Stanley (1963: 39; see also Cook and Campbell 1979: 211) observed that the major threat to validity for the time-series design is history. That is, some event other than the hypothesized event may have caused the change. To check this possibility, we did follow-up case study analysis to verify the consistency of the statistical findings with reality.

Multiple tests of the same stimulus-response relationships greatly increased the strength of our design. Five of the seven agencies under investigation showed a response in the month or quarter after a political appointment. Two of these agencies showed responses to multiple appointments. These appointments all occurred at different times. Finding a plausible alternative explanation for all of these occurrences seems highly implausible.

Notes

CHAPTER 1

1. Throughout this book we take literary license in using the term *preferences* to refer to aggregates of individuals. For example, we often refer to public preferences, majoritarian preferences, democratic preferences, and institutional preferences. The word *preferences* taken in the traditional, rational-choice context means the choice orderings of individual actors. However, we do not mean literally that aggregate actors are rational and have a single set of preferences. We use the term in this context merely as a heuristic device enabling us to ask interesting questions about the relation between politics and bureaucracy in the United States.

2. Consider the following related survey data concerning public attitudes on the bureaucracy. A 1973 University of Michigan Survey Research Center poll found that 78 percent of the respondents agreed that "too many government agencies do the same thing." Likewise, 58 percent expressed the opinion that bureaucrats "gain the most from government services." More than 50 percent said that bureaucrats do not take responsibility for anything, and nearly 50 percent agreed that bureaucrats are not interested in the problems of ordinary people. Substantial percentages also believed that bureaucrats pry into people's personal lives and use their authority to push people around.

The results from a Harris Poll, also conducted in 1973, were only slightly less damning. Nearly 25 percent of all respondents believed that the bureaucracy does things by the book. Nearly 20 percent also believed that bureaucrats play it safe, are just passing time, and are just out for themselves. Surprisingly, only 12 percent described bureaucrats as making red tape, only 10 percent believed bureaucrats only want power, and only 4 percent agreed that bureaucrats are corrupt.

3. For example, 71 percent of the respondents to a poll conducted by the *Washington Post* in the early 1980s said they were pleased with their interactions with federal agencies (Hill 1992: 7). Almost 75 percent of the respondents to a 1973 Harris Poll stated that they found federal bureaucrats helpful, while 66 and 64 percent, respectively, found state and local bureaucrats helpful. In addition, 46 percent of the same poll's respondents said they were "highly satisfied" with their experiences with the federal government, while an additional 29 percent said they were "somewhat satisfied." Only between 25 and 33 percent said they were "not satisfied" with their experiences with the federal, state, or local bureaucracy.

4. Some time ago, citizen perceptions of the bureaucracy became so hostile that some observers characterized them as "bureausis" (Thompson 1977) and a "raging pandemic" (Kaufman 1981).

CHAPTER 2

1. This was indeed the same Wilson who later became president, was also a political scientist, and wrote a book entitled *Congressional Government: A Study in American Politics.*

2. Actually, Wilson recommended some delegation of power by Congress to the bureaucracy in his 1887 article on politics and administration. This, he argued, was necessary for proper policy administration.

3. The form of the triumvirate need not be restricted to only three actors. There can be multiple interest groups, bureaucracies, and congressional committees involved in these so-called subsystems. For a detailed discussion of how policy affects political participation in these systems, see Redford (1969) or Ripley and Franklin (1986).

4. The work by Bentley (1908) and Truman (1951) was seminal in the theory of interest group politics, which preceded the literature on interest groups in the bureaucracy.

5. Arnold (1979) provided a detailed analysis of the self-interested interaction between congressional committees and the bureaucracy. See also Maas's (1951) analysis of the Army Corps of Engineers.

6. Deregulation is the restoration of market mechanisms and the withdrawal of government intervention.

7. See, for example, Randall 1979; Moe 1982, 1985; Stewart and Cromartie 1982; Weingast and Moran 1983; Weingast 1984; Cohen 1985; Brudney and Hebert 1987; Scholz and Wei 1986; Scholz, Twombly, and Headrick 1991; Yantek and Gartrell 1988; Scicchitano, Hedge, and Metz 1991; Hedge and Jallow 1990; Hansen 1990; Wood 1988, 1990, 1991, 1992; Wood and Waterman 1991; 1993; Waterman and Wood 1992, 1993; and Wood and Anderson 1993.

CHAPTER 3

1. Rigorous statistical analysis was used to produce the results discussed in these chapters. However, they were written to be understandable by a general audience. Every effort has been made to simplify the discussion and to avoid unnecessary technical jargon. However, some technical discussion must remain so that we can adequately describe what we did. To those readers who are annoyed by technical discussion, we apologize in advance but ask that attention be directed more toward the substantive results. We report results through both figures and tables. Readers who are uncomfortable with tabular statistical presentations should focus only on the figures, ignoring the tables. The figures contain all essential results and offer a visual presentation of how bureaucratic adaptation processes worked through the period of analysis. Those who want a more technical presentation should examine both the figures and the tables.

2. The term *responsiveness* used here and throughout this chapter means the extent to which outputs from a bureaucracy change with the application of an external political stimulus. Accordingly, we view political appointments, changing budgets, reorganizations, oversight activities, personnel manipulation, and other events as potential stimuli for change.

3. There are two exceptions to the methodological critique offered here. Moe (1985) used quarterly data to evaluate outputs from the National Labor Relations Board. In creating dummy variables for separate presidencies, he assumed that change occurred in the quarter after the first political appointment. This was by assumption, however, and Moe was more concerned with *who* affected policy than with *how*. In contrast, Wood (1988) was concerned with the mechanisms of political-bureaucratic control. Monthly data were used to evaluate responses in EPA's clean air program to various political stimuli. Nevertheless, that study involved only one agency, so it may not be generalizable.

4. There is a disadvantage in using finely divided data. Some process variables (e.g., political ideology or interest group influence) do not lend themselves well to such analysis because there are no monthly measures of these factors. Thus, this analysis is restricted to how events, not processes, affect bureaucracies. Certainly, not all political control mechanisms operate instantaneously (see, e.g., Wood and Waterman 1993). Nevertheless, since many are applied abruptly, many of the mechanisms of political control should still be seen.

5. For the EEOC we had only one measure of outputs that had finely divided time intervals: litigations. The series we report includes litigations for individual cases of employment discrimination but not class action or systemic suits. The series aggregates Title 7, age discrimination, and gender discrimination litigations into one measure. The EEOC was uncooperative in providing additional monthly data.

6. Ferejohn and Shipan (1989) argued the importance of congressional "signals" in their case study of the FCC. They observed that Congress acted in a cohesive and rational fashion to change FCC decisions on user fees after the deregulation of the telephone industry.

7. The FTC suffered budget reductions in March and October 1981 from the Carter-proposed budgets for fiscal years 1981 and 1982. There was no perceptible response to the May reduction. Unfortunately, the October reduction coincided precisely with Miller's arrival at the commission so it is difficult to say with complete confidence that the observed response did not have a fiscal component.

8. Moreover, Goodman and Wrightson (1987: 178–181) asserted, based on a qualitative assessment, that the Reagan administration was unsuccessful in manipulating the NRC's regulatory process through either appointments or the budget so a finding of responsiveness would be interesting.

9. The total change is calculated:

$$change = \frac{\omega_0}{1-\delta_1}$$

10. Technically, the FDA commissioner was appointed by the secretary of the Department of Health and Human Services, Schweiker, not Reagan. Senate confirmation of the appointment was not required.

CHAPTER 4

1. Before proceeding, a word of caution is appropriate here for some readers. The materials presented in this chapter are a bit more technical than those in the

other chapters. The theoretical concepts are more abstract, the methods are more complex, and the presentation is necessarily more difficult to follow. We have moved most mathematical notation to the endnotes, and we have simplified the exposition as much as possible without loss of meaning. However, for some readers it could still be necessary to study this chapter rather than simply read it through once. The effort should produce a deepened understanding of the nature of political-bureaucratic adaptation processes, and we encourage scholars at all levels to do so.

2. A tonal stimulus can be measured more formally as:

$$X_{tonal} = \sum_{l=1}^{L} X_{t-l}$$

where X_t is an event process, L is the number of lagged observations, and 1 is the lag number for a particular observation.

A key feature distinguishes a tonal stimulus measured in this way. The contribution of each lagged observation of X_t to the total stimulus is the same regardless of whether the observation is the first or last observation of the moving average window. Observations distant in time contribute exactly the same amount to the measure as observations recent in time. Note also that the moving average described in the equation simply aggregates a sequence of events to depict this gradually building force that we hypothesize causes a change in bureaucratic behavior.

The tonal stimulus described here is similar to the so-called hysteresis effect in the physical sciences. For example, in an inductive electrical circuit the buildup of electromagnetic force lags the application of voltage with respect to time. Similarly, our tonal stimulus reflects an accumulation of force that follows some time after the application of the actual stimulus.

This is a fairly restrictive definition of what constitutes a tonal stimulus. The measure just discussed considers accumulations of events over time *for single variables only* rather than accumulations of events over time and across all variables. Although it would be interesting to consider the latter concept as a measure of what might be called overall policy tone, we declined to consider such a measure because of the technical difficulty of combining such diverse variables as are in this analysis. An alternative concept, policy mood, has been developed by Stimson (1991), but those data are unavailable with sufficient temporal resolution for our analysis.

3. Time-dominant pools typically have autocorrelation problems much like those associated with a single time series. Also, when the pool contains few individuals, it is more reasonable to think that the relationship between X and Y is the same across individuals. Thus, one would rarely select pure covariance or random effects specifications for estimating time-dominant pools because these specifications ignore problems of autocorrelation and imply greater heterogeneity among committees.

4. Standardizing on the center of the scale, rather than the mean committee LCV score, allowed us to preserve differences among committees.

5. By focusing on the substance of news media coverage, we capture something

from each of the preceding categories. Interest groups use the news media for publicity purposes. Other interest group activities, including litigations and lobbying, are also often reported in news stories. We selected the *New York Times* for this purpose because it is well indexed and does a good job of reporting the national news.

6. We took special care in constructing the news media variable to avoid problems of simultaneity. The measure excluded all news media reports on program activities that occurred in the same time period as the program activities.

7. The model is given in mathematical terms as:

$$Y_{pt} = \beta_0 + \sum_{k=1}^{K} \beta_k X_{kpt} + \varepsilon_{pt} \qquad k, 1 \ldots \ldots K$$

where:
Y_{pt} = *referrals for program p at time t*
β_0 = *constant intercept for all programs*
β_k = *effect parameters for each independent variable k*
X_{kpt} = *independent variable k for program p at time t*
ε_{pt} = *disturbance for program p and time t*

8. Estimates for this most restricted model, and all subsequent models, were obtained using the pooled-time-series cross-section technique discussed in Kmenta (1986: 616–625). The technique employs a Generalized Least Squares (GLS) transformation matrix to improve estimation efficiency, which is limited by residual autocorrelation, heteroscedasticity, and correlation among residuals from different programs. Designing an appropriate GLS transformation matrix requires first obtaining Ordinary Least Squares (OLS) estimates. Based on residual diagnostics from OLS (reported in Table 4.1), the first model was estimated under assumptions of different autocorrelations and variances for each program as well as cross-program residual correlations.

9. The Pooled Q statistic reported in Table 4.1 is the average of the Ljung-Box (1978) Q statistic for each program. This is just a modified Lagrange Multiplier test for autocorrelation. The Breusch-Pagan (1979) Lagrange Multiplier statistic tests the null hypothesis that the residual vector is homoscedastic relative to the independent variables. The test for mutual unit correlation is a Lagrange Multiplier statistic for the diagonality of the cross-covariance matrix of errors after autocorrelation and heteroscedasticity have been corrected for.

10. There are two restrictions that must be applied to the percent change interpretation. First, Tufte (1974: 125) showed that the percent change analogue tends to break down when the natural log estimate is greater than around 0.25. Second, Halvorsen and Palmquist (1980; see also Kennedy 1981) showed that when the natural log estimate pertains to a 0–1 dummy variable, then the estimate should be transformed back into the original metric by the equation:

$$\%change = 100 \, (e^b - 1)$$

In the analyses to follow, the only coefficients that exceeded 0.25 in the natural log metric were those associated with the political appointment dummies. In those instances, we transformed the coefficients back to the original metric using the preceding equation.

11. The distributed lag model is given in mathematical terms as:

$$Y_{pt} = \beta_0 + \sum_{k=1}^{K} \delta_{jk} L^k \beta_k X_{kpt} + \varepsilon_{pt}$$

$j, 0 \ldots J$
$k, 1 \ldots K$

where:
Y_{pt} = *referrals for program p at time t*
β_0 = *constant intercept for all programs*
δ_{jk} = *lag response weights for each lag j of variable k*
L^k = *a backshift algebra polynomial specifying the lag response function*
β_k = *set of effect coefficients for each variable k*
X_{kpt} = *independent variable k for program p at time t*

12. With respect to the budget, it is interesting to speculate that there might be a difference in the speed of responses to the budget depending on the direction of budget changes. Budget reductions should produce faster responses by the bureaucracy than budget increases because it takes little time to reduce the number of personnel and resources in an organization, whereas it takes more time to translate new money into policy actions. This asymmetry could be tested through the use of dummy variables and interaction effects. However, the most significant budget changes during the period of this analysis were downward so we leave this to future research.

13. Terasvirta and Mellin (1983) compared various statistical criteria for specifying distributive lag models in a Monte Carlo study and concluded that Schwarz's (1978) criterion (SC) does quite well. Based on the minimum of SC, we set the maximum lag length for the remaining variables at four and the polynomial degree at two. This least-restricted model assumes a common lag length and polynomial degree for all variables except political appointments and the budget.

14. Also, OLS diagnostics show that residuals are no longer heteroscedastic or correlated among programs. However, the residuals remain autocorrelated, so we used a GLS transformation matrix that assumed separate autocorrelations among programs for estimation.

15. The t statistic on the sum of lag coefficients reported in Table 4.2 is computed using estimates from the variance-covariance matrix of estimates. For any coefficients in general the following identity holds:

$$VAR(A+B) = VAR(A) + 2\,COV(A,B) + VAR(A)$$

16. More precisely, the standard errors for the individual coefficients depend on collinearity between variables in the equation, and collinearity will always increase if the nonrelevant variables are correlated with the other variables. Also, the

probability of accepting a false null hypothesis (Type II error) increases as the degrees of freedom decrease, as shown by any table of t-statistics.

17. Various statistical criteria have been proposed for selecting the relevant set of regressors, but among these SC favors the lowest dimensional model. (See Judge et al. 1985: 869–875; or Ramanathan 1989: 165–167, for a listing of these criteria and their associated references.)

We began with the least-restricted model and estimated all possible versions while eliminating one lag at a time. Using both substantive theory and the minimum of SC, we discarded the Thomas appointment, economy, and group variables as well as several lags for the House and Senate committees and courts.

18. The mean lag is obtained by differentiating the lag polynomial in endnote 11 with respect to L, summing the resultant coefficients, and dividing by the sum.

19. For variables with zero order constraints (i.e., the budget, Burford, and Ruckelshaus), the analogous graphs to those in Figure 4.1 consist of a single spike at lag zero with a probability of 1. Therefore, we omit presenting graphs of the impulse response weights for these variables.

20. An alternative interpretation of the impulse response weights in Figure 4.1 might be that there was a pattern of exponential decay in the first four time periods, with an increase in probability at lag four due to stochastic effects. However, we used various polynomial degrees with longer lags in an effort to eliminate this effect, but with no success. We conclude that the true response is flat from lags one through four.

21. These results on independent presidential influence are consistent with past work suggesting that bureaucratic resistance can thwart efforts at political control. For example, Aberbach and Rockman (1976) argued that presidents are deeply concerned with countering independent power bases within the bureaucracy. Since Reagan employed the various techniques of Nathan's (1983) administrative presidency strategy in almost textbook fashion (Waterman 1989), it is especially interesting that EPA bureaucrats continued to resist the Reagan administration's environmental agenda. This outcome suggests that presidents may have to build support at the bureaucratic level rather than just relying on particular administrative tools.

22. Recall from Equation 2 and the preceding discussion that a tonal measure assumes that the impulse response coefficients for all lags of X_k are equal.

23. We used the minimum SC criterion discussed previously.

24. One version of this model could not be tested. A moving average of news stories and presidential statements from lags zero to four could not be included in the same equation as a distributed lag of these same variables from lags zero to four because of perfect collinearity. We resolved this problem by eliminating lag four from the distributed lags. All lags of presidential statements and the last four lags of news stories were nonsignificant under this specification.

25. The Wald test for the omitted variables was nonsignificant, and SC was substantially lower for the final model.

26. One way of viewing the closeness of the coefficients from the dynamic stimulus-response model and the dynamic response model is as yet another goodness-

of-fit measure. If the tonal specification was inappropriate, then the coefficients would diverge from those of the dynamic response model.

CHAPTER 5

1. The Center for Political Studies conducts an annual General Social Survey that asks citizens each year what the most important problems facing the nation are. There is substantial variation through time on the responses to these questions.

2. This is a subcommittee of the House Committee on Internal and Insular Affairs.

3. In our early research on the NRC, we also identified an immediate and sustained impact to the issuance of the policy statement with regard to the number of enforcements actions taken (Wood and Waterman 1991). The response to the size of the civil penalty then is consistent with our earlier findings.

4. These statements are paraphrased from Kraft (1984: 35–43).

CHAPTER 6

1. Agency loss is the cost difference between the provision of costless information to a principal and the actual costs associated with establishing an effective monitoring capability.

2. To our knowledge there has been little empirical work on the question of how often the goals of principals and their agents actually diverge. Aberbach and Rockman (1976, 1989); Aberbach, Putman, and Rockman (1981); and Cole and Caputo (1979) compared the ideology of bureaucrats to elected officials. Goodsell (1983) and Quirk (1981) examined the attitudes of various public officials. Beyond these studies, which at best only tangentially apply, this basic assumption of the principal-agent model has undergone little empirical analysis.

References

Aberbach, Joel D. 1990. *Keeping a Watchful Eye: The Politics of Congressional Oversight*. Washington, D.C.: Brookings Institution.

Aberbach, Joel D., Robert D. Putman, and Bert A. Rockman. 1981. *Bureaucrats and Politicians in Western Democracies*. Boston: Harvard University Press.

_____. 1976. Clashing Beliefs in the Executive Branch: The Nixon Administration Bureaucracy. *American Political Science Review* 70: 456–468.

Aberbach, Joel D., and Bert A. Rockman. 1989. Administration, Interest Groups and the Changing Political Universe in Washington—Perceptions and Behavior. Paper presented at the annual meeting of the International Political Science Association Conference on the Structure and Organization of Government, Zurich, Switzerland, September 27–30.

_____. 1976. Clashing Beliefs in the Executive Branch: The Nixon Administration Bureaucracy. *American Political Science Review* 70: 456–468.

Akaike, H. 1974. A New Look at Statistical Model Identification. *IEEE Transactions on Automatic Control* AC-19: 716–723.

Almon, Shirley. 1965. The Distributed Lag Between Capital Appropriations and Expenditures. *Econometrica* 33: 178–196.

Andrews, Richard N.L. 1984. Deregulation: The Failure at EPA. In *Environmental Policy in the 1980s: Reagan's New Agenda*, ed. Norman J. Vig and Michael E. Kraft. Washington, D.C.: Congressional Quarterly Press.

Arnold, R. Douglas. 1979. *Congress and the Bureaucracy: A Theory of Influence*. New Haven: Yale University Press.

Arthur Anderson and Co. 1979. *The Cost of Government Regulation Study: Executive Summary*. New York: Business Roundtable.

Bachrach, Peter, and Morton S. Baratz. 1970. *Power and Poverty: Theory and Practice*. New York: Oxford University Press.

Banks, Jeffrey S., and Barry R. Weingast. 1992. The Political Control of Bureaucracies Under Asymmetric Information. *American Journal of Political Science* 36: 509–524.

Bardach, Eugene, and Robert A. Kagan. 1982. *Going by the Book: The Problem of Regulatory Unreasonableness*. Philadelphia: Temple University Press.

Barnard, Chester. 1938. *The Functions of the Executive*. Cambridge, Mass.: Harvard University Press.

Baumgartner, Frank R., and Bryan D. Jones. 1993. *Agendas and Instability in American Politics*. Chicago: University of Chicago Press.

Bendor, Jonathan., Serge Taylor, and Roland Van Gaalen. 1987. Politicians, Bureaucrats, and Asymmetric Information. *American Journal of Political Science* 31: 796–828.

_____. 1985. Bureaucratic Expertise vs. Legislative Authority: A Model of Decep-
tion and Monitoring in Budgeting. *American Political Science Review* 79: 1041–
1060.

Bentley, Arthur F. 1908. *The Process of Government: A Study of Social Pressures.* Chicago: University of Chicago Press.

Bernstein, Marver. 1955. *Regulating Business by Independent Commission.* Princeton:
Princeton University Press.

Bibby, John F., and Roger H. Davidson. 1972. *On Capitol Hill.* Hinsdale, Ill: Dryden
Press.

Box, G.E.P., and G. M. Jenkins. 1976. *Time Series Analysis, Forecasting and Control.*
San Francisco: Holden-Day.

Box, G.E.P., and G. C. Tiao. 1975. Intervention Analysis with Applications to Economic and Environmental Problems. *Journal of American Statistical Association*
70: 70–79.

Breusch, T. S., and A. R. Pagan. 1979. The Lagrange Multiplier Test and Its Applications to Model Specifications in Econometrics. *Review of Economic Studies* 47:
239–254.

Brown, Anthony. 1987. *The Politics of Airline Deregulation.* Knoxville: University of
Tennessee Press.

Brudney, Jeffrey L., and F. Ted Hebert. 1987. State Agencies and Their Environments: Examining the Influence of Important External Actors. *Journal of Politics*
47: 186–206.

Bryner, Gary C. 1987. *Bureaucratic Discretion: Law and Policy in Federal Regulatory
Agencies.* New York: Pergamon Press.

Bullock, Charles S. III., and Charles M. Lamb. 1984. *Implementation of Civil Rights
Policy.* Monterey, Calif.: Brooks-Cole.

Calvert, Randall, Mathew D. McCubbins, and Barry R. Weingast. 1989. A Theory
of Political Control and Agency Discretion. *American Journal of Political Science*
33: 588–611.

Calvert, Randall, Mark J. Moran, and Barry R. Weingast. 1987. Congressional Influence over Policymaking: The Case of the FTC. In *Congress: Structure and Policy,* ed. Mathew D. McCubbins and Terry Sullivan. New York: Cambridge University Press.

Campbell, Donald T., and Julian C. Stanley. 1963. *Experimental and Quasi-experi-
mental Designs for Research.* Chicago: Rand-McNally.

Cater, Douglas. 1964. *Power in Washington: A Critical Look at Today's Struggle to Gov-
ern in the Nation's Capitol.* New York: Random House.

Chubb, John E. 1985. The Political Economy of Federalism. *American Political Science Review* 79: 994–1015.

_____. 1983. *Interest Groups and the Bureaucracy: The Politics of Energy.* Stanford:
Stanford University Press.

Claybrook, Joan. 1984. *Retreat from Safety.* New York: Pantheon Books.

Cohen, Jeffrey E. 1985. Presidential Control of Independent Regulatory Commissions Through Appointment: The Case of the FCC. *Administration and Society*
17: 61–70.

Cole, Richard L., and David A. Caputo. 1979. Presidential Control of the Senior Executive Service: Assessing Strategies for the Nixon Years. *American Political Science Review* 73: 409–432.

Cook, Brian, and B. Dan Wood. 1989. Principal-Agent Models of Political Control of the Bureaucracy. *American Political Science Review* 83: 965–978.

Cook, Thomas D., and Donald T. Campbell. 1979. *Quasiexperimentation: Design and Analysis Issues for Field Settings.* Chicago: Rand-McNally.

Council on Environmental Quality (CEQ). 1984. *Environmental Quality.* Washington, D.C.: GPO.

———. 1981. *Environmental Quality.* Washington, D.C.: GPO.

Crandall, Robert W. 1982. The Environment. *Regulation* 6: 29–32.

Cronin, Thomas E. 1980. *The State of the Presidency.* Boston: Little, Brown.

Culhane, Paul J. 1984. Sagebrush Rebels in Office: Jim Watt's Land and Water Politics. In *Environmental Policy in the 1980s: Reagan's New Agenda*, ed. Norman J. Vig and Michael E. Kraft. Washington, D.C.: Congressional Quarterly Press.

Davis, Glenn, and Gary D. Helfand. 1985. *The Uncertain Balance: Governmental Regulators in the Political Process.* Wayne, N.J.: Avery Press.

Davis, Kenneth Culp. 1969a. *Discretionary Justice: A Preliminary Inquiry.* Baton Rouge: Louisiana State University Press.

———. 1969b. A New Approach to Delegation. *University of Chicago Law Review* 36: 713–725.

Derthick, Martha. 1987. American Federalism: Madison's Middle Ground in the 1980's. *Public Administration Review* 46: 66–74.

Derthick, Martha, and Paul J. Quirk. 1985. *The Politics of Deregulation.* Washington, D.C.: Brookings Institution.

Dodd, Lawrence C., and Richard L. Schott. 1979. *Congress and the Administrative State.* New York: John Wiley and Sons.

Downs, Anthony. 1967. *Inside Bureaucracy.* Boston: Little, Brown.

Ebbin, Steven, and Raphael Kasper. 1974. *Citizen Groups and the Nuclear Power Controversy.* Boston: MIT Press.

Eisner, Marc Allen, and Kenneth J. Meier. 1990. Presidential Control Versus Bureaucratic Power: Explaining the Reagan Revolution in Antitrust. *American Journal of Political Science* 34: 269–287.

Equal Employment Opportunity Commission. 1984. *Equal Employment Opportunity Commission, 19th Annual Report.* Washington, D.C.: GPO.

Fellmeth, Robert. 1970. *The Interstate Commerce Commission: The Public Interest and the ICC.* New York: Grossman.

Fenno, Richard F., Jr. 1966. *The Power of the Purse: Appropriations Politics in Congress.* Boston: Little, Brown.

———. 1959. *The President's Cabinet.* New York: Vintage Books.

Ferejohn, John A., and Charles R. Shipan. 1989. Congressional Influence on Administrative Agencies: A Case Study of Telecommunications Policy. In *Congress Reconsidered*, ed. Lawrence C. Dodd and Bruce I. Oppenheimer. Washington, D.C.: Congressional Quarterly Press.

Fiorina, Morris. 1981. Congressional Control of the Bureaucracy: A Mismatch of Incentives and Capabilities. In *Congress Reconsidered*, ed. Lawrence C. Dodd and Bruce I. Oppenheimer. Washington, D.C.: Congressional Quarterly Press.

Freeman, J. Leiper. 1955. *The Political Process: Executive Bureaus–Legislative Committee Relations.* New York: Random House.

Freudenburg, William R., and Rodney K. Baxter. 1985. Nuclear Reactions: Public Attitudes and Policies Toward Nuclear Power. *Policy Studies Journal* 5: 96–110.

<dd>168</dd>

Fuchs, Edward Paul. 1988. *Presidents, Management, and Regulation.* Englewood Cliffs, N.J.: Prentice-Hall.

Galloway, George B. 1951. The Operation of the Legislative Reorganization Act of 1946. *American Political Science Review* 45: 41–68.

_____. 1946. *Congress at the Crossroads.* New York: Thomas Y. Crowell.

Gerston, Larry N., Cynthia Fraleigh, and Robert Schwab. 1988. *The Deregulated Society.* Pacific Grove, Calif.: Brooks-Cole.

Gerth, H. H., and C. Wright Mills. 1946. *From Max Weber: Essays in Sociology.* New York: Oxford University Press.

Goodman, Marshall, and Margaret Wrightson. 1987. *Managing Regulatory Reform.* New York: Praeger.

Goodnow, Frank J. 1900. *Politics and Administration: A Study in Government.* New York: Russell and Russell.

Goodsell, Charles T. 1983. *The Case for Bureaucracy: A Public Administration Polemic.* Chatham, N.J.: Chatham House.

Gormley, William T. 1989. *Taming the Bureaucracy: Muscles, Prayers, and Other Strategies.* Princeton: University of Princeton Press.

_____. 1983. *The Politics of Public Utility Regulation.* Pittsburgh: University of Pittsburgh Press.

_____. 1982. Alternative Models of Regulatory Process: Public Utility Regulation in the States. *Western Political Quarterly* 35: 297–317.

Gottron, Martha V. 1982. *Regulation: Process and Politics.* Washington, D.C.: Congressional Quarterly Press.

Grace Commission. 1983. *The President's Private Sector Survey on Cost Control: Report on the Department of Energy, the Federal Energy Regulatory Commission, and the Nuclear Regulatory Commission.* Washington, D.C.: GPO.

Greer, Douglas F. 1983. *Business, Government, and Regulation.* New York: Macmillan.

Griffith, Ernest S. 1939. *The Impasse of Democracy.* New York: Harrison-Hilton Books.

Halvorsen, R., and R. Palmquist. 1980. The Interpretation of Dummy Variables in Semilogarithmic Equations. *American Economic Review* 70: 474–475.

Hansen, Wendy L. 1990. The International Trade Commission and the Politics of Protectionism. *American Political Science Review* 84: 21–43.

Harris, Joseph P. 1965. *Congressional Control of Administration.* Washington, D.C.: Brookings Institution.

Harris, Richard A., and Sydney M. Milkis. 1989. *The Politics of Regulatory Change: A Tale of Two Agencies.* New York: Oxford University Press.

Hayes, Michael T. 1992. *Incrementalism and Public Policy.* New York: Longman.

Heclo, Hugh. 1978. Issue Networks and the Executive Establishment. In *The New American Political System,* ed. Anthony A. King. Washington, D.C.: American Enterprise Institute.

_____. 1977. *A Government of Strangers: Executive Politics in Washington.* Washington, D.C.: Brookings Institution.

_____. 1975. OMB and the Presidency—The Problems of Neutral Competence. *Public Interest* 38: 80–98.

Hedge, David, and Saba Jallow. 1990. The Federal Context of Regulation: The Spatial Allocation of Federal Enforcement. *Social Science Quarterly* 70: 285–299.

Hill, Larry B. 1992. Taking Bureaucracy Seriously. In *The State of Public Bureaucracy*, ed. Larry B. Hill. New York: M. E. Sharpe.

Hsiao, Cheng. 1986. *Analysis of Panel Data*. New York: Cambridge University Press.

Hunter, Susan, and Richard W. Waterman. 1992. Determining an Agency's Regulatory Style: How Does the EPA Water Office Enforce the Law? *Western Political Quarterly* 45: 401–417.

Hunter, Susan, Richard W. Waterman, and Robert Wright. 1993. Why Has the EPA Adopted a Negotiated Enforcement Style? Paper presented at the annual meeting of the Southwest Social Science Association, New Orleans, Louisiana, March 17–20.

Huntington, Samuel P. 1952. The Marasmus of the ICC: The Commission, the Railroads, and the Public Interest. *Yale Law Journal* 61: 467–509.

Huzar, Elias. 1942. Legislative Control over Administration: Congress and the WPA. *American Political Science Review* 36: 55–67.

Hyneman, Charles. 1950. *Bureaucracy in a Democracy*. New York: Harper and Row.

Judge, George G., W. E. Griffiths, R. Carter Hill, Helmut Lutkepohl, and Tsoung-Chao Lee. 1985. *The Theory and Practice of Econometrics*. New York: John Wiley and Sons.

Kagan, Robert A. 1980. *Regulatory Justice: Implementing a Wage Price Freeze*. New York: Russell Sage Foundation.

Katzman, Robert A. 1980a. The Federal Trade Commission. In *The Politics of Regulation*, ed. James Q. Wilson. New York: Basic Books.

_____. 1980b. *Regulatory Bureaucracy: The Federal Trade Commission and Antitrust Policy*. Cambridge, Mass.: MIT Press.

Kaufman, Herbert. 1985. *Time, Chance, and Organizations: Natural Selection in a Perilous Environment*. Chatham, N.J.: Chatham House.

_____. 1981. *The Administrative Behavior of Federal Bureau Chiefs*. Washington, D.C.: Brookings Institution.

_____. 1960. *The Forest Ranger*. Baltimore: Johns Hopkins University Press.

Kennedy, Peter E. 1981. Estimation with Correctly Interpreted Dummy Variables in Semilogarithmic Equations. *American Economic Review* 71: 802.

Kiewiet, D. Roderick, and Mathew D. McCubbins. 1991. *The Logic of Delegation*. New York: Prentice-Hall.

Kingdon, John W. 1983. *Agendas, Alternatives, and Public Policies*. Boston: Little, Brown.

Kirschten, Dick. 1983. Administration Using Carter Era Reform to Manipulate Levers of Government. *National Journal* 15: 732–736.

Kmenta, Jan. 1986. *Elements of Econometrics*. New York: Macmillan.

Koenig, Louis. 1975. *The Chief Executive*. New York: Harcourt Brace Jovanovich.

Kohlmeier, Louis M., Jr. 1969. *The Regulators: Watchdog Agencies and the Public Interest*. New York: Harper and Row.

Kolko, Gabriel. 1965. *Railroads and Regulation, 1877–1916*. Princeton: Princeton University Press.

_____. 1963. *The Triumph of Conservatism: A Reinterpretation of American History, 1900–1916.* New York: Macmillan.

Kotowitz, Y. 1989. Moral Hazard. In *Allocation, Information, and Markets,* ed. John Eatwell, Murray Milgate, and Peter Newman. New York: Macmillan.

Kraft, Michael E. 1984. A New Environmental Policy Agenda. In *Environmental Policy in the 1980s,* ed. Norman J. Vig and Michael E. Kraft. Washington, D.C.: Congressional Quarterly Press.

Landis, James. 1939. *The Administrative Process.* New Haven: Yale University Press.

Lanouette, William J. 1983. Reagan's NRC Chairman: Nuclear Power Could Still Be a Valid Option. *National Journal* 15: 1457.

Lindblom, Charles E. 1959. The Science of Muddling Through. *Public Administration Review* 19: 79–88.

Ljung, George, and George E.P. Box. 1978. On a Measure of Lack of Fit in Time Series Models. *Biometrika* 66: 265–270.

Long, Norton E. 1949. Power and Administration. *Public Administration Review* 9: 257–264.

Lowi, Theodore J. 1979. *The End of Liberalism: The Second Republic of the United States.* New York: Norton.

Maas, Arthur. 1951. *Muddy Rivers: The Army Engineers and the Nation's Rivers.* New York: Oxford University Press.

MacAvoy, Paul W. 1979. *The Regulated Industries and the Economy.* New York: Norton.

Mackenzie, G. Calvin, ed. 1987. *The In-and-Outers: Presidential Appointees and Transient Government in Washington.* Baltimore: Johns Hopkins University Press.

March, James G., and Hebert A. Simon 1958. *Organizations.* New York: John Wiley and Sons.

McCleary, Richard, and Richard A. Hay. 1980. *Applied Time Series Analysis.* Beverly Hills, Calif.: Sage.

McConnell, Grant. 1966. *Private Power and American Democracy.* New York: Vintage Books.

McCubbins, Mathew D. 1985. The Legislative Design of Regulatory Structure. *American Journal of Political Science* 29: 721–748.

McCubbins, Mathew, Roger G. Noll, and Barry R. Weingast. 1989. Structure and Process as Solutions to the Politician's Principal-Agency Problem. *Virginia Law Review* 74: 431–482.

McCubbins, Mathew, and Thomas Schwartz. 1984. Congressional Oversight Overlooked: Police Patrols Versus Fire Alarms. *American Journal of Political Science* 28: 165–179.

Meier, Kenneth J. 1993. *Politics and the Bureaucracy: Policymaking in the Fourth Branch of Government.* Pacific Grove, Calif.: Brooks-Cole.

_____. 1985. *Regulation: Politics, Bureaucracy, and Economics.* New York: St. Martin's Press.

Meier, Kenneth J., and David R. Morgan. 1981. Speed Kills: A Longitudinal Analysis of Traffic Fatalities and the 55 MPH Speed Limit. *Policy Studies Review* 1: 157–167.

Melnick, R. Shep. 1983. *Regulation and the Courts.* Washington, D.C.: Brookings Institution.

Mitchell, Robert Cameron. 1984. Public Opinion and Environmental Politics in the 1970s and 1980s. In *Environmental Policy in the 1980s: Reagan's New Agenda*, ed. Norman J. Vig and Michael E. Kraft. Washington, D.C.: Congressional Quarterly Press.

Mitnick, Barry M. 1980. *The Political Economy of Regulation: Creating, Designing, and Removing Regulatory Forms.* New York: Columbia University Press.

Moe, Terry M. 1989. The Politicized Presidency. In *New Directions in American Politics*, ed. John Chubb and Paul E. Peterson. Washington, D.C.: Brookings Institution.

———. 1985. Control and Feedback in Economic Regulation: The Case of the NLRB. *American Political Science Review* 79: 1094–1117.

———. 1984. The New Economics of Organization. *American Journal of Political Science* 28: 739–777.

———. 1982. Regulatory Performance and Presidential Administration. *American Journal of Political Science* 26: 197–224.

Moore, Thomas Gale. 1978. The Beneficiaries of Trucking Regulation. *Journal of Law and Economics.* 21: 327–342.

Morgan, Charles S. 1953. A Critique of the Marasmus of the ICC: The Commission, the Railroads, and the Public Interest. *Yale Law Journal* 62: 171–225.

Mosher, Frederick C. 1968. *Democracy in the Public Service.* New York: Oxford University Press.

Nathan, Richard P. 1983. *The Administrative Presidency.* New York: John Wiley and Sons.

Niskanen, William A. 1971. *Bureaucracy and Representative Government.* Chicago: Aldine.

Noll, Roger G. 1971. *Reforming Regulation.* Washington, D.C.: Brookings Institution.

Nuclear Regulatory Commission (NRC). 1986. *Rules of Practice for Domestic Licensing Proceedings.* Washington, D.C.: GPO.

———. 1980. *Three Mile Island: A Report to the Commissioners and to the Public.* Vols. 1 and 2. Washington, D.C.: GPO.

———. 1979. *Staff Report to the President's Commission on the Accident at Three Mile Island.* Washington, D.C.: GPO.

Office of Management and Budget. 1981. *Budget of the United States Government.* Washington, D.C.: GPO.

Ogul, Morris. 1981. Congressional Oversight: Structures and Incentives. In *Congress Reconsidered*, ed. Lawrence C. Dodd and Bruce I. Oppenheimer. Washington, D.C.: Congressional Quarterly Press.

———. 1976. *Congress Oversees the Bureaucracy.* Pittsburgh: University of Pittsburgh Press.

Pastzor, Andy. 1984. Interior Prepares to Crack Down on States with Deficient Strip Mining Programs. *Wall Street Journal*, February 14.

Patterson, Walter C. 1983. *Nuclear Power.* New York: Penguin Books.

Perrow, Charles. 1986. *Complex Organizations: A Critical Essay.* New York: Random House.

Pfiffner, James P. 1988. *The Strategic Presidency: Hitting the Ground Running.* Chicago: Dorsey Press.

Pratt, John W., and Richard J. Zeckhauser. 1985. Principals and Agents: An Overview. In *Principals and Agents: The Structure of Business*, ed. John W. Pratt and Richard J. Zeckhauser. Cambridge, Mass.: Harvard Business School Press.

President's Commission on the Accident at Three Mile Island. 1979. *The Need for Change—The Legacy of TMI*. Washington, D.C.: GPO.

Posner, Richard A. 1974. Theories of Economic Regulation. *Bell Journal of Economics and Management Sciences* 5: 335–358.

————. 1981. *Industry Influence in Federal Regulatory Agencies*. Princeton: Princeton University Press.

Quirk, Paul. 1980. Food and Drug Administration. In *The Politics of Regulation*, ed. James Q. Wilson. New York: Basic Books.

Ramanathan, Ramu. 1989. *Introductory Econometrics with Applications*. New York: Harcourt Brace Jovanovich.

Randall, Ronald. 1979. Presidential Power Versus Bureaucratic Intransigence. *American Political Science Review* 74: 795–810.

Reagan, Michael. 1987. *Regulation: The Politics of Policy*. Boston: Little, Brown.

Redford, Emmette S. 1969. *Democracy in the Administrative State*. New York: Oxford University Press.

Ripley, Randall B., and Grace A. Franklin. 1986. *Policy Implementation and Bureaucracy*. Chicago: Dorsey Press.

Rosenbaum, Walter A. 1985. *Environmental Politics and Policy*. Washington, D.C.: Congressional Quarterly Press.

Rossiter, Clinton. 1956. *The American Presidency*. New York: Harcourt Brace Jovanovich.

Rourke, Francis E. 1984. *Bureaucracy, Politics, and Public Policy*. 3d ed. Boston: Little, Brown.

Sabatier, Paul A., and Neil Pelkey. 1987. Incorporating Multiple Actors and Guidance Instruments into Models of Regulatory Policymaking: An Advocacy Coalition Framework. *Administration and Society* 19: 236–263.

Sawa, T. 1978. Information Criteria for Discriminating Among Alternative Regression Models. *Econometrica* 46: 1273–1291.

Scher, Seymour. 1960. Congressional Committee Members as Independent Agency Overseers: A Case Study. *American Political Science Review* 54: 911–920.

Scholz, John T., John Twombly, and Barbara Headrick. 1991. Street Level Political Control over the Bureaucracy. *American Political Science Review* 85: 829–851.

Scholz, John T., and Feng Heng Wei. 1986. Regulatory Enforcement in a Federalist System. *American Political Science Review* 80: 1249–1270.

Schwarz, G. 1978. Estimating the Dimension of a Model. *Annals of Statistics* 6: 461–464.

Scicchitano, Michael J., David M. Hedge, and Patricia Metz. 1991. The Principal-Agent Model and Regulatory Federalism. *Western Political Quarterly* 44: 1055–1080.

Selznick, Phillip. 1949. *TVA and Grass Roots*. Berkeley and Los Angeles: University of California Press.

Sharfman, I. L. 1931–1937. *The Interstate Commerce Commission: A Study in Administrative Law and Procedure*. Vols. 1–4. New York: Commonwealth Fund.

Shover, Neal, Donald A. Clelland, and John Lynxwiler. 1986. *Enforcement or Nego-tiation: Constructing a Regulatory Bureaucracy*. Albany: State University of New York Press.

Simon, Herbert. 1947. *Administrative Behavior: A Study of Decisionmaking Processes in Administrative Organizations*. New York: Macmillan.

Stewart, Joseph, Jr., and Jane S. Cromartie. 1982. Partisan Presidential Change and Regulatory Policy: The Case of the FTC Deceptive Practices Cases, 1938–1974. *Presidential Studies Quarterly* 12: 568–573.

Stigler, George. 1975. *The Citizen and the States: Essays on Regulation*. Chicago: University of Chicago Press.

———. 1971. The Theory of Economic Regulation. *Bell Journal of Economics and Management Science* 2: 3–21.

Stimson, James A. 1991. *Public Opinion in America: Moods, Swings, and Cycles*. Boulder: Westview Press.

Stone, Alan. 1982. *Regulation and Its Alternatives*. Washington, D.C.: Congressional Quarterly Press.

———. 1977. *Economic Regulation and the Public Interest: The Federal Trade Commission in Theory and Practice*. Ithaca: Cornell University Press.

Sundquist, James L. 1981. *The Decline and Resurgence of Congress*. Washington, D.C.: Brookings Institution.

Taylor, Frederick W. 1947. *Principles of Scientific Management*. New York: Norton.

Terasvirta, T., and I. Mellin. 1983. *Estimation of Polynomial Distributed Lag Models*. Research Report 41. Helsinki: Department of Statistics, University of Helsinki.

Thompson, James D. 1967. *Organizations in Action: Social Basis of Administrative Theory*. New York: McGraw-Hill.

Thompson, Victor A. 1977. *Modern Organization*. University: University of Alabama Press.

———. 1975. *Without Sympathy or Enthusiasm: The Problem of Administrative Compassion*. University: University of Alabama Press.

Truman, David B. 1951. *The Governmental Process: Political Interests and Public Opinion*. New York: Knopf.

Tufte, Edward R. 1974. *Data Analysis for Politics and Public Policy*. Englewood Cliffs, N.J.: Prentice-Hall.

U.S. Government. 1967. *The Organization and Management of Great Society Programs*. Final report of the President's Task Force on Government Organization. Washington, D.C.: GPO.

U.S. House of Representatives. 1986. *A Report on the Investigation of Civil Rights Enforcement by the Equal Employment Opportunity Commission*. 99th Cong., 2nd sess., Committee on Education and Labor. Washington, D.C.: GPO.

———. 1983. *Oversight Hearings on the Federal Enforcement of Equal Employment Opportunity Laws*. 98th Cong., 1st sess., Subcommittee on Employment Opportunities of the Committee on Education and Labor. Washington, D.C.: GPO.

———. 1982a. *Oversight Hearings Before the Committee on Energy and the Environment of the Committee on Insular Affairs*. 98th Cong., 2nd sess. Washington, D.C.: GPO.

———. 1982b. *Oversight—Motor Carrier Act of 1980*. 97th Cong., 2nd sess., Hearings before the Public Works Committee. Washington, D.C.: GPO.

_____. 1981. *Hearings Before the Subcommittee on Post Office and Civil Service.* 97th Cong., 1st sess. Washington, D.C.: GPO.

_____. 1979. *Nuclear Regulatory Commission Authorizations for Fiscal Year 1980.* 96th Cong., 1st sess., Hearings before the Subcommittee on Energy and Environment of the Committee on Interior and Insular Affairs. Washington, D.C.: GPO.

_____. 1973. *Confidence and Concern: Citizens View American Government.* 93rd Cong., 1st sess., Hearings before the Subcommittee on Intergovernmental Relations to the Senate Committee on Government Operations. Washington, D.C.: GPO.

U.S. Senate. 1986. *Hearing Before the Committee on Labor and Human Resources, United States Senate, on Clarence Thomas of Maryland to Be Chairman of the Equal Employment Opportunity Commission.* 99th Cong., 2nd sess. Washington, D.C.: GPO.

_____. 1982. *Hearing Before the Committee on Labor and Human Resources, United States Senate, on Clarence Thomas of Maryland to Be Chairman of the Equal Employment Opportunity Commission.* 97th Cong., 1st sess. Washington, D.C.: GPO.

_____. 1981a. *Nomination—Chairman of the Interstate Commerce Commission.* 97th Cong., 1st sess., Hearings before the Senate Committee on Commerce, Science, and Transportation. Washington, D.C.: GPO.

_____. 1981b. *Senate Committee on the Environment and Public Works: Nominations of Nunzio Palladino and Thomas M. Roberts.* 97th Cong., 1st sess. Washington, D.C.: GPO.

Vig, Norman J., and Michael E. Kraft. 1984. *Environmental Policy in the 1980s: Reagan's New Agenda.* Washington, D.C.: Congressional Quarterly Press.

Waterman, Richard W. 1989. *Presidential Influence and the Administrative State.* Knoxville: University of Tennessee Press.

Waterman, Richard W., and B. Dan Wood. 1993. Policy Monitoring and Policy Analysis. *Journal of Policy Analysis and Management* 12: 685–689.

_____. 1992. What Do We Do with Applied Research? *PS: Political Science and Politics* (September): 559–564.

_____. 1991. The Politics of Nonrecursive Bureaucratic Adaptation. Paper presented at the Western Political Science Association meetings, Long Beach, California.

Weidenbaum, Murray. 1979. *The Future of Business Regulation.* New York: Amacom.

Weingast, Barry R. 1984. The Congressional-Bureaucratic System: A Principal-Agent Perspective (with Applications to the SEC). *Public Choice* 44: 147–191.

Weingast, Barry R., and Mark J. Moran. 1983. Bureaucratic Discretion or Congressional Control: Regulatory Policymaking by the Federal Trade Commission. *Journal of Political Economy* 91: 756–800.

_____. 1981. Regulation, Reregulation, and Deregulation: The Political Foundations of Agency Clientele Relationships. *Law and Contemporary Problems* 44: 149–177).

Wenner, Lettie M. 1984. Judicial Oversight of Environmental Regulation. In *Environmental Policy in the 1980s: Reagan's New Agenda,* ed. Norman J. Vig and Michael E. Kraft. Washington, D.C.: Congressional Quarterly Press.

White, Leonard D. 1945. Congressional Control of the Public Service. *American Political Science Review* 39: 1–11.

Wildavsky, Aaron. 1964. *The Politics of the Budgetary Process*. Boston: Little, Brown.

Wilson, James Q. 1989. *Bureaucracy: What Government Agencies Do and Why They Do It*. New York: Basic Books.

———. 1980. *The Politics of Regulation*. New York: Basic Books.

———. 1975. The Rise of the Bureaucratic State. *Public Interest* 41: 77–103.

———. 1967. The Bureaucratic Problem. *Public Interest* 6: 3–9.

Wilson, Woodrow. 1987. The Study of Administration. In *Classics of Public Administration*, ed. Jay M. Shafritz and Albert C. Hyde. Chicago: Dorsey Press (originally published June 1887).

Woll, Peter. 1963. *American Bureaucracy*. New York: Norton.

Wood, B. Dan. 1992. Modeling Federal Implementation as a System. *American Journal of Political Science* 36: 40–67.

———. 1991. Federalism and Policy Responsiveness: The Clean Air Case. *Journal of Politics* 53: 851–859.

———. 1990. Does Politics Make a Difference at the EEOC? *American Journal of Political Science* 34: 503–530.

———. 1988. Principals, Bureaucrats, and Responsiveness in Clean Air Enforcements. *American Political Science Review* 82: 213–234.

———. 1987. "Principals, Agents, and Federalism: The Case of Clear Air Enforcements." Ph.D. diss., University of Houston.

Wood, B. Dan, and James Anderson. 1993. The Politics of U.S. Antitrust Regulation. *American Journal of Political Science* 37: 1–39.

Wood, B. Dan, and Richard W. Waterman. 1993. The Dynamics of Political-Bureaucratic Adaptation. *American Journal of Political Science* 37: 497–528.

———. 1991. The Dynamics of Political Control of the Bureaucracy. *American Political Science Review* 85: 801–828.

Yandle, Bruce. 1985. FTC Activity and Presidential Effects. *Presidential Studies Quarterly* 15: 128–135.

Yantek, Thom, and Kenneth D. Gartrell. 1988. Political Climate and Corporate Mergers: When Politics Affects Economics. *Western Political Quarterly* 41: 309–322.

About the Book and Authors

Political control has long been a major theme in the bureaucratic literature. Beginning with the politics-administration dichotomy, scholars have attempted to solve a paradox: How does one grant the bureaucracy enough autonomy and authority to carry out its mandated functions without delegating too much authority to unelected administrators? Most bureaucratic scholars have contended that government has failed in this delicate balancing act. They contend that elected officials have delegated too much authority to the administrative state and have been too inattentive to the bureaucratic process. They have also contended that bureaucrats have abused their power. As a result, the consensus view in the bureaucratic literature is that democracy itself is imperiled by a bureaucratic process that is clearly out of control.

In this book, through an empirical analysis of enforcement outputs from eight different federal agencies, the authors demonstrate that many of these popular ideas about the nature of the bureaucratic process are nothing more than "myths of the bureaucracy." This book demonstrates that elected officials actively seek to control the bureaucratic state, that bureaucrats are indeed responsive to them, and that the bureaucratic process is intensely political, with different political actors and their agents vying for control of the bureaucracy over time. Based on the results of a quantitative analysis, the authors conclude that the bureaucratic process is not out of control. Rather, it is a highly dynamic and democratic process. Despite this optimistic view of the bureaucratic process, the authors also argue that greater bureaucratic accountability is required, but not just from bureaucratic agents. Real bureaucratic accountability requires accountability from both elected officials and their unelected agents. This book therefore introduces a policy analytic reform, called policy monitoring, designed to promote accountability among both principal officeholders and their agents in the bureaucracy.

B. Dan Wood is associate professor of political science, Texas A&M University.
Richard W. Waterman is associate professor of political science, University of New Mexico.

Index